PIDGINIZATION AND CREOLIZATION

AMSTERDAM STUDIES IN THE THEORY AND HISTORY OF LINGUISTIC SCIENCE

General Editor
E.F. KONRAD KOERNER
(University of Ottawa)

Series IV - CURRENT ISSUES IN LINGUISTIC THEORY

Advisory Editorial Board

Henning Andersen (Copenhagen); Raimo Anttila (Los Angeles)
Thomas V.Gamkrelidze (Tbilisi); Hans-Heinrich Lieb (Berlin)
J.Peter Maher (Chicago); Ernst Pulgram (Ann Arbor, Mich.)
E.Wyn Roberts (Vancouver, B.C.); Danny Steinberg (Tokyo)

Volume 33

Kees Versteegh

Pidginization and Creolization:
The Case of Arabic

PIDGINIZATION AND CREOLIZATION: THE CASE OF ARABIC

KEES VERSTEEGH
Katholieke Universiteit, Nijmegen

JOHN BENJAMINS PUBLISHING COMPANY
Amsterdam/Philadelphia

1984

Library of Congress Cataloging in Publication Data

Versteegh, Kees.
Pidginization and creolization.

(Amsterdam studies in the theory and history of linguistic science. Series IV, Current issues in linguistic theory; ISSN 0304-0763; v. 33)
Bibliography: p. 151
Includes indexes.
1. Arabic language -- History. 2. Pidgin languages. 3. Creole dialects. I. Title. II. Series.
PJ6075.V47 1984 492'.77 84-28364
ISBN 90-272-3529-5

Talis enim erat ei loquendi modus semper per infinitivum nec casus servabat; et tamen satis intelligi poterat "For he had this habit of always speaking in infinitives and without declension: and yet, he made himself sufficiently understood" (Giraldus Lambrensis about a Welsh monk, *De rebus a se gestis*, III, ed. by J.S. Brewer, 90.8-10. London: Longmans, 1861.)

TABLE OF CONTENTS

Preface		ix
Chapter I.	The Arabic language in the pre-Islamic period	1
	Notes	14
Chapter II.	The transition from Old Arabic to New Arabic	17
	Notes	32
Chapter III.	Pidginization and creolization	35
	Notes	56
Chapter IV.	The socio-linguistic context of the early period of Islam	59
	Notes	76
Chapter V.	Pidginization and creolization in Arabic	79
	Notes	106
Chapter VI.	Modern Arabic trade-languages, pidgins, and creoles	113
	Notes	127
Chapter VII.	Conclusions and prospects	129
	Notes	148
List of references		151
List of abbreviations		171
Index of names		175
Index of subjects		181

PREFACE

Let us assume that a scholar finds to his surprise that insular dialects of several unrelated languages differ from their continental counterparts in a significant and systematic way. He calls such dialects ‘insulars’ and suggests that a common process — let us call it ‘insularization’ — is responsible for this development. Others are attracted to the idea and start looking for parallels. One scholar asserts that all European ‘insulars’ have a common origin, since they all have preserved the same traces of the language of a Proto-European people that once inhabited all European islands. Clearly, this claim is invalidated by the fact that all African, Asian, and American ‘insulars’ are found to exhibit the same features as the European ones, and nobody seriously believes that the Proto-European people once inhabited all islands in the world. The next contribution comes from a sceptic who points out that we do not have a watertight definition of the notion ‘island’: does it apply to peninsulas, is England an island, what about islands in rivers? Consequently, he denies the value of the notion of ‘insularization’, and claims that there is no such thing as an ‘insular’. But then someone argues that the individual features which are believed to be characteristic of ‘insulars’ are also found in some continental languages. He adds that, after all, every continent might be regarded as an island, so that we are justified in calling all languages ‘insulars’.

Still, this does not explain the fact that the original instances of ‘insularization’ do seem intuitively to exhibit a very characteristic combination of features that is not found anywhere else. One scholar refuses to call any dialect an ‘insular’ until a complete classification of islands is made that takes into account not only the geographical position, but also the vegetation, the temperature of the water, and the presence or absence of certain animals. Still another scholar goes so far as to include mountain dialects, delta dialects, and beach dialects in the group of ‘insulars’, since, so he claims, these dialects are as isolated as the original ‘insulars’. The discussion comes to a point where for some people ‘insulars’ constitute only a very small group of dialects (‘real insulars’), whereas others feel that the term is so vacuous as to include almost any language. Many debates are devoted to the question whether or not Australian English is an 'insular' (or perhaps a 'pseudo-insular'?), and many people vehemently oppose the suggestion that continentals who stay more than a few weeks on an island may be said to 'insularize' their speech.

Finally, a proposal is made that satisfies everyone. It is decided that a combined effort will be made to find out what happens when a group of people is left on an inhabited island. A group of volunteers is selected and dropped and, after fifty years, revisited. It turns out that ...

At this point, it is perhaps preferable to leave the matter to future scholars, who may one day be confronted by the problem of 'insularization'. In what follows I wish to occupy myself with a much less fictitious problem, that of 'pidgins' and 'pidginization', of 'creoles' and 'creolization'. I believe that what went wrong in the approaches sketched above was that they were all based on one implicit assumption, namely that the notion 'insular' corresponded to something in the real world. The discussion concentrated, therefore, on the question whether or not certain dialects or languages could be called 'insulars', instead of trying to determine the nature of the process involved, and the relation between that process and the changes in the languages involved. Thus, what ought to be proved first became the axiomatic point of departure for a very entangled discussion. I intend to look at the discussions about 'pidginization' and 'creolization' in the following chapters from various angles, and to find an approach that connects the nature of the process to the changes involved. Then, I shall try to apply this approach to a concrete example, the history of the Arabic language.

It is, perhaps, superfluous to add that the above considerations are in no way intended as an innovation, in the sense of something that has not been put forth by anyone else. The only reason I did present them was to be absolutely clear about the status of my discussion, which, after all, concerns a language to whose history the notion of 'pidginization' has hardly ever been applied. A further reason for starting at an elementary level is that it is imperative for an outsider to a certain field of research to show exactly where he stands, and to admit right from the beginning that his only attitude can be one of common sense, without any claim to inside knowledge based on personal research. This principle is particularly valid in the case of someone trained in philological methods within a discipline that is by and large still characterized by a certain aloofness from developments in general linguistics. I have tried to use the existing literature on 'pidgins' and 'creoles' as conscientiously as possible, and no statement about any phenomenon linked with these languages should be taken as more than a faithful reproduction of the data collected by others, and interpreted by someone without specialist knowledge. In a somewhat less strict sense this also applies to data from the field of Arabic dialectology, which are not based on any fieldwork, but only on the perusal of the existing literature.

In the first chapter I discuss the linguistic situation in the period before the coming of Islam on the Arabian peninsula, and I conclude that during that period there was essentially one Arabic language, more or less identical with the later standardized form of Classical Arabic. In chapter II I discuss the various theories that have been put forward to explain the emergence of a new type of Arabic, and the use they make of both the common and the divergent features of the modern dialects of Arabic. Chapter III summarizes the current opinions about 'pidginization' and 'creolization', and tries to determine the best vantage point from which to apply these notions to the history of Arabic. Briefly put, my conclusion is that 'pidginization' is a useful label for an incomplete process of second language acquisition in an untutored context of language learning, whereas 'creolization' is a useful label for the construction of a first language from an unnatural input. In the next chapter I study the sociolinguistic context of the early period of Islam in order to analyze the conditions of language learning in the territories conquered by the Arabs. In chapter V I apply my conclusions to the changes between the old and the new type of Arabic, and I compare these changes with those occurring in other languages that have undergone the same process. In chapter VI I present some material concerning some recent 'pidginized' and 'creolized' varieties of Arabic. Finally, chapter VII reformulates my ideas and tentatively connects them with other language areas.

I have alluded above to the feeling of trespassing one has in crossing into an unfamiliar field of research. Unfortunately, it is not always possible to make one's self as inconspicuous as one might wish to, and it is impossible not only to avoid all pitfalls, but also to mask one's unawareness of them. Obviously, the help of others, both in exploring the field, and in helping one on one's way, is indispensable in such an enterprise.

In the first place, I wish to thank all of my colleagues, who probably never wish to hear the word 'pidgin' again. Henk Maier provided interesting material on Indonesian, and Jan Peters read an early version of my ideas. But the brunt of my communicativeness was borne by Erik-Jan Zürcher, whose wish to preserve me from the more daring conjectures I advanced in the course of my research was fairly matched by his willingness to listen to them at all hours.

I take this opportunity to settle a long-standing debt towards Hans Bertens (University of Utrecht), who guided my first efforts in English composition. Whatever merits my English prose possesses are due to him; whatever defects still remain are entirely my own fault. Phil Hyams (University of Nijmegen) very kindly agreed to check the final draft and to correct the most blatant offenses against English grammar.

An early version of my ideas was presented at the 5th Congress of Historical Linguistics at Galway (1981). Elizabeth Traugott (Stanford University) and David Lightfoot (then University of Utrecht) took the trouble of reading my paper, which has been published in the proceedings of the conference.

Several people assisted in obtaining for me materials on Arabic dialects. Bernd Heine (University of Cologne) allowed me to consult the pre-publication version of his manuscript on the Arabic creole Nubi, and let me have a copy of the published book. Robin Thelwall (University of Ulster), Ushari Mahmud (Khartoum International Institute of Arabic) and as-Sayyid Ḥāmid Ḥurreiz (University of Khartoum) sent me material concerning Arabic in the Sudan. Alexander Borg (University of Erlangen) allowed me to use his unpublished habilitation on Cypriot Arabic. Alan Kaye (California State University) kindly sent me a copy of his dictionary of Nigerian Arabic, and corrected some errors. Ernő Csiszár (Várpalota) provided me with information about the phenomenon of Esperanto as a first language and invited me to give a lecture at the 5th *Renkonto de Esperantistaj Familioj* (Sümeg, August 11th, 1983). Ernst Håkon Jahr (Tromsø) sent me his manuscript on Russenorsk.

At the 11th congress of the Union Européenne des Arabisants et des Islamisants at Évora (1982) I was given the opportunity to discuss the analogy between the history of Arabic and the history of the Romance languages in a paper in which I presented the main outlines of my ideas. I wish to thank all those who engaged in this discussion. On the basis of this paper Roger Wright (University of Liverpool) sent me his comments on my theories in a very generous way, and started a most stimulating discussion.

I am particularly grateful to Hartmut Bobzin (University of Erlangen) for having invited me to Erlangen for a visit as a guest-lecturer (December 18th, 1982), and I wish to thank the participants in the ensuing discussion, in particular Wolfdietrich Fischer, Otto Jastrow, Hartmut Bobzin, and Alexander Borg, for their benevolent scepticism, which forced me to reconsider my position in some points.

At the final stage of preparation Pieter Seuren (University of Nijmegen) was kind enough to read the entire manuscript and to give me the much-needed support of a professional linguist, as well as the even more needed advice concerning the presentation of my ideas. At this stage I received a number of general, but very penetrating questions from Georgine Ayoub (Paris), which helped me to reformulate some essential points. After the completion of the manuscript I had a chance to present my ideas as a guest lecturer at the University of Bochum (July 14th, 1983), to which I had been invited by Gerhard Endreß.

Finally, I wish to thank those of my students who took the trouble of following my frequent digressions about those subjects that happened to occupy me, and who had a knack of putting to me precisely those questions to which I had not yet invented an answer.

In a very literal sense this book would not have appeared without the help of the editor of this series, Konrad Koerner (Ottawa), and the publishers, Claire and John Benjamins. I am grateful to them and to Hans Hospers (Groningen) for their warm support.

Nijmegen, December 1983

CHAPTER 1
THE ARABIC LANGUAGE IN THE PRE-ISLAMIC PERIOD

The problem to be discussed here concerns the cause or causes that brought about the transition from the old type of Arabic to the new type of Arabic around the time of the Islamic conquests that founded the empire of the Umayyads and the 'Abbāsids. Although causality has become a rather controversial notion in historical linguistics (cf. e.g. Lass 1980) I believe that a causal model of linguistic change may have more than merely aesthetic value, provided the mechanism of change is identified unequivocally, without the introduction of extra-linguistic factors that are commonly held responsible for changes in the language. As for the two types of Arabic referred to above, I shall define provisionally the new type of Arabic as the sum total of characteristics that set apart the modern Arabic dialects from the Classical standard (these characteristics will be discussed in ch. II). The many senses in which the term 'Old Arabic' has been used have made it rather ambiguous, so that I shall have something to say about it. By 'Old Arabic' I refer to the Arabic used in the Arabian peninsula before Islam. Part of my understanding of the history of the Arabic language concerns precisely the nature of that language, so that I shall devote this first chapter to a discussion of the linguistic situation in the pre-Islamic period (*Ǧāhiliyya*).

It is generally held that before the period of the Islamic conquests, which started after the death of the prophet around 630 A.D., the Arab tribes in the peninsula spoke different dialects. Apart from their own dialects, the Arab tribes shared an intertribal, more or less formal, not directly comprehensible variety of Arabic, which was used for poetry, prophecies, gnomic sayings, etc. This intertribal language — frequently called 'poetic koine' — is believed to have evolved from one of the dialect groups, but not without incorporating features from other dialects, as well as many archaisms (Cohen 1970:105-106; Blau 1965:3; Zwettler 1978:101-103). The extent of the differences between the dialects, as well as the differences between the dialects and the 'poetic koine' is not very well established. Some evidence is furnished by the grammarians (cf. Rabin 1951:6-16 for an enumeration of the sources), and from what little is known about the dialects we may deduce that they were divided into at least two major groups, the Eastern and the Western dialects (Rabin 1951:1ff.; Corriente 1975:43-46; Fischer 1982:40-43).

According to Rabin the division Eastern vs. Western Arabic roughly corresponds to the distinction made by the Arab grammarians between Ḥiğāzī and Tamīmī Arabic. He mentions many differences that are mentioned by the grammarians as typical of the two major groups. To mention only a few examples from the Eastern group: these dialects are characterized *vis-à-vis* the Western group by the following features: the elision of unstressed /i/ and /u/ (e.g., *fa'ila* > *fa'la*; Rabin 1951:97); a certain amount of vocalic assimilation (e.g., *ba'īr* > *bi'īr*; Rabin 1951:99);[1] the preservation of the glottal stop, which had disappeared in the Western dialects (Vollers 1906:83-96; Rabin 1951:130-45); and the phenomenon called *taltala* in later sources, i.e. the use of the prefix-vowel /i/ instead of /a/ in the imperfect (cf. Ferguson 1959:621-22; Rabin 1951:61-63). These examples may serve to give an impression of the kind of difference involved; as far as our sources are concerned, these differences go rarely beyond matters of phonology and lexicon.

As early as 1906 Vollers (1906:171-75) had claimed that the language of the Ğāhilī poems was based on the dialect of one group, which he situated in the Nağd and the Yamāma. This dialect had been changed considerably by the poets, but the result differed even more from the rest of the dialects. These other dialects represented the *Volkssprache* in the title of Vollers' spectacular book. In Rabin's view, too, the early form of Classical Arabic, i.e. the poetic koine, was based on a mixture of Eastern and Western dialects, but one in which the Eastern element dominated, such as it was used in the Nağd (Rabin 1951:1). It was there that both Classical poetry and its language, the Classical standard, originated.

Contrary to the accepted opinion, I do not distinguish between a colloquial and a poetic language: instead, I regard all varieties of Arabic in the pre-Islamic period as one language, comprising — as apparently all languages do — different registers as well as regional varieties. In this view, the poetic koine is nothing but the elevated style or register that happens to be used for poetry, and the dialects are the regional varieties of that same langguage.[2] I believe that one of the motives that have led scholars to posit the existence of a discrete, poetic language may have been a false analogy between the language of the Ğāhilī poems and the Homeric poetic dialect. Without going into the dicussion about the oral nature of Classical Arabic poetry,[3] I maintain that the language of the poems was identical with the colloquial of the tribes.

It is, perhaps, rather arbitrary to speak of two registers rather than two dialects or, for that matter, two different languages. This objection also applies if one views the differences between Old Arabic and New Arabic as fundamental rather than gradual. I shall not attempt here to give a principal answer and I shall base my position on entirely practical considerations. The differences between Old Arabic and New Arabic concern the entire linguistic structure on all levels, they are frequent, and it is not possible to map the new structure onto the old one by one-to-one correspondence rules. Differences of that size and range have never been claimed for any two varieties of Arabic in the *Ǧāhiliyya*. Therefore, it is clear that, whatever term is chosen to indicate the relationship between varieties of Arabic in that period — registers with regional varieties, dialects, languages — the linguistic situation in the *Ǧāhiliyya* was fundamentally different from the later development. I have opted here for the term 'registers' and believe that the use of other, farther reaching terms places the burden of proof on those who wish to use them.

One argument for this view is given by Blau (1981a:219-22): he points to the complete absence of pseudo-correct features in the preserved pre-Classical texts, a phenomenon that in his view cannot be attributed to a gradual polishing of the text in later redactions. Another important argument for the view that there was but one Arabic language prior to the period of the conquests — a view held in the past by orientalists such as Nöldeke (1904), and in essence also by Fück (1950) — is the testimony of the grammarians. If we wish to take their writings seriously, we are actually forced to accept the trustworthiness attributed by them to the Bedouin (*al-ʿArab*). The grammarians used this term not only to refer to their informants in the cities — they might be accused of inaccuracy, whether for financial reasons, or because they had adapted themselves to sedentary speech — but also, and in particular, to the nomadic tribes, whose members continued to speak the older, purer type of Arabic, i.e. the type of Arabic that had been spoken universally in the Arabian peninsula before Islam. No doubt, the romantic idealization of desert life and Bedouin values current in early Islamic sedentary society played an important role in the appreciation of Bedouin linguistic purity, but, on the other hand, the testimonies of the grammarians are too explicit to be ignored.[4] In my view, the only reasonable conclusion to be drawn on the basis of the evidence of grammatical literature is that, essentially, the colloquial and the literary language of the Arab tribes, both before the conquests and for a long time afterwards, were identical.

Almost the only criterion hitherto applied to the distinction between Arabic colloquial and alleged poetic koine is the — in itself controversial — question of the presence or absence of the declensional endings (*iʿrāb*). The discussion about the nature of the poetic koine and the transition from Old Arabic to New Arabic — summarized neatly by Zwettler 1978:97-188 — keeps coming back to the question of whether or not Bedouin speech had lost its declensional endings before the coming of Islam. Several types of evidence have been adduced to prove that the short vowels that indicate the cases of the declined noun in the singular had disappeared from everyday Bedouin speech, as distinct from the literary language, e.g., the rhyming conventions (Zwettler 1978:103-110); the 'functional yield' of declensional endings in literary Arabic (Zwettler 1978:139-49; Corriente 1971-72; and cf. below ch. V, p. 91); and the orthography of the Nabataean inscriptions, as well as the development of the writing system in the early period.[5] But without denying the considerable value of such detailed studies for a better understanding of the history of Arabic, I doubt that they are very relevant to the point at issue, namely the complete modification of the Arabic language. Even for those who hold that the *iʿrāb* was almost absent from the pre-Islamic colloquial dialects, the distinction between these dialects and later forms of Arabic remains a fundamental one. As far as I know, no one claims that most of the characteristics of later Arabic were already present, even latently, in the pre-Islamic dialects. I hope to show below that the loss of the (singular) declensional endings is but a small part of what constituted the transition from Old Arabic to New Arabic, and that the current phonological explanation for this phenomenon is inadequate, if only because of the fact that any explanation in terms of the elision of the short end vowels, or in terms of pausal phenomena, does not take into account the existence of another set of declensional endings, those of the sound plural, that disappeared as well, although they could not have been affected by such phonological phenomena.

I believe, therefore, that the presence or absence of declensional endings as far as they are represented by short vowels in Bedouin speech, before or after Islam, is irrelevant to my purpose, which is to analyze and explain the entire complex of changes which the Arabic language went through during the first century after the conquests. This being so, I may add that I agree with those who claim that the Bedouin continued to use the declensional endings for a few centuries after the conquests (cf., e.g., Fück 1950; Blau 1965; Fleisch 1974), and only lost them under the increasing influence of sedentary civilization, which changed not only their language, but their entire life style as well. I disagree with Fleisch, though, when it comes to the distinction between colloquial and poetic koine he adheres to,[6] and I shall rather follow Fück's implicit theory about the history of the Arabic language, according to which the change from Old Arabic to New Arabic must be explained by the corrupting influence on the part of the population of the conquered territories, or, as Blau formulates it (1977:16), there was no diglossia before Islam. This explains the absence of pseudo-corrections in the preserved pre-Classical texts, and of deviations in the direction of New Arabic. Blau, too, concludes that the changes took place as a result of the conquests (1977:7ff.).

According to the accepted opinion the language of the poems — i.e. in the view taken here, the elevated register of Old Arabic — became the language of the *Qur'ān* as well. The differences between the language used for the two genres are not essential (e.g., the idiosyncratic treatment of the glottal stop in the qur'ānic dialect, as compared with the normal practice in Eastern type dialects to which the poetic dialect belongs). They are to be regarded, not as evidence for a later translation of the text of the *Qur'ān* into Classical Arabic, as Vollers (1906) does, but as regionalisms of the Ḥiǧāzī variety of Old Arabic. According to Rabin (1951:4) the Ḥiǧāzī dialect was not a pure Western type dialect, but profoundly influenced by the Central and the Eastern dialects which formed the basis for later Classical Arabic. It is, however, doubtful whether the nature of the material at our disposal warrants such a conclusion. There can be no doubt that Ḥiǧāzī is the dialect that is best known from all pre-Islamic dialects. This means that we cannot exclude the possibility that the alleged influence of Central-Eastern dialects in Ḥiǧāzī (i.e., the presence of Classical traits) was, indeed, present in all dialects, without our knowing about it through lack of documents. This conclusion could also be formulated in the sense that there was no discrepancy at all between the two types of Arabic.

The poetico-qur'ānic language — and the colloquial as well, if one accepts my thesis — formed the basis for the later Classical norm of the *'Arabiyya* (cf., e.g., Rabin 1955). The Mediaeval philologists and grammarians cultivated and standardized this language at an early date (cf. below, p. 9f.). According to Wansbrough (1977:90-94) the Classical norm must have originated at a much later date (3rd/9th century); this means that he rejects the evidence of the large body of grammatical material concerning the very first period of Islamic history, in which grammarians tried to formulate the rules of the linguistic canon available to them, i.e. both the language of the Bedouin and the language of the poems and the *Qur'ān* (cf. Blau 1981a:216-19). In my view, the opposition between a literary language and a colloquial language did not exist before Islam, but came into being through the emergence of a wholly new variety of Arabic, characterized by a radical departure from the rules of the essentially uniform language of the Ǧāhiliyya. Henceforward, the linguistic history of the Arabs anywhere exhibited the opposition between a high and a low variety with different social and cultural functions, that was to become typical of the linguistic situation in the arabophone world. This situation, in which there are no discrete varieties, but rather a continuum ranging from the deepest dialect to the most elevated style, has been described in detail for Modern Egyptian by Diem (1974), and in somewhat less detail for Moroccan by Forkel (1980).

Our sources for the nature of the changes and their rate of developing and spreading are very meagre, indeed, as long as we do not take fully into account the evidence provided by the modern dialects themselves. The problem with using the evidence of the dialects, which in my view are derived from the early form of the new type of Arabic referred to above, is that, although fairly good descriptions of the major dialects are now available, the authors of such descriptions tend to let the structure of the Classical language interfere with their analysis and evaluation of the dialectal data. What is more, the use of these data is complicated by the inevitable fact that the selection of evidence from them and the acceptance of such evidence as relevant are intimately connected with our own presuppositions concerning the origin of the dialects and the factors contributing to the changes that brought about their evolution. It seems to me, however, that the study of the modern dialects is the only way to find out what actually happened during the first century.

In this respect it may be mentioned that two categories of dialects merit special attention, since their place within the Arabic dialects is unique. In the first place, I wish to emphasize the importance of the so-called *Sprachinsel*, i.e. those dialects whose links with the mainstream of Islamic and Arabic history were severed a long time ago (cf. below, ch. II, p. 29). The Arabic dialects spoken in these areas (Soviet Uzbekistan, Central Anatolia, Afghanistan, Khuzestan, Malta, Cyprus) did not undergo at all, or only to a certain point, the levelling influence of the Classical standard. I shall argue below that their structure is that of the earliest stages in the development of the new type of Arabic. In the second place, I believe that the study of those

Arabic pidgins and trade languages which are spoken in Africa today — e.g., the Juba Arabic of Sudan, the Nubi of Uganda, the Arabic trade language in Ethiopia, and some varieties of Chad Arabic — is of particular interest to the point of view taken here: these pidginized and creolized varieties of Arabic demonstrate both the extent and the rate of decay affecting a language in a specific set of circumstances (cf. below, ch. VI).

Of a different nature is the kind of evidence to be found in the so-called *laḥn al-ʿāmma*-treatises, which list and correct the linguistic mistakes made by various categories of people in their use of Arabic (about these treatises, cf. Molan 1978; Anwar 1981). The authors of these prescriptive treatises are not interested in the structure of the colloquial as such, nor is it their intention to correct the speech of the common people, but they concentrate on the kind of mistake that is likely to occur in written texts (Molan 1978:22-30). They will give, for instance, examples of words to be written with /ḍ/ or /ḏ̣/, since these consonants were frequently used incorrectly. As a matter of fact, the confusion of /ḍ/ and /ḏ̣/ can be explained by the development in the dialects, where the two Classical phonemes had merged at an early date, one of the phenomena included by Ferguson (1959:630) in his list of fourteen features, which are used as evidence for the koine-theory (cf. below, ch. II, p. 20). But obviously, the limitation to those mistakes that occur in written texts prevents us from obtaining a full picture of the colloquial, since many of the characteristics of the colloquial were too stigmatized to be used in writing at all. Therefore, the material of the *laḥn al-ʿāmma*-treatises constitutes only the lower limit of the discrepancy that existed between the literary and the colloquial language.

The same disadvantage attaches to the texts in Middle Arabic. This term is normally used for the language of those texts in which we find an attempt at Classical Arabic with varying degrees of success.[7] The nature of Middle Arabic texts prohibits their use as direct witnesses for the spoken language, but they do provide us with some information about it. The spoken language tends to shine through at every step in the mistakes that occur, but, on the other hand, the most patent mistakes do not appear in these texts. The authors evidently tried to avoid those forms that deviated too obviously from the Classical norm, such as the replacement of /q/ with /'/ in Egyptian Middle Arabic, the use of aspectual prefixes in the verbal system, the use of analytical possessive constructions, or the use of the plural first person *nqtlū* in Maghrebine Middle Arabic (cf. Blau 1965:51ff.). This last example is very enlightening, because it demonstrates that what the authors of these texts tried to avoid most was anything that might offend the reader's eyes: the singular first person *nqtl* does occur in written texts, presumably because it is identical with the Classical first person plural of the imperfect, whereas the form *nqtlū* is non-existent in Classical Arabic (Blau 1965:52-53). In his analysis of Judaeo-Arabic Blau concludes that for this variety of Middle Arabic "true dialectal features ... are of relatively rare occurrence" (1965:67-68), and even if they are found, they can never be regarded as the sum total of dialectal characteristics in the period in which the text originated.[8]

In passing we may mention that a similar methodological problem confronts scholars in Romance linguistics, where apart from the structure of the Romance languages the only evidence for the early stages of the popular language consists in observations by grammarians and texts in so-called Vulgar Latin. In reality these texts (from Plautus' comedies to late treatises about cooking and veterinary medicine) are always written in Classical Latin with only glimmerings of the colloquial language. Many misunderstandings concerning the history of the Romance languages have been the result of attemps to use these testimonies as *termini a quo* for the introduction of some linguistic change.[9]

Another parallel between texts in Middle Arabic and in Vulgar Latin is perhaps that in both cases heterodox groups played a considerable role in the propagation of the varieties in question. We might even say that in the case of Middle Arabic, the existence of texts in this variety could be due to the very fact that they were written by Jews and Cristians, for whom the standard of Classical Arabic did not happen to be such an object of reverence as it was for the Muslims. Therefore, they were not under the same kind of pressure to preserve the purity of the Classical standard, the language of the revealed text. It has even been asserted that in the case of Judaeo-Arabic — and possibly also in the case of Christian Middle Arabic — we are dealing with a discrete variety, insofar as the 'faulty' use of the written language within a group led to its adoption as a new standard by that group (Blau 1965:46-50; 1981:180). It is significant, for instance, that the Jewish writer Maymonides used Classical Arabic in some of his works, but Judaeo-Arabic in his letters to his coreligionists. This is ascribed by Blau to the fact that Jewish authors were able to switch between different levels of Arabic, so that they could adapt their style to their public (Blau 1965:25-27). The mother tongue of Jewish communities all over the Islamic world was a colloquial form of Arabic, which may, however, have undergone quite considerable changes as compared to the Arabic used by the Muslims. On the other hand, we also find documents in Middle Arabic written by Muslims, which exhibit the same types of mistakes as those found in Jewish and Christian Middle Arabic documents.[10]

Summing up, I repeat that both the *laḥn al-'āmma*-treatises and the Middle Arabic texts may give us an idea of the minimal discrepancy between Classical language and colloquial, but they can never be used as reliable or exclusive witnesses to the full extent of that discrepancy, nor, for that matter, to the exact chronology of the changes in question. The first attested use in written documents of a linguistic change will always be subsequent to its occurrence in speech, quite apart from the fact that many of the irregularities that occur in texts may never have occurred in the colloquial at all, being only the result of a tendency towards hyper-correction that is very typical of this kind of text (cf. Blau 1965:27ff.). I believe that any attempt to set up a chronology of the evolution of an Arabic dialect with the help of documents is doomed to failure. One such attempt has been made by Garbell (1958), who argues that there were different stages in the development of the phonology of what she calls EMA, i.e. the sedentary dialects of Syria, the Lebanon, and Palestine. With regard to its historical component her paper is largely based on the evidence of documents in which mistakes are mentioned (e.g. a treatise by Saadya Gaon), but there is absolutely no guarantee that the changes mentioned in these documents did not occur earlier. Garbell mentions the levelling influence of the great cultural centres on or near the Eastern shore of the Mediterranean without, however, taking into account the fact that this influence must have been operative from the very beginning of the Islamic period, at least if one accepts the normative status of the *'Arabiyya*. This means that we can never trust the contemporary written texts, and, consequently, that it is very doubtful whether we can set up a satisfactory chronology with their help.

There is one source, however, that provides us, so to speak, with an eye-witness account of the changes that occurred in Arabic. I have stated above that the testimony of the grammarians is a very strong argument for the thesis that the Bedouin continued to speak their pre-Islamic dialects with its 'Classical' features. The traditional account of the development of the science of grammar in Islamic culture (cf. Semaan 1968:21ff.; Versteegh 1977:5-7) — which is normally rejected in Western histories of Arabic grammar — states that after the period of the conquests the Arabic language was corrupted by the new speakers, especially in the cities, and that this threatened to affect the recitation of the *Qur'ān*. It was therefore decided to codify the Classical language. We do not know for sure on whose initiative this step was taken, but most sources mention the role of Abū l-Aswad ad-Du'alī (d. 69/688?) in combination with that of the fourth caliph, 'Alī (cf. the above mentioned sources and Carter 1968:1-2). Two problems confronted the early grammarians: the existence of numerous variant readings of the *Qur'ān* and of the classical poems; and the mistakes made by the new converts who tried, without much success, to speak the language of their rulers, that was at the same time the language of their new religion.

The grammarians attempted to solve the problems of the variant readings by developing criteria that might help them to select the 'correct' ones from among the multitude of only slightly differing readings. Their most important criterion was the living language, i.e. the language of the pure Bedouin who had not yet been corrupted by contact with the sedentary population. This development was interrupted when the authoritative edition of the *Qur'ān*, which had been ordered by the third caliph, 'Uṯmān, gained general acceptance around the end of the 1st century of the Hiğra, i.e. 1st half of the 8th century A.D. (cf. Beck 1945; 1946). From now on, *verbatim* transmission of the *Qur'ān* became imperative, and the grammarians had to divert their attention elsewhere. This partially motivated them to engage in the theoretical study of language and this in turn led to the development of the system of grammar as we know it from the times of al-Ḫalīl (d. 175/791) and Sībawayhi (d. 177/793) onwards.[11]

The second problem, that of the mistakes against correct speech on the part of the new converts, led to an awareness of the need to protect the Classical language against what was termed *laḥn*, i.e. in general any mistake against the rules of grammar, but specifically the incorrect use of the case-endings, which became, as it were, the *shibboleth* of bad education and bad manners (for the term *laḥn*, cf. Fück 1950:128-35; Corriente 1976:71, n. 2; Versteegh *forthcoming* a).

The details of this early development have been set forth elsewhere; here I wish to emphasize the importance of data drawn from the history of Arabic grammar to the history of the Arabic language. Unless we reject the testimony of the Arab grammarians as a body, we have to accept their judgment about the opposition of pure Bedouin speech to corrupted urban speech. To put it more bluntly: when Abū 'Amr ibn al-'Alā' (d. 154/770) asserts that only by living for forty years on and off among the nomadic tribes did he succeed in learning the living Classical language with case-endings and all, we either have to call him a liar, or to accept that throughout the first centuries of Islam the Bedouin tribes did indeed preserve the Classical language as it had been spoken before the period of the conquests. This is confirmed by the reports in the sources according to which aristocrats, even caliphs, sent their sons into the desert to learn pure Arabic (Danner 1975:579ff.): although in themselves these reports may be the reflection of the idealization of Bedouin society and culture, combined with the other data they warrant the conclusion that the Bedouin did not lose their Classical Arabic until after a few centuries. We have seen above that this view has far-reaching consequences for our understanding of the history of Arabic before the coming of Islam.

A further corroboration of the conclusion that even after the period of the conquests the Old Arabic of the Ǧāhiliyya — i.e. in my definition the Classical language — was still used in everyday intercourse, may be found in the numerous anecdotes that are transmitted concerning the speech of the new converts. Normally, these anecdotes, which make fun of the new converts' mistakes in Arabic grammar, are used as evidence for the inability on their part to speak Arabic properly, and, of course, they do show that the new speakers of Arabic modified the language to a considerable degree. But these anecdotes also show something else: it is inconceivable that the new speakers should have gone to the trouble of attempting to use the case-endings, if they had not heard those endings being used in normal speech by their masters. The sentence *tuwuffiya abānā wa-taraka banūna* "our father [acc.] has died and left sons [nom.]" in the mouth of a convert (Sīrāfī, *Aḫbār* 17-18) proves not only that this man did not know the rules of the nominal case-endings, but also that these rules were still in force for at least some of the Arabs, and the Old Arabic norms were at that time still alive.

Although it is obvious that in the long run the Bedouin did not preserve their purity of speech, their dialects have retained more conservative features than those of the sedentary population, as will be apparent from the following list of features that are typical of modern Bedouin dialects. It must be remembered, though, that in many cases Bedouin dialects have been affected by prolonged contact with urban centres.[12] In the peninsula, where the conservative character of the Bedouin dialects is most pronounced, we find the following features:[13]

- no *imāla* or *tafḫīm* in inlaut (Fischer & Jastrow 1980:103);
- in many areas preservation of the diphthongs *ay* and *aw* instead of *e* and *o* (Fischer & Jastrow 1980:103);
- the original *a*, *i*, *u* are preserved as independent phonemes in the West

and the South-West of the peninsula (Fischer & Jastrow 1980:104);
- almost everywhere the interdentals remain, with the exception of cities such as Mecca and Aden (Fischer & Jastrow 1980:104-105); in one area, Daṯīna, we do not even find the general merger of /ḍ/ (> /l/) and /ḏ̣/ (Fischer & Jastrow 1980:106);
- the Bedouin dialects of the peninsula show an extremely conservative syllable structure (Fischer & Jastrow 1980:107-108), except in Ḏofarī and Ristāq;
- the accentual system is conservative (Fischer & Jastrow 1980:109);
- there is gender distinction in the 2nd and 3rd person plural of the pronouns and the verbs (Fischer & Jastrow 1980:111-12), except in the cities Mecca, Aden, and Riyad;
- in the Bedouin dialects and in Yemenite Arabic the IVth verbal measure is still productive (Fischer & Jastrow 1980:116-17);
- the internal passive of the Ist measure is preserved in Ristāq, as well as in some Bedouin dialects of North-Africa (Fischer & Jastrow 1980:117), and in the Ḥassāniyya dialect of Mauretania (Zavadovskij 1981:35-36);
- the Bedouin dialects are in general distinguished by their preservation of the inflectional endings *-īn* and *-ūn* as against the sedentary dialects (Fischer & Jastrow 1980:118);
- the use of the verbal preformatives is very limited (cf. below, ch. II, p. 18), so much so that in some areas the presence or absence of the preformative may be regarded as the most important distinctive feature between sedentary and nomadic dialects (cf. for the Syro-Palestinian and North-Arabian area Palva 1969a:15);
- the use of the *status constructus* is much more widespread than in the sedentary dialects; in fact, most Bedouin dialects ignore the analytical possessive construction (Harning 1980:158-81);
- there are vestiges of nunation, the old inflectional ending that indicated indetermination (Fischer & Jastrow 1980:120).[14].

At first sight, it might seem contradictory that we also find innovatory features in Bedouin dialects, but the fact that they are in general more conservative does not prevent them, of course, from following their own independent development, and single features that are characteristic of language change in New Arabic may occur in Bedouin language as well. It is often difficult in the case of dialect innovation to determine whether we are dealing with an independent internal development, or with the result of the inevitable attraction of the urban centres, which has always been strong in the Arab world. The cultural importance of the Bedouin groups, particularly those who had remained in the peninsula, used to be much less strongly felt.

In the foregoing I have attempted to sketch briefly my understanding of the first stage of the history of the Arabic language, and to survey the sources at our disposal for its subsequent development. In what follows I shall set forth some ideas that might help to elucidate the causes or mechanisms that brought about the new dialects. Chapter II briefly discusses the common characteristics of these dialects as against the Classical language, and surveys the most important theories that have been advanced so far in order to explain the transition from Old Arabic to New Arabic. Chapter III introduces some basic notions from the field of pidgin- and creole-studies, which, it is suggested, may contribute towards a better understanding of the nature of the process the Arabic language underwent in the early stages of its development. Chapter IV discusses the socio-linguistic context of the Arab conquests. The next chapter explores the possibilities of applying the concepts of pidginization and creolization to the history of the Arabic dialects, and provides some examples of pidginizing tendencies in these dialects. The possible contribution in this respect of modern Arabic pidgins and creoles is discussed in chapter VI. Finally, chapter VII summarizes my conclusions and seeks to compare the history of the Arabic language with parallels elsewhere, notably in the history of the Romance languages.

Obviously, my view of the history of the Arabic language and the origin of the Arabic dialects is not in line with most contemporary thinking on this subject. Still, the introduction of the concept of pidginization is not as novel as one might believe, since it was already used by Fück in his seminal book on the *ʿArabiyya* (1950). In this connection I may also mention that the study of the Arabic dialects has received a new impetus through a recent publication on an Arabic creole in Africa, Nubi, by Heine (1982). What is more, there is some poetic justice in defending almost exactly the same position as that held by one of the eminent historians of the Arabs, Ibn H̲aldūn (d. 808/1406) in his *Muqaddima*. As I shall more than once have to point out below, I reject the prevalent attitude towards the Arabic sources. I concede that these sources contain exaggerations, biased selections, omissions, sometimes even slanderous and tendentious reports — just as any other kind of source — but to assert that all Islamic historiography is a mere fake — as, for instance, Crone & Cook (1977) come very close to saying — is counter-effective and downright unfair to Arab scholars of earlier times, most of whom tried to document the sources of their knowledge as conscientiously and as fully as possible.

I should like, therefore, to conclude this introductory chapter by quoting Ibn Ḫaldūn's views on what happened during that first century of the Muslim era. After having explained that language is a habit, he says:[15]

> When Islam came and they [sc. the Arabs] left the Ḥiğāz ... and started to mingle with the non-Arabs, their [linguistic] habit began to change as the result of the different ways of speaking they heard from those who tried to learn Arabic, for hearing is the source of linguistic habits. As a result of this influence, Arabic became corrupt ... Their scholars began to fear, lest the [linguistic] habit should become completely corrupted, and lest people should grow used to it, so that the *Qur'ān* and the Tradition would become incomprehensible. Consequently, they deduced laws from their [sc. of the Arabs] ways of speaking, that were universally valid for this habit ..., and that could be used as a canon for the rest of their speech.

I believe that if we disregard the ethical overtones of the notion 'corruption', this is a fair account of the development of Arabic, and in the next pages I shall try to revindicate Ibn Ḫaldūn's opinion.

NOTES

1) Cf. the contrast between Eastern *min-him* and Western *bi-ġulāmuhum* mentioned already by Sībawayhi, *Kitāb* II, 321.

2) Cf. also Versteegh *forthcoming* b. A similar conclusion concerning the distinction between colloquial and literary language in the Ǧāhiliyya is reached by Wansbrough (1977:85-118); his arguments, however, differ completely from mine.

3) Cf. Zwettler (1978) and the reviews of this work by Schippers (1980) and Heinrichs (1982). The arguments for and against are summarized by Fischer (1982:86-89). For an early reference to the analogy between poetic koine and Homeric dialect cf. Fischer 1905:662, n.4.

4) Cf. Fleisch 1974:22; for a general discussion of the attitude of early grammarians towards 'corruption of speech', cf. Versteegh *forthcoming* a. Rabin's remark (1951:18) that it is hard to understand why the Arab grammarians never realized that their judgments about the language of the Bedouin were influenced by the current fashion begs the question of the value of these judgments.

5) Cf. Diem 1973; a much more careful conclusion concerning the possibility of using the spelling conventions in the early qur'ānic manuscripts is given by the same author in a later publication (1981:381); cf. also Zwettler 1978:149-51. On the value of the Nabataean and other inscriptions for the determination of the case-system in the Ǧāhiliyya, and the chronology of its change, cf. Blau 1977:9ff., who underlines the fact that these were border-dialects, influenced by Aramaic, and as such not very reliable as evidence.

6) Cf. Fleisch 1974:14, n. 2: "Différences évidemment moins grandes que maintenant après des siècles d'évolution du langage arabe, mais différences réelles".

7) For the terminology cf. Blau 1981a:215. Blau proposes to use 'Middle Arabic' for the language of texts with a varying mixture of Neo-Arabic, Classical Arabic, and pseudo-corrections. 'Neo-Arabic' is his term for what is called here 'New Arabic'.

8) In connection with the chronology the study of the language of the earliest papyri is of the utmost importance. I have not been able to consult the unpublished thesis by Hopkins (1978) on this subject, but from the quotations by Fischer (1982:90) and Blau (1981a:239) it appears that the analysis of the language of the papyri confirms the early date of the changes.

9) About the analogies between the study of the history of the Arabic dialects and of the Romance languages, cf. below, ch. VII, p. 133ff., and Versteegh *forthcoming* b. For an analysis of the sources of 'Vulgar Latin' that is interesting to arabists as well, cf. Maurer 1962:15-34; 74: "Os plebeísmos encontrados nos textos e nas censuras dos retores e gramáticos são geralmente os que conseguiram penetrar camadas sociais mais altas, ameaçando corromper o latim mais puro dos círculos cultos de Roma", a conclusion that seems to be valid for Middle Arabic texts as well.

10) Cf. Blau 1965:123-32. General information about the Jewish and Christian forms of Middle Arabic in Blau 1966-67; 1972-73; 1980.

11) Cf. Versteegh 1982:41f and *forthcoming*. For a different view cf. Carter (1968) who stresses the intimate connection between the development of the study of law and the study of grammar.

12) A good example is mentioned by Blau 1977:24, and n. 121, quoting Boris 1958 s.v.: the verb *šāf* — typical of sedentary dialects — occurs in Marazig Arabic in the speech of the men, but not in that of the women; here we see the influence of sedentary culture and language actually at work. At times, the influence was the other way round, one famous example being that of the dialect of Bagdad, where the Muslims adopted a Bedouin type of dialect of the *gilit*-group, whereas the Baġdādī Jews and Christians retained their *qəltu* type of 'Irāqī Arabic, cf. Blanc 1964.

13) Cf. also Johnstone (1967) for relevant data from the Bedouin and the sedentary dialects in the Gulf states; examples of linguistic conservatism from North-east Arabian dialects are given by Ingham 1982:35ff.

14) But cf. Blau 1965:167-212, who is rather sceptical; about the development of the *tanwīn*-ending into a connective element *-an* in Spanish Arabic, cf. Corriente 1977:121-22. According to Ingham (1982:53-56) the indefinite marker *-in* in rural Naǧdī Arabic is characteristic for Bedouin speech.

15) Ibn H̱aldūn, *Muqaddima* 546: *fa-lammā ǧā'a l-Islām wa-fāraqū l-Ḥiǧāz ... wa-ḫālaṭū l-'Aǧam taġayyarat tilka l-malaka bimā alqā ilayhā s-sam' min al-musta'ribīna wa-s-sam' abū l-malakāt al-lisāniyya wa-fasadat bimā ulqiya ilayhā ... wa-ḫašiya ahl al-'ulūm minhum an tafsuda tilka l-malaka ra'san wa-yaṭūla l-'ahd bihā fa-yanġaliqa l-Qur'ān wa-l-Ḥadīṯ 'alā l-mafhūm fa-stanbaṭū min maǧārī kalāmihim qawānīn li-tilka l-malaka muṭṭaridatan ... yaqīsūna 'alayhā sā'ir anwā' al-kalām.*

CHAPTER II

THE TRANSITION FROM OLD ARABIC TO NEW ARABIC

In the preceding chapter I have attempted to show that before the coming of Islam there was a single Arabic language, which was used both as a colloquial and as a 'literary' language. After the conquest this unity was broken: Old Arabic continued to be used as the prestige language of literature and scholarship, and possibly as the language of the court and of high society. This variety is variably called Classical Arabic, Classical Standard, or *al-'Arabiyya*. Alongside this literary language there arose a multitude of urban colloquials, normally referred to as 'Arabic dialects'. We have seen above that at least during the first period of Islam the Bedouin retained the Old Arabic language as colloquial. In the modern world the Arabic dialects contrast with the modern form of the Classical standard (referred to as Modern Standard Arabic, Modern Classical Arabic, or Modern Arabic), which serves as the high variety in the Arabic diglossia as described by Ferguson (1959a). Although it is true that the present socio-linguistic and political situation in the arabophone world exerts a constant pressure on the Modern Standard, which leads to the development of regional varieties of this language, it still remains unquestionably a highly uniform language that is essentially identical with the Classical language.

The differences between dialects and (Modern) Standard manifest themselves in different ways. In the first place, the dialects exhibit common deviations from the Classical norm, ranging from very general identical trends, such as the loss of the case-endings and the reduction of the opposition /i/ - /u/, to highly specific similarities, such as the replacement of Classical *ra'ā* with dialectal *šāf* "to see". In the second place there are many points in which the dialects differ from both the Classical language and from each other. This is the case with many items in the lexicon — although most of the dialects share a considerable part of their vocabulary, there are even in the basic vocabulary list items for which they differ (cf. Cadora 1976) — but also with other parts of the linguistic structure. Some of these differences characterize an entire dialect area (e.g., the use of the 1st person singular prefix

MSA

?

?

not in references.

n-, which is typical for Maghrebine Arabic), whereas others are idiosyncrasies of one single dialect. In the third place, there are those cases where all dialects share a tendency that moves them away from the Classical Standard, but select different ways to find a replacement device. It goes without saying that these cases are very important for any theory that wishes to explain the origin of the dialects: they show a combination of divergence and convergence that is one of the fundamental matters to be explained in this connection. Before discussing the current theories, I shall first give a few examples of the third category.

With the disappearance of the case-endings the need arose for a new possessive construction as a replacement for the Classical *status constructus*. Virtually all urban dialects replaced this synthetic construction *kitābu r-rağuli* "book the-man [gen.]" with an analytical one containing a genitive exponent, e.g. (Moroccan) *le-ktab dyal ṛ-ṛažel* "the-book poss. the-man". The interesting point is that many different genitive exponents were selected by the various dialects, so much so that the choice of a specific genitive exponent is highly characteristic of a particular dialect or dialect group (for a list of exponents and an analysis of the construction cf. below, ch. V, p. 92f.). The second example concerns the verbal system. Just as the case-endings disappeared in the dialects, the old distinction between indicative, subjunctive and jussive was no longer operative. In all dialects the resulting form was used in combination with a prefix to indicate various aspects, such as durative or irrealis. But again, each dialect chose different prefixes, e.g., (Egyptian) *b-yiktib* present durative, *ḥa-yiktib* future; (Moroccan) *ka-nekteb* present durative, *ġa-nekteb* future. Again, the choice of a particular combination of aspectual prefixes is characteristic for individual dialects or dialect groups (for an analysis of these combinations of aspectual prefixes, and their aspects, cf. below, ch. V, p. 84ff.). A third example concerns the interrogative adverbs and pronouns. In all modern dialects many Classical adverbs and pronouns have disappeared, and have been replaced by a nominal periphrastic* expression with the meaning of, for instance, "what thing?", "what time?", "what colour?", instead of "what?", "when?", "how?". We shall see below (ch. V, p. 96f.) that this phenomenon is connected with the origins and development of the dialects. Here, I wish to emphasize the fact that, whereas the dialects agree in replacing the interrogative adverbs and pronouns with nominal periphrases, they differ in the specific result. A similar development may be mentioned for the demonstrative adverbs, such as *al-āna* "now" that is replaced by a multitide of demonstrative periphrases (cf. Fischer 1959:143-56).

*use of particle or aux instead of inflection ("did sing" for "sang")

Most theories about the origin of the Arabic dialects limit themselves to an explanation of either the differences or the similarities between the dialects. A major problem in the evaluation of these theories is the complete lack of agreement on the question of chronology, specifically, whether the transition from Old Arabic to New Arabic must be viewed as a sudden break, or as a gradual development already prepared by latent tendencies in an older stage of the language. As we have seen above, most of the discussion concerning the history of the Arabic language concentrates on the presence or the absence of the declensional endings in the pre-Islamic Bedouin dialects. Those who hold that the declensional endings were already in the process of disappearing before the period of the conquests, also situate the beginning of the transition process before the conquests. For them, a sudden break is, therefore, out of the question, as is the attribution of a major role in the development of Arabic to the inhabitants of the conquered territories. On the other hand, those who hold that the Bedouin not only used the inflectional endings before the period of the conquests, but also continued to use them for some time afterwards, are more willing to regard the transition as a sudden break, and to acknowledge some measure of influence on the part of the new speakers of Arabic in the creation of the urban colloquials.

The disappearance of the declensional endings is, however, only part of the picture. As far as I know, nobody has yet asserted that the more spectacular innovations that we find in the modern dialects already existed in the dialects of the Ǧāhiliyya. Here, I am thinking of features such as the replacement of synthetic constructions with analytical ones, the development of a new aspectual system, the reduction or disappearance of a large number of grammatical categories, the reduction of the phonemic inventory, and the introduction of new rules of agreement, etc. While it is true that for many of the features mentioned attempts have been made to point out pre-Islamic precedents, nevertheless, even if it can be shown, for instance that the pre-Islamic synthetic case-system was largely redundant (cf. Corriente 1971-71), or that the reduction of the vocalism in the modern dialects was foreshadowed by the limited contrast of some of the vocalic oppositions in Old Arabic (cf. Ambros 1973-74), the question still remains why these tendencies were actualized in the period after the conquests. For the moment, therefore, I shall leave aside the relatively irrelevant question of whether or not the loss of some of the inflectional endings was already under way during the period of the Ǧāhiliyya (cf. Zwettler 1978:116-56 for a summary of the current opinions on this point), and concentrate here on the explanations that have been put forward for the differences and the similarities of the modern dialects.

According to Ferguson (1959) the common characteristics of the modern dialects as against the Classical Standard can only be explained if we assume that at one time during the period of the conquests there was an interdialectal koine in which the differences between the pre-Islamic dialects had largely disappeared. This post-Islamic koine must, of course, be sharply distinguished from the supposed intertribal language in the Ǧāhiliyya, which is often called the 'poetic koine' (cf. above, ch. I, p. 1ff.). Ferguson's koine resembles much more the linguistic result of the campaigns of Alexander the Great, from which the technical term 'koine' is derived (cf., e.g., Browning 1969:27-58). Ferguson's koine might be called the 'military koine', since it is supposed to have originated in the military settlements of Syria and Egypt, where the intercourse of members from all tribes resulted in the abandonment of the most typical features of each dialect and the subsequent adoption of some kind of intertribal colloquial that was to serve as the basis for the modern dialects. Only thus, Ferguson believes, can we explain the fact that the modern dialects share a number of common innovations, represented by the fourteen features he lists:

1. the loss of the dual in the verbs and the pronouns;
2. the sound shift *a* > *i* in prefixes (*taltala*);
3. the merger of the IIIw and IIIy verbs;
4. the analogous treatment of the geminate verbs, which made them indistinguishable from the IInd measure of IIIw/y verbs;
5. the use of *li-* affixed to the verbs for indirect objects;
6. the loss of polarity in the cardinal numbers 13-19;
7. the velarization of the /t/ in the cardinal numbers 13-19;
8. the disappearance of the feminine elative *fu'lā*;
9. the adjective plural *fu'āl* < *fi'āl*;
10. the suffix for denominal adjectives (nisbe) *-ī* < *-iyy*;
11. the use of the verb *ǧāb* < *ǧā'a bi-* "to bring";
12. the use of the verb *šāf* instead of *ra'ā* "to see";
13. the use of the indeclinable relative marker *illī*;
14. the merger of /ḍ/ and /ḏ̣/.

In his discussion of Ferguson's theory — which, for reasons to be analyzed below, he rejects — Cohen (1970) adds a few common features along similar lines:

15. the occlusive realization of the interdental spirants;
16. the partial or complete disappearance of the *-h-* in the pronominal suffix of the 3rd person masc after consonants;
17. the loss of the gender distinction in the plural of pronouns and verbs;
18. the quadriliteral plural patterns *f‘ālil* instead of *f(a)‘ālīl*;
19. the diminutive pattern *f(u)‘ayyal*;
20. the use of a verbal particle with the imperfect verb to indicate a present durative;
21. the use of an analytical possessive construction.

From the discussion in Fischer & Jastrow (1980:39-48) I add some more common features:

22. the loss of the glottal stop;
23. the reduction of short vowels in open syllables;
24. the reduction of the opposition /i/ - /u/;
25. the assimilation of the feminine endings *-at*, *-ā*, *-ā’* > *-a*;
26. the disappearance of the internal passive;
27. the assimilation of the verbal patterns *fa‘ula* and *fa‘ila*;
28. the tendency to re-analyze biradical nouns as triradical nouns;
29. the loss of the IVth measure;
30. the agreement in number between subject and verbal predicate.
31. the nominal periphrasis of interrogative adverbs.

Although, as Fischer & Jastrow emphasize, there has been very little research into the syntactic differences between dialects and Classical language, these differences are remarkably uniform. It is precisely these syntactic differences that play an important role in my explanation of the process of change, and they will, accordingly, be dealt with in greater detail below (cf. V, p. 99ff.). Here, I shall limit myself to an enumeration of the most important common deviations that have not yet been mentioned:

32. the word order SVO instead of VSO;
33. the use of serial verbs such as *qa‘ada*, *qāma*, *ǧā’a*, etc.;
34. the tendency to use asyndetic constructions with expressions with a modal meaning, such as *lāzim* “must”, *bədd* “want to”, etc.

It is obvious that any theory which tries to explain the origin of the modern Arabic dialects, must minimally explain the similarities represented by these features. In chapter V I shall try to do so for some of them within the framework proposed in this book; in this chapter I shall survey the most important contributions towards an explanation that have been advanced so far. But first, we must ask ourselves, what exactly is the status of these common features? Within the context of Ferguson's theory the fourteen features are the result of a search for similarities shared by the modern dialects against the literary language: they are present in all dialects, but absent in the language of the poems and the *Qur'ān*. Moreover, they must not be explainable by reference to a 'general drift' that operates in every language, irrespective of the socio-linguistic context. To these two conditions Cohen (1970:109) adds a third: the common features must be shared by the sedentary dialects alone, and set them apart from the Bedouin dialects, for which a different origin is claimed. However, the force of the third condition, though it is quite sound from a methodological point of view, is considerably weakened by the fact that we do not know enough about the history of the dialects to be able to cancel out secondary bedouinization of sedentary dialects, or sedentarization of nomadic dialects. There are, of course, features that are very characteristic of Bedouin dialects, in particular their shared conservatism in most points of linguistic structure (cf. above, ch. I, p. 11-13), but even in the case of the most widely cited *shibboleth* — the voiced realization of the /q/ — there are counter-examples, where secondary bedouinization has led to a voiced realization of /q/ even in sedentary dialects, such as Muslim Baġdādī Arabic (on [q] vs. [g] see Blanc 1969; Cohen 1970:111-15). This means that we can never rule out the possibility of Bedouin influence in other cases which are less well documented. It is true, though, that the relative conservatism of the Bedouin dialects is something that has to be explained in any general theory concerning the origin of the modern dialects.

As for Ferguson's conditions, they are of unequal value. Every theory about the origin of the modern dialects has to take into account those features that set apart the modern dialects from the literary language. I should like to add — in view of what has been said above — that within the context of my approach the common features of the modern dialects must differentiate them from the Arabic language in the Ǧāhiliyya as a whole, not just from the language of the poems and the *Qur'ān*. At this point, one possible misunderstanding should be avoided. I have stated above that in my view the pre-Islamic colloquial and the poetic koine were essentially one and the same language. This does, however, not exclude the existence of regional or social variants. Obviously, whatever our views on the nature of the colloquial of the tribes, whether we regard it as identical with the poetic koine or not, it must have been that very same colloquial that constituted the basis for the

Arabic language as it was taken over by the inhabitants of the conquered territories. In some instances there may well have been differences between that colloquial and the poetic koine on some minor point of grammar, in spite of their basic identity. In such cases, the modern dialects must, of course, agree with the colloquial, and not with the poetic koine. One possible instance of such a case may be that of the so-called *taltala* (above, feature 2), for which, as far as we know, the colloquial agreed with the later dialects, whereas the literary koine, or at least the language of the *Qur'ān*, differed from them (cf. Cohen 1970:120-121; Kaye 1976:137ff.).

Ferguson's exclusion of those features that might be explained by reference to a 'general drift' is more problematic. It is certainly relevant to point out that the phenomenon of the disappearance of morphological categories such as the dual is found in other languages as well,[1] but this does not tell us why the loss of the dual took place in Arabic at this particular point in its history, in such a short time, and — to reverse Ferguson's argument — why its loss was incomplete. Likewise, it is relevant to compare the merger of the IIIw and the IIIy verbs in modern Arabic dialects with similar developments in Hebrew and Syriac (Kaye 1976:148), or to compare the behaviour of /i/ and /u/ in Arabic with general Semitic or even 'Proto-Semitic' trends (Ambros 1973-74:91, n. 36, also 82, n.9), but neither comparison can explain the particular combination of changes that took place in Arabic, nor do these and similar comparisons tell us anything about the predictability of these phenomena.

Using the notion of 'general drift' actually boils down to the assertion that because some particular change has taken place there must have been a latent tendency in the language concerned to bring about such a change, in other words: a change has taken place, because it has taken place.[2] Explanations in terms of inherent mechanisms in the languages concerned are used for the history of other languages as well, and they have never led to any tangible results, as long as the mechanisms were not identified. Moreover, as I shall try to show below, the opposition 'common descent' vs. 'independent development' — in which the second member is usually associated with some kind of 'general drift' — is not a very helpful one in discussions concerning the origin of the type of languages or dialects we are dealing with here.

Returning to Ferguson's theory I repeat that any general explanation of the present state of the Arabic dialects must, as he does, take into account the similarities between them. On the other hand, Ferguson's theory does not seem to be equipped to explain the fact that alongside the similarities, the dialects show many differences, not only 'independent differences' — these could be explained with substratal influence, cf. below — but also 'related differences', i.e. those instances where dialects chose different solutions for one and the same tendency, for instance, the substitution of an analytical possessive construction for the Classical *status constructus*. In his critical analysis of the koine-theory Cohen (1970) demonstrates convincingly that there can be no monogenetic explanation for all modern dialects. He concludes that, instead of Ferguson's military koine as a single basis for all dialects, there must have been various centres, from which the innovations spread in a wave-like movement to the surrounding areas: "En somme, on peut bien parler de koinès à propos de dialectes: mais ce sont celles qui se sont constituées indépendamment dans divers centres et qui s'étendent encore sous nos yeux dans diverses régions du monde arabe" (1970:124). Cohen's explanation accounts for the differences between the dialect areas with regard to innovatory features, and for the fact that the dialects do not have all the same replacement device for the Classical synthetic genitive construction, or the same aspectual verbal particles. But the uniformity in purpose and the similarity in tendencies exhibited by the dialects remain unexplained in his modification of the koine-theory. According to Blau (1977:21ff.) the sedentary koine is not the starting point for the modern sedentary dialects, but the final result of linguistic development, homogeneity emerging because of intensive contact between dialects (wave-theory, cf. Bailey 1973:99-101), and because of parallel development (general drift). Both Cohen and Blau concentrate on the differences and do not give an explanation for the similar tendencies in the modern dialects.

In order to explain the differences between the dialects Cohen takes recourse to a substratal theory, and supposes that the differences between the dialect areas were caused by the fact that in these areas there were different substratal areas. Such an explanation only complicates the problem on hand, that of the similar tendencies, since the difference between the various substratal languages makes the identical tendencies even harder to explain (Cohen 1970:124). As a matter of fact, substratal influence is a very convenient way of explaining the existing differences between the modern dialects: the cause of the innovations occurring in these dialects is, according to those theories which base themselves on substratal influence, to be sought in the structure of the languages that were spoken originally by the inhabitants of the conquered territories, for instance, Syriac, Coptic, Persian, Berber, etc. The speakers of these languages, so the substratal theory states, were not able to free themselves completely from the structure of their mother tongues and, consequently, took some of it with them into their new language. As a result, Arabic started to change, and it changed in different ways according to the structure of the substratal language concerned. According to Garbell (1958:304) this influence was not — contrary to what one might believe — stronger at the beginning and weaker in the course of time but, as the newly conquered population learned Arabic, the influence of their substratal languages become increasingly important. In Garbell's view, this process took a long time. In the case of the Mediterranean dialect she describes there was a long period of time in which the two languages, Aramaic and Arabic, coexisted, the structure of the former constantly influencing the speech habits of those who attempted to speak the latter. In my view, it is undoubtedly true that there were areas in which a stable situation of bilingualism obtained — after all there still are some small pockets where Neo-Aramaic has remained in use. But it is doubtful whether in the large cities the original languages stood much chance against the predominance of the Arabic language. I shall come back to this point below (ch. IV, p. 73) but wish to emphasize here that even where the two languages coexisted the 'substratal language' did not automatically put its stamp on the brand of Arabic spoken locally.

As a matter of fact, recent research in the field of Arabic seems to show that this influence should not be overestimated.[3] The position of Diem (1979) is particularly negative: he only recognizes those cases where no parallels for the innovatory features concerned can be adduced from elsewhere in the Arab world, and concludes that substratal influence, at least in the restricted sense of his article, has been exaggerated in the past, and that on the whole its role as a formative factor in the development of the dialects should be minimized. We should take into account that Diem's method is probably too severe: if we exclude all instances of similarities between Arabic and alleged substrates, we completely disregard the possibility of a catalyzing function of the substratal language.[4] But even so, the fact remains that the sum total of demonstrable substratal influence is very small, and that its role as an explanatory factor in a theory concerning the origin of the Arabic dialects is, consequently, not very important.

All theories and issues discussed so far — koine vs. substratal influence, monogenesis vs. parallel development, foreign influence vs. general drift — could be regarded as reflections of the existing convergence and simultaneous divergence of the modern dialects. These terms are used by Diem (1978), who does not regard the development of the Arabic language as very spectacular or revolutionary as compared to, for instance, the development of the Aramaic dialects. We have seen that it is rather difficult to combine within one single theory all features of the modern dialects: the existing theories seem to cancel each other out, independent changes being undermined by the occurrence of so many common innovations, and a common descent being ruled out by the existence of so many differences between the dialects. Nor does it do to attempt to explain the course of the changes by some kind of universal law, a general process of decay that will affect any language (a good example of such an explanation in Blau 1965:14-15): those who take this position must show the universality of each and every feature in the dialects, otherwise they will have to concede in principle the validity of other explanations.[5]

If we now start looking at the other end of the development, and ask ourselves what the linguistic input was for those who wished to learn Arabic in the first period of the Islamic conquests, we are confronted again by the problem of the Arabic language in the Ǧāhiliyya. Theoretically, those who hold that there was a great difference between the colloquial of the tribes and the 'literary' koine have two alternatives in determining the linguistic input for the new kind of Arabic: either the colloquial or the koine. But, whatever our opinion about the linguistic situation in the Arabian peninsula before the conquests, one can hardly believe — with Birkeland (1952:7), Rabin (1955:26), and Cohen (1970:108) — that the poetic koine was the variety of Arabic with which the inhabitants of the conquered territories first became acquainted. Still reasoning along the lines of the accepted theory of pre-Islamic diglossia, one would rather expect the colloquial variety to have been at the basis of the approximations of Arabic produced by the new speakers. I have tried to show above (ch. I) that before Islam there were no essential linguistic differences in the Arabian peninsula — apart from normal regional and stylistic variation — and I believe, therefore, that the question is largely academic.

What is more, it does not even matter very much whether or not the existing minimal differences between the pre-Islamic dialects were koineized (as Fück 1950:4-28 asserts) before the new speakers got the chance to become acquainted with them. The important point is that there were a large mass of people who had to learn Arabic fast without losing too much time. The most salient feature in the history of the Arabic language is that, having been the language of the Bedouin in the Arabian peninsula, it became adopted eventually by the entire population of the conquered territories, in spite of the fact that this population was vastly superior in number to the Arabs who were taking part in the campaigns (cf. below, ch. IV, p. 63ff.). Still, in most studies on the history of the Arabic language, only the Arabs themselves are represented as changing their own language for one reason or another and then handing it down in its new appearance to the non-arabophones within the empire. The latter took it from them exactly as it had been given to them, in spite of the fact that there was nowhere in the provinces a formal system of education to teach everyone Arabic in a systematic manner. When Cohen (1970:108) makes allowances for the corrupting influence of the sedentary population in the provinces that manifested itself in the changes the Arabic language underwent — he even uses the term 'pidgins' for the varieties of Arabic spoken by some groups within that population — he assumes that the normative force of the Classical language was, in the end, strong enough to counter any corrupting influence. In other words, the non-arabophones eventually dropped their old speech habits in order to adopt those of the pure Arabs, never the other way round.[6]

In this connection it is important to emphasize the fact that the differences between the dialects and the Classical language have often been played down. Arabophones themselves frequently either deny the existence of dialects, and regard them as merely occasional mistakes, or they define them as debased varieties of the Classical language only used by women and children, but even then not differing fundamentally from the Classical Standard. They consider the *'Arabiyya* to be the mother tongue of all Arabs, and in this perspective the dialects constitute a corruption of the Classical rules (cf. Ferguson 1968; Diem 1974:1-9). From a synchronic point of view, this attitude is, of course, absurd, since the dialects are in fact everyone's mother tongue, irrespective of social background, education or intelligence, whereas the Classical language is only a learned language, at best incompletely mastered by those who had the chance to go to school. From a diachronic point of view, however, there is much truth in the conception of the dialects as a corruption of the Classical language. The rather harsh term 'corruption' here and elsewhere must, of course, be taken as a descriptive term for the language learning and language change process Arabic underwent, not as an evaluative term for the modern dialects.

For the Arab grammarians, the transition from the old type of Arabic to the new type, i.e. the colloquials, was brought about by the new speakers in the cities, who learned the language of their new masters, but did so imperfectly, and thus succeeded in corrupting the speech habits of the pure Arabs, at least of those who stayed in the cities. In this view, only the Bedouin managed to stay clear of the corrupting decadence of town speech and to preserve the pure Arabic language, at least for a while (cf. above, ch. I, p. 10f.). Obviously, 'corruption' in the terminology of the grammarians was a derogatory term by which they referred not only to the history of the language, but to the development of society as a whole. But I do believe that they were right in one point, namely, that the colloquial of post-Islamic times was not a continuation of a pre-existing *Volkssprache* — as Vollers (1906) asserted — but a 'corruption' of the Classical language, in this view the only variety that had been in use in pre-Islamic times. I differ from the Arab grammarians, though, in that I regard the difference between the two types of Arabic as fundamental, rather than as a collection of mistakes. It goes without saying that both the notion of 'corruption' and that of 'fundamental differences' are useless without any further definition. Both expressions will become clearer when I connect them with the notion of 'pidginization'. The notion 'corruption of speech' has become obsolete in Western studies of the history of the Arabic language, but nevertheless Western Arabists do tend to interpret the data of the dialects in terms of the *'Arabiyya*, either because unconsciously they follow the opinion of the arabophones that the distance between dialect and Classical Standard is not very great, or because they concentrate on a comparison of dialects and *'Arabiyya* on the basis of a historical-comparative method. I believe that it is legitimate to ask whether this method is universally valid, irrespective of the process the language(s) in question underwent.

If one follows the historical-comparative method, research in the field of dialectology — insofar as it does not limit itself to the gathering of data or the drawing up of inventories — will tend to concentrate on the reconstruction of the 'underlying form', i.e. in this context the reflexes of the dialectal forms in the Classical language. Such a reconstruction, even if it is carried out for contrastive purposes, always brings out the genealogical relatedness of the two varieties, and obscures the differences. Moreover, it is largely limited to more directly accessible parts of the language, particularly in phonology and morphology, whereas syntax is mostly left out (although there are important exceptions, e.g. Bloch 1965; Denz 1971). The results of these reconstructions are often very atomistic, stressing the survival of isolated elements of the Classical language in the dialects, and neglecting the fundamental differences.

Inevitably, on the basis of such a method, there will be a tendency to conclude, for instance, that no radical change in the verbal system has taken place. In this view, a form such as Egyptian *b-yiḍrib* "he is hitting" can only be analyzed as the Classical imperfect indicative, minus the ending and plus a prefix *b(i)-* that does not add very much to the meaning of the verb form. Or, to take another example, in this view the active participle used to indicate the perfective aspect, e.g., in Uzbekistan Arabic, will always be analyzed as just that: it remains a participle with a somewhat idiosyncratic construction. Thus, the structure of the verbal system as a whole in the modern dialects becomes obscured, as well as the importance of the fact that a complete transformation of the verbal system has taken place.

Similarly, the preservation of synthetic possessive constructions for some categories of words in a dialect — e.g. for nouns denoting kinship or periods of time (cf. Harrell 1962:194-201 for Moroccan; Harning 1980) — is thought to be more important and more relevant to the study of the modern dialects than the wholesale introduction of replacement devices of an analytical nature, such as *bitā'*, *dyal*, *māl*, *taba'*, etc. (for a more extensive discussion of the analytical construction, see below, ch. V, p. 92f.). Typical of this point of view is also the assertion that the disappearance of the inflectional endings was caused by the elision of the short vowels at the end of words. The fact that in the sound masculine plural the use of the case-endings has been abandoned as well — the former oblique ending *-īn* serving as a plural ending for all grammatical functions — is then regarded as a phenomenon caused by analogy. If one reasons along such lines, one does not feel obliged to explain why it happened to be the accusative ending that took over the functions of the other cases, and not the other way round. Generally speaking, one can say that hardly any explanation is offered at all for the fact that this or that specific change has taken place, and in most cases an inventory of preserved Classical elements is thought to be a sufficient analysis of the relations between dialects and Classical language.[7] This impression of relatedness between dialects and Classical language is strengthened by the fact that for those instances where the two differ, parallels from the pre-Islamic dialects are often pointed out in order to show that the changes concerned were already foreshadowed in an earlier stage of the language before the period of the conquests.

It is also typical of this point of view to state that the isolated dialects of the so-called *Sprachinsel* are good examples of hypertrophied Arabic: being cut off from any contact with the central areas of Arabic culture and Arabic language they seized their chance, so to speak, and developed into wild caricatures of the *'Arabiyya*. The dialects concerned are Maltese, Uzbekistan and Afghanistan Arabic, Cypriot Maronite Arabic, and the Arabic dialects of Central Anatolia.[8] Undoubtedly, in the case of these dialects the influence of the substrate or the adstrate languages, such as Tajik, Persian, Uzbek, Kurdish, Italian, Greek, etc., may be expected to have been stronger than in other dialects.[9] But even in these dialects we should not lose sight of the fact that most phenomena found in them are essentially identical with those found in other modern dialects which had not become isolated at an early time. I prefer, therefore, not to compare the development of dialects spoken in the *Sprachinsel* to that of a living organism or a garden, but to follow the old dictum of areal dialectology, according to which the varieties at the periphery always preserve the oldest forms, which were more difficult to affect by subsequent innovations. Innovations in this case would consist especially in a growing influence of the Classical Standard, which could not reach the isolated dialects outside the sphere of influence of the Islamic empire.[10]

These considerations lead me to regard the peripheral dialects of the arabophone world as representatives of an early stage of the transition from Old Arabic to New Arabic, a stage, in fact, that the other dialects also went through prior to their becoming affected by the normative pressure of the Classical language, which caused their development into their modern form. The only difference between the *Sprachinsel* and the 'central' Arabic dialects is that the isolation of the *Sprachinsel* to some degree prevented — according to the date of the rupture between these dialects and the central area — the kind of levelling towards the Classical Standard that took place in the case of the 'central' dialects, which could hardly escape the influence of the *'Arabiyya*. Consequently, I cannot agree with Diem, when he says (1978:133): "Es ist dem mangelnden Kontakt mit dem arabischen Sprachgebiet zuzuschreiben, wenn diese Dialekte signifikante Sonderentwicklungen akkumulieren und andererseits signifikante Konvergenzerscheinungen mit den nichtarabischen Adstrat- und Superstratsprachen entwickelt haben, beides Faktoren, durch welche sie sich aus der Hauptentwicklungslinie des Arabischen ausgegliedert haben". I should like to argue the contrary that there is no reason at all to suppose that dialects left to their own fate suddenly degenerate,[11] as if the speakers of a language that becomes isolated should gradually forget their former speech habits and change them drastically.

One may perfectly well concede that in cases such as these extensive borrowing from neighbouring languages took place, that perhaps even some grammatical and syntactic calques found their way into the language, but the fact that a language is cut of from its target language (for this expression, cf. below, ch. III, p. 38), as the *Sprachinsel* dialects were cut of from Classical Arabic, can only bring about the discontinuation of a process of levelling, and it can never bring about a degeneration that had not already been present. This is also shown by other cases of linguistic enclaves: the dialects concerned preserve archaic features that have long been abandoned by the mainstream of the language, but they never degenerate in the way the Arabic dialects mentioned above are claimed to have degenerated. The term *Sprachinsel* is derived from the linguistic enclaves in Central and Eastern Europe where German was spoken, mostly among Slavonic languages, and the study of these enclaves reveals that there is no degeneration at all to be found in them.[12] I hope to show below (ch. VI) that the situation of the isolated Arabic dialects is not dissimilar to that of the Arabic creoles that originated in the last century in Central and Eastern Africa, such as Nubi Arabic.

One of the criteria to determine whether we are dealing with an isolated dialect of Arabic is the presence or absence of loans from the Classical language. Dialects that have been in constant contact with the Classical Standard always contain such loans, which present some characteristic features that set them apart from the inherited stock, similar to the *formation populaire* vs. the *formation savante* in the Romance languages: lengthened vowels in pretonic open syllables contrasting with the elision of vowels in this position in the inherited words, e.g. *mūdīr* "director" as against *kbīr* "large" in Syrian Arabic (Grotzfeld 1965:13); the use of sibilants instead of interdentals contrasting with the dialectal shift of interdentals to dentals in those dialects that did not preserve the interdentals, e.g. *sanya* ("second (of time)" as against *tāni* "second" (Grotzfeld 1965:7), both reflexes of the Classical *ṯāni(ya)*. The presence of such doublets is highly characteristic of dialects that have remained within the sphere of influence of the Classical language. A similar criterion is the use of hyperurbanisms which will be conspicuously absent in the speech of those who speak one of the isolated dialects, whereas they form an integral part of the socio-linguistic make-up of the 'normal', i.e. 'classicizing' dialects (cf. Diem 1974:29-30; 107-108; for a discussion of hyperurbanisms in Middle Arabic, cf. Blau 1965:27ff.). These criteria will be discussed again in connection with the notion of 'decreolization', one of the decisive factors in the development of the Arabic dialects (cf. below, ch. III, p. 41; ch. IV, p. 76; ch. VI, p. 125f., ch. VII, p. 138). One final point needs to be mentioned here. If we regard the 'central' dialects, i.e., all dialects outside the periphery which lie within the sphere of influence of the social, political, and cultural centres of the Arab world, as 'classicizing', a certain circularity is involved, when we start to analyze the 'pure' dialect. Dialect speakers move about on a continuum that stretches from low to high, and it is impossible to divide this continuum into discrete, pre-constituted varieties, as for instance, Badawī's (1973) five levels of Egyptian Arabic. This means that the definition of pure dialect is a theoretical construct, an artificial cutting up of a continuous scale. A similar problem attaches to the distinction between Standard English and Jamaican Creole to mention an example from outside the Arab world (cf. Sutcliffe 1982:113-19). The status of 'pure' dialect becomes even more urgent in those cases where decreolization is posited as a factor in the past which is supposed to have led to the actual disappearance of basilectal traits or the emergence and subsequent predominance of acrolectal traits (e.g., the synthetic genitive, cf. below, ch. V, p. 94f.). Several answers may be given to this objection. In the first place, new methods of fact finding in Arabic dialectology may lead to a more realistic picture of the actual usage than the existing dialect grammars which all too often represent a type of speech that has been influenced demonstrably by the wish of the informants to embellish their speech. In the second place, new models of linguistic description may be applied to the dialect material. Recent research (cf. below, ch. III, n. 7) has shown that it is possible to divide the continuum not into discrete varieties, but according to a hierarchy of features produced by the speakers themselves, in which the co-occurrence of certain features determines their position on the linguistic scale. Finally, observation of actual patterns of classicization may lead to the identification of those classicizing traits which are used as markers of upgrading (cf. below, ch. VI, n. 11). Similarly, a comparison with non-decreolized varieties of Arabic may give an idea of the extent to which the factor of classicization operates in the Arabic dialects (cf. below, ch. VI, p. 117).

NOTES

1) For instance, in Hebrew (Blau 1961:130ff.; 1977:19-20), not to mention the case of the Indo-European languages, which, with very few exceptions, such as Lithuanian and Slovenian, have completely lost the category of the dual in their present form.

2) For a discussion of the notion of 'drift' in connection with Sapir's theory of language history, see Bynon 1977:250; for a comparison with the use of this notion in Romance linguistics, see Versteegh *forthcoming* b. A similar tendency to explain language change in terms of 'general drift' is found in the study of the history of Afrikaans: its development has frequently been attributed to a 'general drift' in the West-Germanic languages that was held responsible for all changes in Afrikaans *vis-à-vis* its Dutch ancestor, with the exclusion of any other influence, cf. below, ch. III, p. 52.

3) See, for example, Bishai 1960; 1961; 1962 on Coptic influence in Egyptian Arabic; Diem 1979, especially about South Arabic influence in Yemenite Arabic.

4) Diem 1979:15-17. A similar methodological problem is found in pidgin studies; one example is that given by Valdman (1977a:175) who refuses to explain the use of possessive determiners as postpositions in French-based creoles exclusively in terms of either French possessive constructions in popular French, or the syntactic sttructure of many West African languages, but tries to combine both explanations: one influence, that of the constructions in French colloquial speech, reinforcing the other, the substratal influence of West African languages; cf. also Valkhoff 1972:79. On multiple conditioning see below, ch. III, p. 59.

5) This argument is borrowed from Bickerton 1977:65, who applies it in a different, yet in some ways similar context.

6) A similar one-sided view of the socio-linguistic context in which second language learning takes place prevailed for a long time in pidgin studies, witness the many attemps to reduce all differences between pidgin languages and relate them all to a common ancestor, cf. below, ch. III, p. 49ff.

7) Thus, one often finds in dialect grammars the statement that most of the derived forms of the Classical verb are present in a particular dialect, whereas the list of the derived forms shows clearly enough that in most cases they are 'represented' by a few lexicalized items, or borrowings from the Classical Standard. In the dialect of Daragözü, for instance, Jastrow (1973:44) says: "Belegt sind alle Stämme mit Ausnahme des IV ...", but for the IIIrd and Xth measure he quotes only one example, which makes the status of these categories very doubtful; cf. also Fischer & Jastrow 1980:70 "Die neuarabischen Dialekte haben die bekannten, durch ihre Häufigkeit herausragenden 10 Verbalstämme des Altarabischen als Typen verbaler Stammbildung übernommen. Nur der IV. Stamm *'afʿala* ist in vielen Dialekten verloren gegangen". It seems preferable to follow the more careful statement about the dialect of Tetuan by Singer (1958:249), and treat the various verbal types not as direct continuants of the Classical measures, except in the case of borrowings from the Classical language, cf. also Borg 1982:137.

8) On Maltese: Aquilina 1970; on Uzbekistan Arabic: Fischer 1961; Tsereteli 1956; on Afghanistan Arabic: Sīrat 1973; Kieffer 1980; on Cypriot Maronite Arabic: Tsiapera 1969 in combination with the very thorough and devastating review of this book by Jastrow 1977; Newton 1964; Borg 1982; the Arabic dialects of Central Anatolia: Sasse 1971; Jastrow 1973; 1978.

9) Cf. Diem 1978:133-34. As an example I may mention the use of the Persian *izafet*-construction in Uzbekistan Arabic, cf. Fischer 1961:244, but even there this construction is rare. For the influence of Greek in Cypriot Maronite Arabic, see Jastrow 1977:260, and n. 3, and especially Borg 1982:223-25. One should be careful not to attribute every similarity between the Arabic dialect and an adstratal language to external influence; in some cases the presence of the adstratal language may have acted as a catalyzer, as for instance in the case of the indefinite article in Cypriot Arabic: in view of the fact that the development of an indefinite article is common to many Arabic dialects (e.g., Moroccan, 'Irāqī, Uzbekistan Arabic) it is hardly necessary to attribute this development in Cypriot Arabic to the exclusive influence of Cypriot Greek, cf. Borg 1982:218.

10) Cf. Valdman 1977a:164-65 for a parallel from the history of French creoles.

11) Such a degeneration is implied, for instance, by Jastrow (1973:6) who speaks of "Anzeichen einer beginnenden Verwilderung, wie sie nur in wenigen, extrem isolierten Sprachinseln Platz gegriffen hat".

12) Cf. Kuhn 1934; for the German dialects in Slovakia see Valiska 1980; for the German dialects in the U.S. see Gilbert 1971; for the effects of isolation in general see Weinreich 1953:90. A good example of an isolated dialect is provided by a recent study of the Albanian dialect of Mandrica (Bulgaria) by Sokolova (1983); the author shows that after several centuries of isolation in which it underwent the influence of Greek, Turkish, and Bulgarian, this dialect still retains its archaic form.

CHAPTER III
PIDGINIZATION AND CREOLIZATION

In the preceding chapters I have asserted, firstly, that the role of the new speakers of Arabic in the conquered territories is consistently underestimated or neglected by most theories that attempt to explain the origin of the Arabic dialects and, secondly, that the differences between the old and the new types of Arabic do not consist only in a few modifications of the sound system and the morphology of the language, sometimes predetermined by latent tendencies in the pre-Islamic dialects, but, on the contrary, in a radical restructuring of the entire linguistic structure of the Arabic language. In order to find a satisfactory explanation for the changes that came to differentiate the new colloquials from the Classical Standard, we shall have to account for both the divergent and the convergent features of the dialects. In the preceding chapters I have occasionally pointed out the methodological similarities between the theories with which arabists attempt to explain the origin and development of the Arabic dialects and, on the other hand, the theories that have been advanced by specialists in the field of pidgin studies. In my view, we can find an explanation for the problem on hand by using the results of recent research in the origin of pidgin languages, transferring these results to the field of Arabic and applying them to the problem of the relationship between Classical Arabic and the dialects. This implies that in my view there is a correlation between the socio-linguistic situation accompanying the growth of a pidgin language and the situation that obtained during the early period of the Islamic conquests, in which we have to situate the origin of the modern dialects. The next step will be to correlate this situation with the ensuing linguistic changes in both pidgin languages and Arabic dialects. In this chapter I should like to summarize relevant data from pidgin linguistics. In the next two chapters I shall try to demonstrate that these data can be applied successfully to the study of the history of Arabic.

Within the last years, the problem of linguistic change has become a highly controversial topic, not only of historical linguistics, but also of socio-linguistics and psycho-linguistics. The description of change and variability, as well as research into the mechanisms that bring about changes in a language are issues on which there seems to be less agreement than ever. Let us simply assume that there is such a thing as a normal type of linguistic change in a language that develops gradually while undergoing the effects of the process of language acquisition by first language learners in a given linguistic community with limited foreign influence where the language is handed down from generation to generation.[1] Let us further assume that such a language typically undergoes certain gradual, from time to time maybe even abrupt changes, without, however, being affected by a process of reduction or simplification, or by a complete restructuring on all linguistic levels. We know, empirically, that there are languages that have been affected by just such a process. There are situations in which certain sudden political and/or social events take place, resulting in a mass process of second language acquisition by people from outside the original linguistic community within a short period of time and without formal linguistic instruction. The hypothesis is that a language when subjected to such a process is affected by it drastically.

There are doubtless many situations of the type sketched above, and one could classify them along a scale, according to various parameters, such as the intensity with which the cultures involved meet or clash, or the length of time during which the members of one culture are exposed to the language of another culture. One might even deny the possibility of distinguishing at all between discrete types of language encounters, and consequently treat the kind of situation described above, instead, as part of a continuum of language contact. The common factor in all these situations is that language learning is always involved and, given the present state of our knowledge of the underlying mechanisms, it does not seem advisable at this moment to go beyond the observation that we are dealing here with a special case of language learning in a special situation.

If we accept that there is a strong correlation between the type of language encounter and the changes affecting the languages concerned, we must then find out what is the common denominator connecting all those instances of languages being changed radically in a period of social, cultural, or political upheaval. Obviously, the degree of intensity of the contact between two languages will exert some influence on the nature of the changes (cf. Rickford 1977:193), but the main point is that in spite of the differences that may exist between various situations of the type we are discussing here, they are all connected by the one fact that is directly relevant to linguistic structure, namely that they involve a mass process of second language learning. I argue that in all those cases where such a process has taken place there is a corresponding similarity in the linguistic changes at work in the languages involved, and that consequently, whenever such drastic changes are found in a given language, and whenever we can prove that a mass process of second language learning has taken place in the history of that language, we are dealing with the same phenomenon. For this phenomenon I shall use the term 'pidginization'. In his study of Marathi Southworth (1971:255) poses the question of whether there is a difference between extensive borrowing and pidginization. He is concerned with finding out if Marathi is a pidginized variety of an Indo-Aryan language, or an Indo-Aryan language with many elements from the neighbouring Dravidian languages. I believe that such a question cannot be answered by linguistic criteria alone, but only by a combination of historical and linguistic data. Southworth's article is relevant to the history of Arabic for more than one reason: as we shall see below, the case of the Arabic dialects, too, is one in which we must decide whether or not the language ever underwent a sharp break in its history. I believe that the answer in both cases is the same: in accordance with the definition given above, I shall use the term 'pidginization' only when it is possible to prove that (a large number of) speakers of another language had to learn the language in question in a short time without any formal instruction.

Whether or not we shall call the resulting language a 'pidgin' is hardly relevant. The term 'pidgin' has become the current designation for a number of specific languages, and it should perhaps remain reserved for those languages. Typically, the languages that are referred to by this name are reduced varieties of languages of major European nations that were broken down in a fairly specific way within the characteristic socio-cultural setting of a 'plantocracy', i.e. a large plantation with a mixed population and a very marked barrier between the masters and the slaves. Other current terms — 'language of contact', 'lingua franca', 'sabir', 'trade language', 'koine' — could then be used for other specific types of linguistic environment or linguistic encounter (cf. Ferguson & DeBose 1977). But the important thing is that we do not need a taxonomy of contact situations before we can start comparing with each other complexes of changes that have taken place in languages which originated as a result of historically unrelated events. Nor do we have to demand a complete analogy between the historical events that helped shape the languages we wish to compare, as Schlieben-Lange (1977) does in her discussion of pidginization/creolization in the Romance languages.

It is possible to make long lists of differences or similarities between chains of events that have led to the development of languages that are commonly referred to as 'pidgin languages' or 'creoles', but, unless we identify within the complex of events the relevant circumstances — the causes of pidginization/creolization — we do not know what we are comparing, since we have no way of distinguishing between significant and accidental circumstances. A condition of complete analogy without the identification of relevant factors — i.e. factors that can be related to the process of change — only leads to the kind of discussion in which we start asking whether or not a given language is a pidgin, instead of finding out if it ever underwent the above mentioned process of second language learning. In my view, the term 'pidgin' is a convenient label for the result of a certain type of process in which languages are broken down in an abnormal situation of acquisition, and not something a language as such can be. I therefore agree with Bickerton's remark, made in a study of the development of Hawaiian Pidgin English, but useful in any discussion of pidginization in which the term 'pidgin' is used (1977:52): "True understanding of these phases has thus far been inhibited by an outmoded form of thinking that treats 'pidgins' as *states* or *entities* rather than processes. To reify is to falsify ...".[2]

As soon as children start using the pidginized version of a language as their first language, we say that the language is creolized. In this definition the two processes of pidginization and creolization are closely related, as well as distinct. The basic similarity between them is that in both cases a language is learnt from a limited input. In the case of pidginization the exposure of the learners to the target language, i.e. the language they wish to learn, is limited, either because of the socio-cultural distance or the infrequency of contacts between them and the speakers of the target language, or because of the removal of the target language, or maybe even because of an intentional limited supply on the part of the speakers of the target language, who use some kind of 'foreigner talk' in their intercourse with the new speakers.[3] In the case of creolization it is the inherently limited pidginized version of a language that serves as input. The basic differences between the two processes is that essentially pidginization is a subcategory of second language learning, whereas creolization is a subcategory of first language learning.

In my view, therefore, the term 'creolization' should be reserved for those cases where a pidginized variety of language — or in general an unnatural language[4] — becomes the mother tongue for a number of speakers. Such a definition is based on historical circumstances: at the most we can show that a process of creolization correlates with certain phenomena in the resulting language, but without knowing the history of the language in question we can never determine its creolizing nature from its structure alone. This does not, of course, exclude the possibility that in the future support may be found for the much stronger claim that creolized (and pidginized) varieties exhibit distinctive features that can be detected without having recourse to the study of the history of those languages. In itself this claim has some plausibility: I shall discuss below the assumption that both pidginization and creolization are governed by universal strategies that — irrespective of the source material produced for the benefit of the new language learners — will operate on the limited input, and seek to replace it with a new system, in the case of pidginized languages a reduced system with limited possibilities of communication, in the case of creolized varieties an expanded version of the pidginized variety that can serve as a natural mother tongue. It must be emphasized, though, that at the moment there is no such test available (cf. below, ch. VII, p. 142).

It would be simplifying matters to distinguish between a pidginizing stage in which a language is broken down and reduced, and a subsequent stage of creolization in which the pidgin is subjected to complication and expansion of the linguistic resources. It is obvious that the speech habits of the first language learners, who are receiving the pidginized variety from their parents as their first language, are bound to have a profound effect on the speech habits of those for whom the language continues to be a second language.[5] In many areas these two stages will be simultaneous within the same linguistic community, albeit not for the individual speaker, who is either speaking an approximation of some target language, or reconstructing a mother tongue from a simplified input. But for the community as a whole these different approaches coexist and result in the presence of a range of varieties which are constantly being subjected to new processes of pidginization and creolization. Thus, while the individual speaker experiences the process only once in his life, the process of creolization does not have to be limited to one single period in the history of a language, as Bickerton implies (1981:6).

According to Valdman (1977a:175) a contact situation may lead in a one-step restructuring process to a relatively stable and elaborated system or, in the terminology of Bollée (1977; 1977a), a contact situation may give rise to a creole without an intermediate stage of pidginization. Taking a look at the situation in the Arabic-speaking countries, we see that almost right from the beginning of the Arab conquests there were children who received the limited variety of their non-Arab mothers as input and construed their own (native) variety of Arabic out of it. But this does not mean that there was no intermediate stage as far as the language is concerned. In the approach taken by Valdman and Bollée there seems to be a confusion between pidginization as a process and a pidgin as a stable variety. As soon as people start to speak their own approximation of a given language — as soon as they apply their universal second language learning strategies to the language they hear — we are dealing with a process of pidginization, whether or not this leads to a discrete variety which is used for some time and which might be termed a 'pidgin'. If the input of the children in our example had been the Arabic of a native speaker, there is no reason at all to assume that they would have started to treat it in the same way as creolizing speakers treat a limited input; on the contrary, they would have acquired Arabic as a perfectly normal mother tongue. In Mühlhäusler's discussion of the terms 'pidginization' and 'creolization' (1974:12-13) there is a similar problem: according to him it is not always easy to distinguish between pidgins and creoles. Against this I should like to say that it is certainly possible to determine for any individual speaker whether the language he speaks was learnt as a first or as a second language — leaving aside the case of bilingual education — and, accordingly, whether the adjustments he makes in his speech belong to a process of pidginization or of creolization. The common factor in both situations is that all adjustments that are being made have to do with the fact that the language is being learnt in a handicapped situation from a restricted input. For the community as a whole, the two processes may well be — and probably often are — concurrent.

In the linguistic community where a pidginized version of a given language is used, new speakers will always have to start afresh and construe an approximation of either the creolized variety of the target language (if there are already first speakers of that language) or of the target language itself (if it has not been removed from that community), or of the broken down versions of those who have learnt the language themselves as a second language (cf. Mühlhäusler 1974:34-35, referring to Labov 1971:60).[6] This means that new generations constantly repeat the process of creolization until there are no more second language speakers left, and the linguistic community has replaced the pidgin variety with a creole, i.e. a new mother tongue. From then on, natural processes of language change — whatever they may be — will take the place of earlier processes of pidginization and creolization.

In other communities the broken down version of the target language never goes beyond the stage of a *lingua franca* used as a means of communication between different groups who each retain their own first language. The pidginized variety may then become a stable variety (cf. Mühlhäusler 1981:46), spoken more or less accurately by its users, and new generations will always learn it as a second language, without showing any tendency to creolize it. If such a pidginized variety turns out to be a successful means of communication, there will be a constant expansion of functions and, consequently, an expansion of structure and grammatical means, not unlike the expansion within a process of creolization which also serves to turn a restricted input into a useful means of communication. On the other hand, when the political and/or social situation changes, such a variety may lose its usefulness and disappear without leaving a trace, except in some fossilized items that were borrowed by the first languages in the area. Such was the fate of those trade languages we know about, e.g. Chinook Jargon, Russenorsk, Russo-Chinese, and it may one day be the case with the pidginized varieties of Arabic that are still being used as trade languages in Central Africa (cf. below, ch. VI, p. 114f.).

Tutoring and formal instruction play an important role in those cases where the influence of the target language — the standard language of that community — gradually increases, so that a process of decreolization sets in which causes the existing varieties to level towards the standard. The most salient pidgin features disappear and the differences between the creole and the standard are spread out on a continuous scale ranging from perfect standard to deep creole, and it is left to the speaker to make his choice along this continuous scale. Such a linguistic landscape is normally referred to as a 'post-creole continuum', as, for instance, in the case of Jamaica (cf. Bickerton 1975). It is impossible to distinguish between discrete varieties in such a system, given the variability within the system of an individual speaker. Low variety (basilect), intermediate variety (mesolect), and high variety (acrolect) do not exist otherwise than as a cluster of features, the predictability of which is determined by selectional criteria.

The analysis of the selectional criteria is still a controversial issue; in particular, it is not clear whether the selection should be viewed as a process governed by linguistic rules, or as a correlation between linguistic features and extra-linguistic factors, including the use of linguistic variation as a means for stylistic variation.[7] The discussion about variation in a post-creole continuum has a special relevance for the linguistic situation in the arabophone world. The co-occurrence of high and low features in the speech of individual speakers in Arab countries would seem to bear a close resemblance to the one described, for instance, for Jamaica. Unfortunately, the only descriptions of such a situation in any Arab country limit themselves to an analysis of transcribed texts (mostly broadcast interviews) without going into the theoretical implications of the analysis (cf. the description of Egyptian Arabic by Diem 1974; and of Moroccan Arabic by Forkel 1980), with one exception, Mahmud's (1979) analysis of the interaction between Juba Arabic and the Arabic of Khartoum in the Southern provinces of the Sudan (cf. below, ch. VI, p. 125f.). Obviously, a post-creole continuum develops only when the target language is both available and accepted as a norm. Such a situation will, therefore, not arise in those parts of the arabophone world where the contact with the cultural and linguistic centres was lost at an early date, i.e. in the *Sprachinsel* (cf. above, ch. II, p. 29-31). Here too, the analysis of the historical events is a prerequisite to the analysis of the development of the varieties in question.

We have seen that the specifics of each contact area must always be taken into account, if we wish to explain the socio-linguistic development of a given linguistic community. In each area the frequency and the intensity of the contacts between the different groups within the linguistic community differ, and so does the degree of exposure to the target language. In each case, therefore, the resulting situation is a different one. In the case of the *Sprachinsel* in the arabophone world the loss of contact with the target language prevented the same levelling towards it that took place in the other dialect areas (cf. also Rickford 1977:193). In the same way, the religious composition of a community may determine its socio-linguistic development, since, generally speaking, the standard language does not necessarily exert the same influence on speakers of different denominations. In the arabophone world, for instance, Muslim speakers react differently towards the standard language than Jewish and Christian speakers do (cf. Blau 1965:23). In many cases the speech of non-Muslims was much more innovative than the surrounding Muslim dialects — or rather, Jewish and Christian Arabic was much more conservative in the sense that it preserved the original radical innovations of the language that had been introduced after the conquests, instead of giving them up under the influence of the Classical, as the Muslim dialects often did, either because of the Muslims' greater sensitiveness to the influence of the Classical standard, or in some instances because of a subsequent bedouinization with a similar result, as seems to be the case with the Muslim dialect of Baghdad (cf. Blanc 1965). A similar distinction has developed in Baḥraynī Arabic between the speech of the Shi'ites and the Sunnites. According to Holes (1983) the latter underwent secondary bedouinization in their speech, whereas the former — a sectarian minority just as the Christians and the Jews — retained the sedentary features.

Within the general picture of the development of a language through pidginization and creolization there seem to be two major types of language encounter that meet the definition. In both of them we find a mass process of second language acquisition, followed by a process of nativization of the pidginized variety in most instances, but there is a difference with regard to the migratory movement of the new speakers. It has often been assumed that there is a direct correlation between such types of encounters and the specific changes the languages in question undergo. We shall see below (p. 53) that the assumption of such a correlation — the 'sociological parameters' of Mühlhäusler (1974) — does not help in explaining the linguistic structure. On the other hand, a taxonomy of situations may help in explaining the development of a pidginized variety, its acceptance or rejection as a means of communication, and its chances of being creolized.

According to Valdman (1977:264ff.) we may distinguish between endogenous creoles arising from the contact between an indigenous population — whether they are slaves or not — and an invading (European) group whose activity was commercial, rather than agricultural and, on the other hand, exogenous creoles, often insular, arising in geographical areas from which, generally speaking, none of the population groups in contact originate. A similar distinction is made by Bickerton (1977) who asserts that there is a large difference between the pidgins/creoles of those areas where the second language learners remained sedentary, and those of areas to which they were transplanted: in the latter areas there never arose stable, 'effable' pidgins, but the resulting language experiments were soon transformed into creoles. Bickerton claims (1977:58-60) that creoles that arose under such circumstances share a number of characteristics. One of the characteristics may be mentioned here, that of the aspectual markers in the verbal system of these 'early-creolized creoles': they use the zero form of the verb for 'simple past' of action verbs, and for 'non-past' of state verbs; they have a marker for anteriority, a marker for irrealis aspect, a marker for non-punctual aspect; all these markers are used in pre-verbal position, and can combine in a number of ways. This system of aspectual markers will be discussed in more detail below (ch. V, p. 84ff.).

According to Bickerton these shared characteristics may be attributed to the fact that the speakers of the 'early-creolized creoles' used certain innate strategies for second language learning under specific handicapped circumstances: "It is obvious that the process must consist of internalizing linguistic rules for which there is no evidence in terms of linguistic outputs".[8] The use of 'innate strategies' in the learning situations that lead to the origin not only of creolized, but also of pidginized varieties, will be discussed below. Here I only wish to point out that the introduction of innate strategies confirms the absence of a direct correlation between circumstances and linguistic features. The circumstances may trigger the use of certain strategies, and these in their turn may determine the changes in a language, but the circumstances in themselves cannot influence directly the linguistic structure of the language.

The discussion above leads to the conclusion that when we wish to study the development of a pidginized variety, the analysis of the linguistic features must go hand in hand with the analysis of the historical circumstances. The linguistic changes are determined by the language learning process, which in itself is the result of a historical process, and the socio-linguistic position of the pidginized variety is determined by the historical context and the evolution of the community. We shall see below (ch. IV) that the situation in the territories conquered by the Arabs during the seventh and eighth centuries corresponds closely to the type of endogenous pidgins/creoles. Some features of this type of situation are given by Heine (1973:67-68) who characterizes it as follows:

1. there is a revolutionary change in the relations between groups which had hardly had any contact beforehand;
2. there is at the beginning only limited communication that is almost completely restricted to certain areas of social life (e.g. commerce, army, taxation);
3. the encounters between members of the two groups tend to be limited in frequency as well as duration;
4. there tends to be a social and/or cultural distance between the two groups;
5. the medium of communication is almost always the spoken language and there is no educational system in which the language can be formally taught to new speakers.

The discussion of the Arab conquests in the next chapter will concentrate on these features in order to find out how far the social context in the conquered territories conforms to the characterization given by Heine. The discussion in chapter V of the traces of pidginization/creolization in the Arabic dialects will also include the typical features of endogenous creoles.

In the discussion of endogenous and exogenous creoles I have already referred to Bickerton's concept of universal strategies of second language learning, which in his view are responsible for the uniformity of the processes that take place in specific types of situation and are not related historically. The similarities between these processes can be explained either by assuming a common descent (monogenesis), or by assuming an underlying universal tendency. The concept of 'universality' is a very ambiguous one (cf. Comrie 1981:1-29), since it is not always clear what is regarded as universal: in the case of the process of pidginization it may be applied to the universality of the result (all known pidgin languages exhibit feature x), or it may be applied to the universality of the changes (in every process of pidginization there is a tendency towards bisyllabicity), or it may be applied to the universality of those elements of the target language that are preserved (processes of pidginization generate structures that are closer to the deep structures of the target language), or, finally, it may be applied to the processes or strategies of language learning that are involved in pidginization. In the last case mentioned it is assumed that all human beings share certain universal strategies that enable them to cope with a situation in which language learning is extremely difficult, because of the infrequency of contacts with the model, for example, or because of the limited input provided by the speakers of the target language ('foreigner talk'). These strategies react to properties of the information supplied by the speakers of the target language, and aid the learner in construing a means of communication out of fragmentary bits of knowledge. This can involve a regularization of the system, uniformity of paradigms, reduction of redundancy, and the establishment of one-to-one relations between form and meaning where these were absent in the target language.

Explaining the way in which the language learner arrives at the expression of his semantic intentions in a conventional linguistic medium in terms of strategies has become a normal procedure in studies on first language learning. Slobin (1973) and Clark & Clark (1977) have set up a series of what they call 'operating principles' that perform this function of guiding the language learner in the case of the language learning process of children. In Slobin's analysis of this process the following 'operating principles' are posited:

1. pay attention to the end of words;
2. the phonological form of words can be systematically modified;
3. pay attention to the order of words and morphemes;
4. avoid interruption or rearrangement of linguistic units;
5. underlying semantic relations should be overtly marked and clearly;
6. avoid exceptions;
7. the use of grammatical markers should make semantic sense.

Some of these principles are quite similar to the strategies posited for the language learning process of the pidgin learner, only these are formulated (below, ch. V, p. 81) in terms of the resulting changes in the target language, i.e. in tendencies manifesting themselves in the language that is being learnt, instead of instructions guiding the learner.

The similarity in itself is hardly unexpected, since — as Slobin (1973:195-96) remarks — it would be illogical to suppose that the operating principles used by adults and by children differ in kind, although quite obviously, owing to the difference in brain capacity between adults and children, there is a large difference in degree.[9] A further difference is that, in their application of operating principles to the linguistic input they receive from the adults around them, children are constantly being checked by the confrontation with their model, and very often also by explicit and systematic correction (except, of course, those children whose input is not constituted by a natural language, as in the case of a pidginized language). Pidgin learners, on the other hand, normally do not have such a friendly model at their disposal, although they do have a different advantage, namely their experience with their first language, which they can use in their learning of the target language.

The most important difference between pidgin learners and learners of a second language under classroom conditions is that in most cases the latter is not confronted with what Slobin calls a "rapidly fading modality". He uses this term in connection with first language learning: children are forced to try and find some order in an incomprehensible mass of sound. But the same thing applies to the pidgin learner: he has no one to assist him in the analysis of the foreign language (apart from 'foreigner talk', and apart from the exceptional cases mentioned by Naro 1978), and he just has to grope around for some meaning. This is precisely what untutored language learning is all about: confrontation with a "rapidly fading modality" without the assistance a second language learner normally expects to receive.[10] The presence or absence of a permanent target and model determines the extent to which these new speakers may generalize their conclusions on the basis of the material they have been exposed to. In other words: when the model is not available for long periods of time, there is no check on the application of the operating principles or strategies of language learning, and the learner is left free to apply them in a systematic and consistent way, without having to bother with the constraints of the specific language he happens to be learning.

Explanations in terms of innate strategies do not rule out the possibility of influence through other factors. In his discussion of the process of creolization Bickerton concedes that there may occur phenomena in creole languages — defined as languages which, having undergone a process of pidginization, become the mother tongue of a linguistic community — that may be explained by substratal influence, or phenomena that occur outside creoles as well. But, he continues, the expansion of a pidginized language into a creole is more easily explained by the fact that "there can be rules of language that are not derived from any linguistic input" (1977:65). I take this to mean that there are certain universals, not of language, but of language learning strategies in a handicapped situation, when there is only very limited linguistic input. In my view, this explanation of certain phenomena in creolization may be applied to the process of pidginization as well. Pidginizing a language thus implies the application of certain universal devices of linguistic restructuring to the process of second language learning, corresponding to Bickerton's explanation of the expansion of a pidginized variety into a creole in terms of certain universal devices that aid the first language learner in turning a limited input into a full-fledged language.

Obviously, in the case of a pidginizing process the same proviso must be applied to the introduction of universal strategies into the theory as the one mentioned above, namely that apart from the effects of these universal devices there may also be additional, in many cases reinforcing, influences from substratal languages. Consequently, the occurrence of one individual feature can never be a sufficient condition for pidginization. To what extent individual features are necessary conditions for the process remains to be seen; in view of the extreme variation with regard to the effects of the process, it would seem unlikely that such necessary features exist. In other words, pidgin languages may — and actually do — share features with other languages. It should also be pointed out that the combination of devices typical for pidginization is, apparently, only operative in certain specific types of language learning in which the process of acquisition takes place wholesale, quickly, and without formal training.[11]

It has been emphasized above that there are no distinctive features of pidginization, and that the linguistic structure of languages that have been through a process of pidginization may very well share features with other languages that are not claimed to have undergone such a process. Consequently, I cannot go along with Woolford's repeated insistence on the similarity between creolization and natural change.[12] She emphasizes that there is nothing specific about particular features of Tok Pisin, the pidginized variety of English that is used in New Guinea, because similar restructuring is found in other languages as well. The main problem with this comparison is that it compares a process with a state (cf. Mühlhäusler 1981:39ff., and above, p. 38). Such a comparison is not valid, because it does not take into account the fact that the essence of pidginization lies in the reanalysis that takes place; the result in itself is not significant. But even if it can be shown that the non-pidginized language did go through an identical change, this does not invalidate the claim, which is that under some circumstances the pidginization or the nativization of a language is accompanied by certain changes in the linguistic structure. This does not, of course, preclude the occurrence of similar changes under normal circumstances as well, although it does preclude the attribution of such changes to the same causes.

It is not surprising to find that the innovations which occur in the course of nativization differ in frequency and applicability for each speaker. Each speaker makes his own choices, depending on his familiarity with the target language and his use of the strategies involved for the elaboration of the material on hand. The subsequent development of a standard language and the disappearance of individual deviations and choices is a matter of socio-linguistics. Socio-cultural factors gradually do away with the differences between the pidginized variety and the evolving standard.[13] This seems to be the normal picture for a linguistic community that is in a transient stage between pidginized variety and creolized first language.

In conclusion I should like to say that I do not claim that some of the characteristic changes resulting from the application of universal strategies might not emerge in normal processes of language learning as well: obviously, the supposed universality of the strategies involved makes it even more likely for them to emerge in such processes as well. I do claim, however, that it is at the moment inadvisable to attempt to generalize the conclusions, and furthermore, that the type of situation sketched above is accompanied by a strong concentration of such characteristics. It should also be borne in mind that universality in this sense concerns the strategies that operate under such circumstances, not universal features in the target language. This point must be made, since according to the theory advanced by Kay & Sankoff (1974) the similarity between pidgin languages can be explained by assuming that the second language learners first and most easily pick up alleged 'universal' features in the target language (cf. Bickerton's criticism 1977:50). Finally, it should be noted that the 'amount of strategy' the second language learner needs in order to overcome the difficult situation in which he finds himself may vary from situation to situation, and that the results of applying a strategy may vary from case to case. To mention one example: the widely attested tendency in pidginization towards the creation of two-syllable words (Heine 1973:226-27) may lead in one language to the lengthening, in another to the shortening of the average word in the target language. The actual results are, therefore, not significant in themselves, but are always related to the structure of the target language. Or, to put it very simply, pidginizing Chinese may involve the same strategies on the part of the new speakers as pidginizing Hausa, but the results will in all probability differ widely.

As we have seen, the hypothesis that pidginization involves rules for which there is no linguistic input leaves entirely open the question how far substratal influence plays an additional or reinforcing role in the formation of a given pidginized variety. Similarly, the possibility of monogenesis in a number of cases remains, not as an alternative, but as a subsequent stage: a common origin for a given group of pidgin languages can quite easily be assumed. Out of an existing pidginized or creolized variety there may arise a new pidgin or pidgins through subsequent stages of pidginization. Proving such a common origin must of course involve more than just pointing out structural similarities, since these may be the result of the application of identical strategies. The only evidence that can help us to decide whether or not a common origin exists is an analysis of the historical data that elucidate the history of the language or the languages involved.

It is interesting to note that both in the case of the European-based pidgins and in that of the Arabic dialects, theories of monogenesis have been advanced, primarily on the basis of structural similarities such as these. At first sight, the often striking similarity between the resulting languages may, indeed, seem inexplicable except in terms of a theory of monogenesis, unless one is prepared to acknowledge the universal character of the language learning strategies involved. In the case of the European-based pidgins, Whinnom's theory (1971; 1977; cf. Todd 1974:33-42; Bollée 1977:18-20; Granda 1978:335) looks for a common basis in the *lingua franca* known as Sabir, which was used in the Mediterranean area during the Middle Ages. According to Whinnom, this Sabir developed into a Portuguese pidgin, which through subsequent stages of reflexification — a renewal of the vocabulary in which the structure of the language remains intact — became diversified into the pidgins now known. Whinnom based his research mainly on the English- and French-based pidgins of the Caribbean, and later research has used precisely the evidence of the French creoles in the Indian Ocean to argue against his theory of monogenesis (cf. Bollée 1977): these creoles are not related historically with the Caribbean creoles, and yet, they bear a striking resemblance to them. But the strongest evidence against Whinnom's theory is provided by studies on pidgins that are not based on a European language and that cannot in any way be connected with his supposed Portuguese pidgin (cf. especially Heine 1973, Manessy 1977, and the evidence of the Arabic pidgins, cf. below, ch. VI).

In the case of the Arabic dialects, Ferguson's theory of a military koine (cf. above, ch. II, p. 20f.) aims at the same conclusion as Whinnom's theory of Sabir: by pointing out the common developments that took place in the Arabic dialects as against the Classical Standard, Ferguson attempts to prove that all modern dialects have a common ancestor. This, however, does not take into account the existing differences between the dialects, and overemphasizes the importance of similarities in a theory of common descent. Later research has modified the theory by assuming more centres from which koineized varieties of Arabic could have spread in a wave-like movement over the arabophone world, thus providing the impetus for subsequent innovations.[14]

In the case of substratal influence the difficulty lies in its probabilistic character: even if we can show that dialect A is spoken in the same area as substratal language A', and that it shows a linguistic change which resembles a phenomenon present in A', we never have any absolute certainty that the existence of the phenomenon in A' actually triggered the linguistic innovation in A. The theory of substratal influence has been discredited in the past, mainly because of this difficulty in obtaining water-tight proof, and because of the sometimes far-fetched analogies that have been posited between innovations and substratal languages. Recent research tends to minimize the influence of the substratum, at least as a single cause.[15]

On the other hand, it is of course unsatisfactory to demand a one-to-one relation between causes and effects in the development of a language. This applies, again, both to the history of pidginized languages and to the history of the Arabic dialects. In both cases, many wild claims have been made concerning substratal influence — in the Arabic dialects we have to put up with such improbable substrates as Phoenician or Akkadian, and in the case of the European-based pidgins the rather vague notion of West-African languages has been used as an explanation for almost any innovation in pidgin languages. As a result, many discussions have been devoted to the question of whether or not pidgin languages are to be regarded as Indo-European languages. It might be noted in passing that in Romance linguistics there has from the beginning been a quite different tradition in which the use of substratal influence belonged to the accepted types of evidence. This tradition has persisted until modern times, so much so that even superstratal evidence is accepted by some as explanation of various developments (cf. Wartburg 1967).

A more promising approach to the phenomenon of pidginization might be one in which innovations are regarded as essentially multi-causal, or, in the formulation of Samuels (1972:3): "An insistence on a single cause ... has been, in the past, one of the main obstacles to progress in diachronic linguistics". In many instances, it is impossible to attribute an innovation to one cause exclusively, and it must be recognized that there are several factors contributing to the final result, one reinforcing the other. In spite of Mühlhäusler's caution (1981:39ff.) that many of the remarkable similarities between pidgins and source languages (i.e., substratal languages) can be shown to be purely accidental when viewed within the development of the pidgin, it is nevertheless tempting to maintain that even in cases where a particular pidgin feature evolves from something quite different from the substratum, the substratal language may still have been a reinforcing factor in the development towards the final result, if only in the selection of one variant from alternative choices. Thus, elements of a target language may gain or lose importance according to the existence or non-existence of similar elements in the substratal language acting as catalyst in the development of the pidginized variety.[16]

Obviously, what we gain here in probable answers, we lose in explanatory power and certainty. The acceptance of multi-causal explanations entails the impossibility of identifying significant factors among the many probable influences. On the other hand, extreme methodological rigour, such as found for instance in Diem's conditions for substratal influence (cf. above, ch. II, p. 25ff.) almost certainly excludes some real instances of the reinforcing contribution of substratal languages towards linguistic innovation in the dialects. I believe that the conflict between theories that try to explain a change or an innovation in terms of latent tendencies in the target language, and theories that try to explain them in terms of elements in the substratal language often turns out to be an artificial one, since in many cases both theories are partly right in that they point out an additional factor, and partly wrong in that they neglect alternatives and, especially, because they do not account for the universality of the processes in question.

Valkhoff's concept of 'linguistic encounter' is an example of a theory that hinges on the multi-causality of innovations. In discussing the opposing theories of spontaneous development and linguistic interaction that have been advanced to explain the development from Dutch to Afrikaans, he proposes his own principle that "if, in the field of linguistic adaptation from Dutch, some sound, form, word, idiom, or construction is rare in Dutch or Low German (dialects) but has become popular in Afrikaans, it may have been assisted and 'acclimatized' through the influence of similar phenomena used by the languages of the Cape Colony" (1972:79).[17] The conflicting theories about the development of Afrikaans are interesting for more than one reason: they also demonstrate the connection between scientific theories about linguistic innovations and political or social attitudes. A similar connection exists in the case of the Arabic dialects, so that it is worthwhile pointing out here that chauvinism or, in the worst cases, downright racism, is one of the factors that dominate discussions about pidginization. Obviously, this interference of outside interests in scholarly discussions is very strong in the case of Afrikaans, as becomes immediately apparent to a reader of Valkhoff's book, which abounds with examples of the kind of interference against which he has to defend his theories.

After this short survey of the various explanations that have been advanced for the origin of pidgins and creoles I wish to restate my own point of view. I define a language as pidginized when it is acquired in an untutored process of language learning as a second language; and I define a language as creolized when it is acquired as a first language, a pidginized variety acting as input. The underlying hypothesis is, of course, that the two processes are always accompanied by certain changes in the linguistic structure. A fuller discussion of the tendencies represented by those changes will be postponed till chapter V in connection with a discussion of the tendencies in the Arabic dialects.

As a conclusion to this chapter I should like to make a few observations about the status of the concomitant social and cultural context. As we have seen above, there have been various attempts to establish a correlation between specific types of language encounter and specific changes. There have also been general descriptions of the conditions supposed to be necessary for pidginization/creolization. Whinnom, for instance, states (1971:104) that the process of breaking down a language can only occur in a multilingual community. The multilinguality of a community is certainly one of the factors that determine the extent of pidginization. When a community is multilingual, it is less likely for elements from the underlying languages to play a major role in the development of the pidginized version of the target language, whereas the continued use of only one underlying language, especially when it carries with it a certain prestige, enhances its chances of influencing the process of pidginization. In the same way, the survival of a substantial number of speakers of the underlying language(s) or the availability of a certain amount of formal instruction in the target language are factors that influence the results of the process. But we are dealing here with factors that influence the development of the pidginized variety, not its origin. What then is the status of the 'sociological parameters'?

In his discussion of pidgin languages Mühlhäusler (1974:60 and elsewhere) distinguishes between a pidginized language (i.e. a variety defined in terms of the mode of transmission (limited input)) and a pidgin (i.e. a language that has been accepted as a means of communication). In doing so he introduces Labov's distinction (1971:15ff.) between a social and an individual solution for any particular socio-linguistic problem, and applies it to the problem in hand. According to this distinction only the social solutions to the handicapped situation in which a new speaker may find himself are linguistically relevant. The individual solutions, so Mühlhäusler seems to assert, are only short-lived and without relevance. It is doubtless possible to establish sociological parameters for the social acceptance of a pidginized variety in terms of the social class of the speakers, for instance, or the isolation from the target language, the multilinguality of the linguistic community, the numerical relations between the groups of speakers, etc. But this is not a linguistic matter, at least not in the sense of its being relevant to the process of linguistic change the language undergoes.

The only categorization that can possibly result from such distinctions and parameters is one into languages that have become accepted as standard for a given community and languages that have not: in other words, we obtain at best a prediction concerning the success of a certain variety in a certain context. Such an instrument for the prediction of success may also be applied to non-standard dialects or sociolects of perfectly 'normal' languages that have nothing to do with pidginization or creolization. But with the help of these parameters we can never determine whether or not the language in question has ever been pidginized in the course of its history (or, in Mühlhäusler's terms, whether it is a pidgin or not), let alone predict something about its linguistic structure. The sociological or cultural parameters do not tell us anything at all about the linguistic changes since there is no connection between them: sociological circumstances in themselves cannot cause linguistic changes. Thus, Mühlhäusler's in itself unobjectionable distinction of various parameters cannot be applied to the measurement of the extent of simplification in a pidgin — a pidgin being in his definition a pidginized variety that has met with social approval, I believe that it is very well possible to correlate the social approval of a language with the proposed socio-cultural parameters, but the causes for the process of simplifying the target language must be sought in the imperfect language learning process that led to the origin of a pidginized variety.

As a matter of fact, 'imperfect learning' does not seem to be the exact term for the cause of pidginization. There are many areas where a foreign language was learnt more or less efficiently, resulting in a regional variety, for instance, of French, or English, or Spanish that while sounding perhaps quaint to the native ear was certainly not simplified in any way at all. Examples one thinks of are the English language in India, and the regional French (Pataouète) that is (was?) spoken in North Africa, both by French colonists and the autochthonous population (cf. Lanly 1970). In both cases the language spoken in the colony clearly differs from the standard varieties of English and French, in pronunciation, vocabulary, and syntax. Some of the tendencies at work in these regional varieties may even remind us of the processes at work in languages that are being simplified. But there is no wholesale breaking down of the target language, as in pidginization. Both in India and in North Africa there must have been a whole range of contact languages used by the colonists and the indigenous population alike, consisting in simplified versions of English and French, somewhat similar to the contact languages that originated in other parts of the world in similar situations. They also resemble, one might add, the contact languages that must have been used in the contact between Arabs and Syrians, Copts, Berbers, etc. in the early period after the conquests. Such pidginized varieties never were to become popular in India or in North Africa, and they just disappeared. The most probable cause of this lack of success was the enormous prestige of the colonial languages together with the fact that there was an educational system that propagated and furthered the correct use of English and French. The pidginized varieties that became unpopular probably exerted a certain degree of influence on the regional standard, which in the course of time began to incorporate some of the characteristic elements of the early contact languages.

If the presence of an educational system of some kind does not prevent the development of an 'imperfectly' learned regional variety, even though it does lead to the disappearance of the pidginized variety, then we can imagine what happens in a situation where there is no such system at all. I have stated above that in a case like that we are dealing with a process of untutored language learning that necessarily leads to a drastic structural change in the language being subjected to it. The need to communicate in a language that has to be picked up in bits and pieces, and must be reconstructed by the new speakers from scratch, calls for the help of strategies that render the material that is available easier to handle. According to Bickerton, these strategies are universally present in all human beings, and they do not have to be learnt. Thus, we have to distinguish between the structural changes that occur during the process of pidginization and are to be attributed to the process of acquisition by which the language in question was learnt as a second language, and the process by which the resulting speech variety becomes standardized and accepted. It is perfectly legitimate, in my view, to look for sociological parameters correlating with the second process. One may, for instance, show that the resulting speech variety becomes stable only in such-and-such circumstances, or that nativization only ensues when such-and-such a situation obtains. But there is no way of correlating the structural changes with sociological factors in any other than a statistical sense. There is, in other words, no way of finding in the sociological and cultural situation some hidden mechanism that affects the language structure. Such a view typically leads to statements that, for instance, attribute the instability of a language to instability in the political and social context.[18] It is, of course, also legitimate to ask why it is that in certain situations the new speakers had no opportunity to learn the new language properly — although a better way of stating this question would perhaps be to ask why it is that in certain situations people actually go to the trouble of learning to speak another language correctly (cf. below, ch. IV, p. 68). Whatever the answer to questions like these may be, it is obvious that there is no need for a taxonomy of situations of contact before we can start to analyze the structural changes that have occurred as the result of untutored language learning.

In the same way, I cannot go along with Mühlhäusler's distinction of a 'creolization[1]' and a 'creolization[2]', according to the situation in which a stable or minimal pidgin is being restructured and expanded. In 'creolization[2]', he says, "rules of the target language replace and supersede the rules of the unstable simplified pidgin". But this is tantamount to asserting that languages lead an autonomous life of their own.[19]. Surely, rules are not being replaced by some mechanical force coming from outside which has nothing to do with the speakers of the language but, on the contrary, those who learn the language as their mother tongue, being confronted with a restricted input, whether a stable or an unstable 'pidgin', have to use their wits (or their innate programme, or whatever name one might care to give this faculty) in order to recreate a natural language.

NOTES

1) For a discussion of the role of acquisition in linguistic change see Samuels 1972:111ff., 135-44; Traugott 1977:79-85.

2)It is not clear why Bickerton himself uses the expression 'true creoles' (e.g. 1981:82) which seems to run counter to this warning.

3) Cf. Ferguson & DeBose 1977; for a special case of instruction in simplified language by the Portuguese who used it to train African interpreters, see Naro 1978.

4) It is, of course, possible to nativize an artificial language. In that case there is a restricted input with the same consequences for the learning process and the subsequent adjustments in the language structure as in those cases where the restricted input is constituted by a pidginized variety, although there is a difference in that those who teach the artificial language to the children normally have a rather good command of the language. An example of this is Ivrit, the official language of Israel, which does show some tendencies towards expansion, just as creolized languages do *vis-à-vis* their pidginized input. It, too, shows the need to create registers, slang, etc., cf. Kornblueth & Aynor 1974. Remarks in this direction are made by Givón (1979:32-33); according to him the degree of coherence in the learning model is reflected by the amount of specific — as against 'universal' — typological features in the resulting language. As far as I know there has never been any serious research into another phenomenon of the same kind, that of *denaskaj esperantistoj*, i.e. native speakers of the artificial language Esperanto. *A priori*, one might assume that if this phenomenon really exists, it might provide interesting insights into the effects of a restricted or unnatural input, cf. some information collected by Declerck 1969; also Csiszár ms.

5) And *vice versa*, cf. Mühlhäusler 1981:57-58; for a special case of influence by creole speakers on the establishment of norms for a written standard of the pidginized version, Tok Pisin, cf. Siegel 1981.

6) A special case of the coexistence of first language and second language versions might be Singapore, where Singapore English — jokingly called 'Singlish' — is at the same time first

language and second language for different groups of speakers, cf. Platt 1975:370. Platt asserts that Singapore provides an example of a creole that did not develop from a pidgin, in his terms a 'creoloid' (1975:366). But, following his account, Singaporean children who contributed to the development of Singlish by transferring features from their respective mother tongues (Malay, Indian languages, Chinese dialects) learnt this variety at school. The point to be taken from the Singaporean situation is, therefore, not that we can find there a creole without a pidgin ancestor, but that in some versions of Singapore English a certain amount of pidginization is to be found in spite of the fact that the process of acquisition happens largely by way of tutored language learning.

7) See the discussion between Washabaugh 1977 and Bickerton 1977a; also Seuren 1982. For a discussion of the notational devices to be introduced for the description of stylistic variation, in particular the 'implicational scale' proposed by DeCamp (1971) see Dittmar 1973:185-95. The need for a polylectal grammar and the technical aspects connected with its use and formulation are discussed by Bailey (1973).

8) Bickerton 1977:64, cf. ib. 55: "One is forced to conclude that a pidgin can creolize at any stage of its development, and that the period at which this step takes place will be decided, not by internal development in the pidgin, but by the communicational needs of children".

9) Slobin 1973:195-96; the differences and similarities of pidginization and first language learning are discussed by Mühlhäusler 1981:75-79.

10) Schuman (1978) proposes to use the pidginization process as a model for second language learning in other more general situations. He explains the reduced and simplified character of the second language in some circumstances as a product of social and/or psychological distance, which in its turn leads to a restricted functioning of the language. However, in their review of Schuman's work, Washabaugh & Eckman (1980) point out that all he shows is that there exists a correlation between the two without proving the directionality of the process.

11) Cf. Bickerton (1977:55): "The difference between arriving at a pidgin and arriving at a reasonably accurate version of a standard language lies mainly in the availability of target models and the amount of interaction with speakers of the target language"; for a discussion of untutored language learning, see also below, ch. IV, p. 68ff.

12) Cf. Woolford (1981:137): "All of the changes involved in the development of a complementizer system in Tok Pisin are quite ordinary processes of language change. There is nothing involved that is unique to creolization". The particular feature she refers to is the syntactic reanalysis of complementizers in sentences such as *yu no ken ting olsem mipela i lusim tingting long yu pinis* "you must not think thus/that we have forgotten you" (1981:133).

13) The role of the written standard in this process is discussed by Siegel (1981) who claims that by virtue of its need for unambiguity and explicitness the written form of Tok Pisin uses phenomena from creolized varieties, such as the perfective marker *pinis*, which has become obligatory in the creolized variety, and the use of marked subordinate clauses. For the nativization of Tok Pisin see Sankoff & Laberge 1974.

14) For a discussion of the methodological difficulties connected with the hypothesis that Vulgar Latin is the common ancestor of the Romance languages see Versteegh *forthcoming* b, where it is argued that a comparison of the theories in Arabic and Romance linguistics may be useful to both disciplines.

15) For recent research concerning this problem in New Guinea see Mosel (1980), who compares Tok Pisin with a local language, Tolai, and demonstrates the absence of interference from

the substratum in the pidgin that is used in the same region. A similar conclusion is reached by Diem (1979) in a study on the various substratal languages and their influence on the Arabic dialects.

16) One instance of such a catalyzing function is that mentioned by Goodman (1964:53) who points out that the use in Haitian Creole of the postposed demonstratives *sa*, *sila* — derived from French *ça*, *cela* or *celui-là* — was probably reinforced by the existence of almost exactly identical forms of a postposed demonstrative in Ewe (cf. the discussion by Bollée 1977:40-41), provided of course that the historical connection between Ewe-speaking slaves and Haiti can be proved. A similar case is that of the object pronouns in Réunion French Creole (*atwe*, *ali*, *anu*, etc.), which, though also explicable in terms of internal French developments alone, probably owe their existence at least partly to similar oblique pronominal forms in Malagassy, as Bollée (1977:54) remarks.

17) Concrete examples of relatively rare elements in Dutch dialects that, according to Valkhoff, have been reinforced by elements in Khoisan languages or Malay are mentioned by him (1972:25, 81).

18) Cf. Togeby 1957:277, who draws an analogy between the decline of the Roman empire and the history of the Latin language. One could say that this view regards language as an organism that somehow adapts to its surroundings, cf. Turner 1966:208, quoted by Mühlhäusler 1974:49. Another instance of this tendency to regard language as an organism has been discussed above, ch. II, p. 30.

19) Schmeck, for instance, says (1955:16) that a spoken language, in this case Latin, "sich nach den ewigen Gesetzen des lebenden Sprachkörpers stets fortentwickelt".

CHAPTER IV
THE SOCIO-LINGUISTIC CONTEXT OF THE EARLY PERIOD OF ISLAM

Nowadays, Arabic is spoken by some 180 million people as their first language in arabophone countries in Northern Africa and the Middle East. Apart from that it is used as a religious language in Muslim countries and countries with a Muslim minority all over Africa and Asia. The knowledge of the language of the *Qur'ān* in those countries may vary from a very limited level of ritual use of qur'ānic texts to an elaborate educational system for Islamic sciences, in which the use of the Classical language is prescribed for religious discussion, for instance in Pakistan and Indonesia. In this chapter I am concerned with the use of Arabic as a first language, one of the most striking effects of the Arab conquests being that all inhabitants of the empire eventually adopted the Arabic language. I shall discuss briefly the chronological and geographical details of the conquests, the number of people involved, the pattern of settlement in the conquered territories, and the development of social relations between conquerors and conquered. I shall then try to sketch the sociolinguistic situation in the early empire, the stages in the development of linguistic relations, and the position of the substratal languages.

From the very complex and at times obscure history of the Islamic conquests I can do no more than pick out a few points that seem to be relevant to our subject, that of the adoption of the Arabic language on the part of the conquered population (for general information see Mantran 1979, and especially Donner 1981). The conquests started immediately after the death of the prophet in 632. There is no agreement on the motives that led the first caliphs to this enterprise, and the prophet himself does not seem to have envisaged a large-scale conquest of the lands beyond Arabia. Probably, several factors contributed to the initiative (Donner 1981:3-9, 267-71). Under the combined command of young enthusiastic Muslim generals and experienced tribal chieftains the Arab armies swept over large parts of the civilized world, aided by the general malaise in the two great powers of the Mediterranean and Middle Eastern area, the Persian and the Byzantine empire. In a few decisive battles enormous areas fell to the Arabs: after the battle at the Yarmūk (636) Syria was torn from the Byzantine empire, and in the same year most of Iraq was conquered. From 639 till 642 campaigns were held in Egypt; Persia was conquered between 640 and 642, the decisive battle being that of Nihāwand (641). Between 644 and 656 further campaigns in Iraq and North Africa expanded the Islamic empire, which culminated in the West with the conquest of Spain (*al-Andalus*) in 711. In the East, the province of H̱urāsān was the starting point for further conquests in the East (Transoxania, India).

In the reign of the first Umayyad caliphs, when the military side of the conquests had been completed the first efforts were made to consolidate the empire, and to work out the complicated system of administrative rules by which it could be handled by the general government, at that time residing in Damascus, the Syrian capital. After the fall of the Umayyad dynasty (750), the ʻAbbāsid caliphs in some areas tried to continue the movement of conquests but, after its first momentum, the signs of decay became apparent at the fringes of the empire: in the periphery parts of provinces, or even entire provinces achieved some measure of independence under petty rulers (for instance, in North Africa and in H̱urāsān) and, of course, Spain had become independent right after the victory of the ʻAbbāsids. The centralism of the ʻAbbāsid government at Baghdad (founded in 762) was threatened by various civil wars that all but divided the empire into two parts: the conflict between al-Ma'mūn and his brother al-Amīn, for instance, which was at the same time a conflict between the Eastern and the Western part of the empire, as well as a conflict between central government and periphery.

Because of their inexperience in administrative matters the Arabs had been confronted from the beginning with various problems, not all of which they could solve with the help of their holy Book. Particularly during the first decades they managed, nevertheless, through a combination of collaboration with the native population and a marvellous sense of improvisation to set up a fairly efficient system of rules, which served in the first place to control taxation, one of the essential aims of their early policy. Many fundamental problems were taken care of provisionally in these early years, but not in all cases were the Arabs successful in finding a definitive solution. These problems concerned in the first place the relations between themselves as Arabs and Muslims and the inhabitants of their new territories. The Muslims had to learn to live with large communities of other religions, after it had become clear to them that any attempt to reconcile Islam with Judaism and Christianism doctrinally was doomed to failure. Luckily for the other religions, the prophet had already laid down — in the course of his expedition to Tabūk (cf. Watt 1956:115ff., 362ff.) — the first rules of conduct towards members of other religions: they were to be regarded as enemies, but could obtain protection in exchange for the payment of a special tax (*ğizya*, cf. *Qur'ān* 9/29). This policy was institutionalized by the early caliphs, who left their new Christian and Jewish subjects free in their choice of religion and awarded the status of *ḏimmī* to those who wished to retain their old religion and pay the taxes that were imposed on them. This remained the normal form of coexistence between Muslims and members of other (established) religions: although there were certain restrictions concerning conduct, clothing, and the professions Jews and Christians were allowed to have, and although there were from time to time persecutions, one can safely say that in general there was freedom of religion. Still, even in the absence of forced conversions, there was a steady flow of people who wished to embrace Islam. Perhaps, the levying of the poll-tax (*ğizya*) had something to do with this tendency (but cf. Dennett 1950:3-13), or — which is more probable — the prestige of the new rulers and their religion made converting the natural reaction to the social situation.[1] A point I shall come back to later is the Islamic marriage law with regard to non-Muslims: according to this law a Muslim may take a non-Muslim wife, who does not need to be converted, but a Muslim woman may never marry a non-Muslim.

A much more serious problem for the government was constituted by the influx of neophytes. Theoretically, the new converts had to be regarded as true believers with just as much influence and value as the pure Arab believers — many of whom, especially those who belonged to the ruling elite of Meccan aristocrats, had fought the prophet and his religion bitterly — but in practice they had to be content with a position as second-rate citizens. In integrating them into Muslim society the Arabs followed the old system of clientage: new Muslims who had no ties with any of the old Arab tribes were adopted by a tribe or a family, and in exchange for their services as client they received the protection of their patron. This system worked well for individuals, but it could, of course, not cope with the reality of tens of thousands of converts who, especially in the provinces, began to resent their treatment as inferior citizens by the Arab Muslims. This animosity towards the Arabs led to serious unrest, especially in those areas where it coincided with the opposition of the periphery towards the central government, who tried to unsurp as much of the autonomy of the provinces as they could. According to Shaban (1970) the opposition towards the central government in a province such as Ḫurāsān was conducted by Arabs and non-Arabs alike, so that race relations became secondary to the cohesive power of anti-government feelings: the Arab settlers were as dissatisfied with their loss of control over the provincial taxes and the booty as the non-Arabs were in protesting against their loss of autonomy. But in a later period racial feeling did become an important issue, especially in the movement of the Šu'ūbiyya, which may be regarded as the non-Arabs' protest against Arab arrogance and pride (cf. Enderwitz 1979).

The frustrations of the non-Arabs must have been reinforced by the fact that by virtue of their cultural superiority they were often needed for the administration of the empire, since the Arabs themselves simply lacked the skills and the knowledge for the management of complicated matters such as taxation and registration, at least in this early period. Although writing was not completely unknown in the Ǧāhiliyya, most Arabs did not regard intellectual achievements, including the manipulation of the writing reed, as something to be aspired to by a real man, so that they were forced to leave these matters to their new subjects. The tax register (*dīwān*), for instance, for a long time employed Christian scribes. We shall see below (p. 66) that the Arabs also depended on a special class of interpreters for their contacts with the local inhabitants. One thing is clear, though: in spite of their cultural and scientific underdevelopment as compared with the Syrians, Persians, Copts, etc., the Arabs were the dominating class in early Islamic society, and they set the tone for the rest of society. It is, therefore, no surprise that the Arabic language ended up by becoming the only means of communication in the Arab world.

In order to understand the development of social relations between the Arabs and their subjects, we have to know more about the pattern of settlement in the conquered territories — as distinct from the conquests themselves. Contrary to the popular image of the Arab conquests, these were not a matter of migratory movement, but a strictly military operation, rather in the way of the pre-Islamic *ġazw*, but on a larger and more organized scale.[2] The total number of men involved, although considerable for Ǧāhiliyya standards, was relatively small. Donner estimates a total of 6000 to 12,000 for the battle of al-Qādisiyya, a total of 20,000 to 40,000 for the battle at the Yarmūk, and a total of active soldiers in Southern Iraq of 2,000 to 4,000

(1981:221). The armies probably did not include the families of the tribesmen, so that it became common practice for the men to marry women from the "people of the Book" (*ahl al-Kitāb*), i.e. probably Christian and Jewish women (Donner 1981:222, quoting from Ṭabarī, *Ta'rīḫ* I, 2375). After a while, the first settlements became populated with Arabs, but the details of many stages of this process are still unclear, in particular because each area presents its own picture, and what is valid for Syria does not have to be the rule for Iraq, or for any other area.

The general picture that emerges, though, is that in most cases the rural population of the conquered territories were left alone: I have stated above that taxation was the principal aim of the Muslim administrators, and the best way of getting high returns for their efforts was to let the local peasants continue to till their soil and harvest their crops. As for the settlement of the Arabs themselves, the regions differ. In Iraq the first settlements at Kūfa (638) and Baṣra (635) were garrisons for the troops who prepared themselves for further campaigning. Partly, these garrison towns also served as dwelling-places for those Bedouin who wished to settle down — or who were urged to settle down by the Muslim rulers who wished to keep the nomads under control. The Bedouin who went to live there had been fighting in the armies, or belonged to the Arab tribes who were living in Mesopotamia before the conquests. Settlement took place largely tribe by tribe, with estimates for Kūfa of about 20,000 persons, and for Baṣra at the beginning no more than about 1000 persons (Donner 1981:226ff.). After the conquests migration of tribesmen from the peninsula to Iraq did take place, but on a modest scale (Donner 1981:231ff.), and others took part in the settlement, for instance Persians who had fought together with the Arabs, landed Persian gentry, etc. Smaller concentrations were housed in the less important towns for garrison duties. In the abandoned land, and in individual allotments from the caliphal share in the uncultivated land (*qaṭā'i'*) some people were allowed to start their own farms (Poliak 1938:42). Generally speaking, most soldiers tried to stay as near as possible to the garrison towns.

In Syria the majority of the Arabs settled in the cities, rather than in the countryside (Donner 1981:245ff.), because many of the inhabitants, especially those with ties with the Byzantine administration, had left their houses. In some cities the distribution of billets for the soldiers was arranged by treaty with the inhabitants. There must have been some settlement of Arabs in the Syrian countryside, but considerably less than in Iraq. The Syrian peasants did not flee like the urban elite, and their share in taxation was valued here as much as in Iraq. In Syria, too, contacts with the indigenous population were almost completely restricted to the cities: the countryside was all but divided into Arab country and *arḍ al-ʿağam* "the land of the non-Arabs". There is no certain information about the total number of Arabs who settled in Syria, but educated guesses show for this area between 200,000 and 400,000 Arabs during the first century of the Hiğra after the consolidation of the caliphate in Damascus, as against 4,000,000 non-Arabs (Poliak 1938:43-44, 48).

Information about the pattern of migration and settlement in Egypt and North Africa is even scarcer. For Egypt there are many accounts of the earliest campaigns and the final victory of the Arabs, as well as about the establishment of a military centre at Fusṭāṭ (cf. Butler 1978), but there are no data about the final settlement and the demography of the migration. For the conquest of Egypt the sources mention a number of 4000 for the original army of invaders under ʿAmr ibn al-ʿĀṣ, which was reinforced soon with a contingent of 12,000 men in 640 (Anawati 1975:31). In 664 the *dīwān* of Alexandria contained the names of 12,000 soldiers for that city alone. In Egypt, too, most settlers were found in the cities and in the garrisons, with only one exception, a settlement of some 3000 families in Bilbays (Poliak 1938:41-42): the rest of the countryside was left to the indigenous peasants. In view of the numbers quoted for Egypt the total of 150,000 mentioned for the originally invading armies in North Africa (Marçais 1961:177) in the Umayyad and the early ʿAbbāsid period seems to be somewhat too high, particularly when we take into account that this does not include the accompanying women, traders, and missionaries. We do know that in North Africa settlement followed the same pattern as elsewhere, since the Arabs were only found in the cities, with Qayrawān (founded in 670) as the most obvious example of the Arabs' tendency to settle down in a city, preferably in a city they had founded themselves. This situation obtained until the invasion of the Banū Hilāl and Sulaym in the 11th century. Probably, this invasion involved more people than the original conquests, but again certain information about the figures is lacking (cf. Marçais 1961:186-87). The total number of 1,000,000 mentioned by contemporary sources — on a total population of about 5,000,000 at that time — is probably exaggerated.

In Syria and Egypt the tribesmen did not start to spread over the countryside until after the Umayyad period (Poliak 1938:54). Where before Bedouin had been discouraged from occupying the countryside, and had been more or less forced to settle down in the newly founded cities, they were now given the opportunity to become the owners of allotments of land, in particular uncultivated land. This process was reinforced by the fact that due to the lamentable economic situation most of the indigenous farmers had started to leave their home villages and to evacuate their lands in search of better conditions of living somewhere else. This led to a massive process of migration, in which entire groups of people went to settle in another area, and in which evacuated villages were resettled with Arab tribesmen. Another result of this process may have been the intensified contact between various heterolingual groups which had never been in contact with one another before and which were now forced to communicate in the only *lingua franca* at their disposal, Arabic, because their own mother-tongue, whether it was Aramaic or Coptic or another language, was no longer of use to them.

The development of settlement in H̱urāsān was in many respects different from that in other provinces. After the initial conquest some 50,000 Arab families from Kūfa and Baṣra were transported to the villages around the city of Merw, where they were allowed to stay among the Iranian population (Shaban 1970:32ff.; Zarrinkūb 1975:28). It had never been the intention of the authorities to use these Arabs as settlers in a larger scheme of colonization, their only use being to serve as a reservoir of manpower for the ongoing campaigns in the East. It is, therefore, quite understandable that the two groups, the Arab settlers and the Iranian population were kept apart (Shaban 1970:96-97). Within the structure of Iranian society that was preserved intact the local aristocracy, the *dahāqīn*, retained their power and even collaborated quite amiably with the Arab administration for the purpose of collecting taxes (Zarrinkūb 1975:43-48). The Arabs were kept busy with the battlefield and when they started to tire from fighting their only possibilities of earning a living was in the trading business. For a later period — around 730 — Shaban (1970:115ff.) mentions the fact that the principle of segregation was abandoned. Those Arabs who did not want to serve as soldiers were left alone, and could assimilate with the Iranian population, with whom they had in common that they were both subjected to the power of the *dahāqīn*. In this respect H̱urāsān is, indeed, completely different from the other provinces, since nowhere else do we find the phenomenon of indigenous local rulers having power over Arab settlers. According to Shaban the 'Abbāsid revolution was supported in H̱urāsān by all those who wished to make an end to the authority of the old aristocracy, i.e. not only by the Iranian peasants, but by the Arab settlers as well. This common interest may have resulted in a less sharp division between the two groups.

For the whole of the Iranian area a process of merging must be assumed by which the Arab invaders or settlers were slowly iranicized.[3] After a few centuries Persian was reinstated as the national language, and Arabic disappeared as a colloquial, although it retained its position as language of religion, science and, in the beginning, of the administration (cf. Spuler 1952; Lazard 1975). Maybe, the infrequency of intermarriage between Arabs and Persian women during the early period of the Islamic conquest of Persia was a factor in this development. Another factor, at least in Ḫurāsān, may have been the pattern of settlement: the early settlers were concentrated here in the villages, not in the cities as in other provinces.

What becomes apparent from all the data available is that we must look to the cities for the most direct contact between Arabs and non-Arabs. The garrison towns that had been founded in the course of the early campaigns grew into large centres of social attraction and civilization to which people flocked in order to participate in the prestigious new order. Here, the necessity of learning as quickly as possible the language of the new masters was felt acutely; here, too, the polyglot society that is typical of early Islamic urban civilization developed.[4] How and where the process of acquisition of Arabic took place remains largely unknown. In the beginning, when contact between the Arab armies and the indigenous population was very limited, and the Arabs remained most of the time within their camps, there probably arose a special class of interpreters, amateurs who spoke Syriac — or whatever language happened to be spoken in a particular area — and Arabic sufficiently well to be able to serve as intermediaries in the contacts between the rulers and their own compatriots. It is a general phenomenon that in situations such as these there are always individuals who specialize in the technique of 'talking to strangers'.[5] Such a class of interpreters must have existed even before the Arab conquests in order to provide for the necessary communication between the local population and the Byzantine administration (cf. Peeters 1950:165ff.). Possibly, some of the Christian Arab tribes living in the Syrian desert and in Mesopotamia long before the period of the conquests provided people who were bilingual in Syriac and Arabic. There are a few curious references to some Arab dignitaries who — at a slightly later period — sent their children to Christian schools in order to learn Arabic, but apart from that nothing much is known about the Christian Arab tribes and their role in the adoption of Arabic by the local population. We have seen above that for some decades the entire system of taxation in the *dīwān* remained in the hands of Greek and Syriac-speaking clerks (cf. also

Versteegh 1977:1-9), and these people must have had a good knowledge of Arabic as well in order to make themselves understood to the new masters.

After a while, though, these interpreters had served their purpose and, especially in the cities, people began to learn Arabic themselves. In order to compare the situation in the early empire with other instances let us go back first to the distinction between endogenous and exogenous creoles, i.e., between creoles that originated with and without a massive transmigration of the new speakers (cf. above, ch. III, p. 43ff.). In the case of exogenous creoles, a mostly multilingual group is transferred to another area, and forced to take over the language of the dominating group, changing it in the process. Their children learn this broken variety as their first language, and a creole is born. Depending on the duration of contact with the language of the masters, and the influence of the norm of that language, a diglottic situation or a post-creole continuum will develop.

In the case of endogenous creoles, no transmigration takes place, and the speakers stay in their original area. In this situation we have to take into account various other circumstances, in particular with regard to the relationship between native speakers and new speakers. In the first place, we must allow for the possibility that the two groups in contact have equal prestige and will, therefore, have to learn each other's language, so to speak. The result is what is often called a 'trade jargon'.[6] If there is a sharp distinction between a target language and a source language (the original language of the new speakers), i.e. if the prestige of one of the two groups is much greater than that of the other, the subordinate group is forced to learn the language of the dominating group. The case of Arabic demonstrates that the degree of domination is not only determined by cultural factors, but may be the result of religious or military factors as well; the case of the Franks or the Normans shows that the conquering group does not always win in this respect: in some cases the conquerors do not force the conquered to take over their language, but decide to learn the language of their new subjects instead. But, of course, the religious fervour and the pride and self-awareness of the Arabs made such a result impossible in the case of the Islamic conquests.

The early contacts between masters and conquered people will almost always result in a primitive means of communication that — given a certain amount of time and contact — may become stable and standardized, once an agreement is reached on how to communicate with each other. If the original population is multilingual, the chances are that they will start using the newly discovered means of communication even among themselves, so that the developing pidginized variety of the language of the conquerors will remain in use even after the disappearance of the target. Given a certain amount of intermarriage among the different heterolingual groups that form the linguistic community, the pidginized language may even become the mother tongue of the next generation, and a creolized version of the target language. This brings us to the position of the native speakers of the target language: they may be traders whose contacts with the local population are mainly practical, ephemeral, and infrequent. They may, however, also be invaders who intend to stay in the conquered area and to incorporate it into their empire permanently. In that case, the prolonged contact with the target language will not fail to influence the development of the pidginized or creolized variety.

In all the situations mentioned there is a common denominator: everywhere people had to learn a language other than their own. The proper way to formulate the problem appears to be: why do people go to the trouble of learning another language than their own more or less correctly, when a much lower degree of knowledge evidently does not prevent them from communicating with the native speakers of that language? Apparently, in our society social pressure or expectations on the part of the native speakers, or a combination of both, force us to try our utmost to constantly correct and improve our versions of a foreign language: speaking it well becomes a matter of prestige. If on the other hand, those same native speakers are convinced anyway that no degree of fluency in their language can ever be attained by a foreigner, and when, moreover, they make this very obvious (for instance, by talking to the learners of their language in a broken version of it) the motivation to learn it correctly diminishes accordingly, and all interest on the part of the learner is lost. This process is reinforced, of course, by the absence of any system of formal education. I believe that in such cases the learners invoke the help of facilitating strategies: given the absence of any pressure to learn the language correctly, all they wish to do is to learn to speak it as quickly as possible with a maximum of efficient communication and a minimum of exertion. I should like to emphasize the difference between facilitation and simplification. Obviously, the net result of the use of facilitating strategies will be a simplified version of the target language, but simplifying the language can be regarded as only one of the possible means towards the primary aim of the learners.

In most cases, the native speaker will continue to speak his mother tongue along with the broken down version — provided he takes the trouble of learning it, which is not at all certain. As the broken down version becomes standardized, the distance between it and the target language may be such that successful communication is no longer possible. Only a few residents of the British East Asian colonies will have been able to speak correctly the Chinese Pidgin English current in those parts, and in New Guinea, speakers of Tok Pisin have to use a special register (called Tok Masta, cf. Mühlhäusler 1981a) in their contacts with white residents, who would not understand them otherwise. This means that the combination of a prolonged stay of the native speakers — and, consequently, of prolonged exposure to a correct version of the language — and an improved system of schooling will prevent the emergence of a creole version of the existing pidgin, as the children will have the chance to hear the correct model over and over again. However, when the invaders leave, it depends on the situation in the area involved whether or not the pidginized variety will disappear, and whether or not a creole will emerge. In some cases, for instance Bamboo-English in Korea (Algee 1960; Webster 1960) and Vietnamese Pidgin French or Tây Bồi in Vietnam (Reinecke 1971; Liem 1979) there was no more need for a pidgin after the disappearance of the target language, because the population was not multilingual and the pidginized variety had served exclusively as a means of communication between them and the invaders. In other cases, the pidgin remained a useful means of communication between the various constituent groups of the community, as for instance, Krio in Sierra Leone, and other varieties of English in West Africa. And in still other cases, the socio-linguistic situation that obtained brought about favourable conditions for the development of a creolized version, for instance, Tok Pisin in New Guinea (Sankoff & Laberge 1974).

In a few exceptional cases, the invaders imposed their language on the conquered population, and then, surprisingly, finished by taking over the broken down version that had developed as a result of the contacts. In my view, a typical instance of such a development — apart from the case of Arabic! — is that of the Latin language in the various provinces of the Roman empire. I believe that what is called in Romance linguistics Vulgar Latin is nothing else than a reflection of the debased variety of Latin in the mouths of the non-Romans, which was imported to Rome and became the normal means of communication for the multilingual society in that city, and in the end even for the Romans themselves.[7] What are the prerequisites for such a development? In the first place, it seems that there must be a certain amount of isolation of the settlers from their home-country, or at least, only minimal possibilities for them of preserving the purity of their children's colloquial by means of schooling. In the second place, the numerical superiority of the conquered population must be overwhelming. And in the third place, there must be a certain amount of intermarriage (for the importance of mixed marriages see Valkhoff 1972:99-118). As I have stated above, I believe that these factors led to a similar development in the countries conquered by the Arabs in the seventh century A.D. Before going into the analysis of this development further, I shall first recapitulate the results of the discussion so far.

Stated paradoxically, these results could be summarized as follows: pidginizing a language is the normal procedure in a process of second language learning. Learners are only prevented from doing so by certain cultural or social inhibitions, the most important of which is the presence of formal education and the opportunity of being guided by a teacher throughout the first attempts to speak a foreign language. A modern example shows very convincingly what happens when this opportunity is not available, namely that of the foreign workers in Western European industrialized countries, in particular France, Belgium, Holland, and the Federal Republic of Germany. During the last twenty years a massive immigration of foreign workers to these countries has taken place, mostly from the countries around the Mediterranean. These immigrants came to their new jobs with hardly any knowledge of the language, and it turned out soon they could do their jobs without learning the language (cf. Bodemann & Ostow 1975), or by learning only a rudimentary version of it (called in West Germany 'Gastarbeiterdeutsch'), various discussions have been devoted to the question of whether or not the resulting variety of German, Dutch, French deserves the name of 'pidgin'.[8] One of the points raised in these discussions is that we cannot regard Gastarbeiterdeutsch as a pidgin, because there is no standardized form, each idiolect representing, in fact, a different version of the supposed pidgin.

On the other hand, it is obvious that the various versions of the target language that are produced by the foreign workers do have many traits in common with each other (cf. Heidelberger Forschungsprojekt 1975). It is equally obvious that when we define 'pidginization' as a process of learning a second language by applying certain strategies that cannot be used in a situation of formal learning, the different versions of Gastarbeiterdeutsch may well be regarded as a pidginized form of German. The question of its status as a 'real pidgin' then becomes irrelevant (cf. above, ch. III, p. 37ff.). Being deprived — generally speaking — of the opportunity of formal education, the foreign workers have to make do with what they can pick up of the language they are constantly being exposed to in their social life. The permanent day-to-day contact with the model of the target language prevents the emergence of an accepted norm of Gastarbeiterdeutsch.[9] What is more, a fluent and correct command of the foreign language brings with it substantial rewards (cf. Bodemann & Ostow 1975:123). The development of a standardized pidgin is furthermore inhibited by the fact that the children of the second generation normally go to school and are expected to learn the foreign language in question in a formal way, so that they are not likely to speak any kind of creolized version of it. Contacts between different ethnic groups are so infrequent as to be of no importance for the development of an inter-ethnic means of communication.

Another point to be made in connection with the emergence of contact jargons concerns the role of 'foreigner talk' in the formation of simplified varieties of the target language (cf. Ferguson & DeBose 1977; Ferguson 1981; Valdman 1981). Apparently, in the case of 'Gastarbeiter' versions of Western European languages the 'foreigner talk' register is rather important (cf. Heidelberger Forschungsprojekt 1975; Werkgroep 1978; Bodemann & Ostow 1975:141-46). But with regard to other pidginized varieties a serious objection to the role of the 'foreigner talk' register in the process of pidginization is raised by Alleyne (1980:125-26). In his view, it is most improbable that Europeans wilfully simplified their own speech in order to be understood by the 'natives'. The existence of many fossilized forms in the resulting creoles — even in those cases where decreolization under the influence of the norms of the target language is excluded — proves that the 'natives' must have heard at least fragments of the entire morphological inventory of the target language, irregular plurals, for instance, and strong preterites in the case of English as a target language. Perhaps, a better approach to the phenomenon of 'foreigner talk' is to assume that the native speakers of the target language anticipate the application of strategies for the facilitation of learning on the part of the new speakers by applying the same strategies themselves to their own language, thus producing their own approximation of the target language which, without being the cause of the emergence of a pidginized variety merely converges with it because of the identity of the strategies used by the two groups. A different matter is, of course, the role the approximation of the pidginized variety by the speakers of the target language may play in the establishment of a more or less stable norm of the pidginized variety. During the formative period of this pidgin norm the approximative version of the native speakers of the target language may constitute an important source of innovations (cf. Mühlhäusler 1981:101), which, however, decreases as the use of the pidginized language as an intertribal means of communication becomes more important. The native speakers of the target language who try to speak the pidginized variety of their own mother tongue contribute to a decreolization of that variety that is both quicker and more complete than it would have been without the exposure of the pidgin speakers to the approximative version.[10]

Let us now go back to the case of Arabic. Applying the results of the foregoing discussion to the situation in the first century of the Hiğra, I wish to deal with the following points in particular: 1) the absence or presence of a system of education as a formal opportunity to learn Arabic in a non-improvised way; 2) the role of the substratal languages; and 3) the importance of mixed marriages and the language of the second generation. Although information is scarce, this last point is particularly important, since I assume that the Classical language was first pidginized, and then became the mother tongue for all speakers. Often, though not always, this creolized version was decreolized afterwards as the result of the influence of the Classical norm. In my argumentation the crucial point is, therefore, that the native speakers of Arabic or rather, their children, took over the debased versions that were developed by the inhabitants of the conquered territories. I repeat that, as far as the 'accepted' pidgins and creoles are concerned, this is not the normal development, but it is by no means an unparallelled one, witness the case of Afrikaans, for instance.

Can the inhabitants of Syria, Iraq, Egypt have learnt the established norm of Classical Arabic at school? We know that in the Hellenistic cultural area there was a dense network of schools; even in the smallest settlements there were elementary schools for instruction in reading and writing (cf. Marrou 1948:460-76; Versteegh 1980a:10-11). Schools may be said to have played an important role in everyday life, especially in Syria. On the other hand, illiteracy must have been the rule, and education the prerogative of a cultural elite that was oriented towards Byzantine civilization. After the conquests, the schools remained important as intermediaries in the process of borrowing by which the Arabs learnt the rudiments of science and philosophy. But for the overwhelming majority of the population there was no way of participating in this intellectual movement. After the general upheaval of the conquests the elementary schools had all but disappeared, except perhaps for the convent schools which were allowed to continue their work.

The Arabic school system cannot be called a true successor to the Hellenistic tradition, at least not as far as the elementary schools are concerned. It is true that most children participated in one way or another in the instruction in religion and recitation of the *Qur'ān* that was offered in the *kuttāb*, the lowest elementary school, but reading and writing was something that only a few could achieve. The schools did help to propagate the language of the *Qur'ān*, and this was an important factor in the development of the Arabic language and the Arabic dialects, but they could not — nor were they expected to — provide language-courses for the non-Arabs who wished to learn the language. The statistics of illiteracy even in the 20th century (cf. Diem 1974:10) make abundantly clear that the Classical culture remained reserved for a dwindling minority, whereas the masses, especially in the countryside, had nothing to do with that culture. The generally higher level of the schools in the cities and the better opportunities for urban children in this regard somewhat bridged the gap between conservative Bedouin dialects in the countryside and innovatory urban dialects mentioned above.

My second point concerns the position of the substratal languages, the languages originally spoken in the area that was overrun by the Arabs. The most important of these are Syriac and Aramaic dialects, with Syriac as a flourishing literary language that had begun to be the language of a rich literature; Persian; Coptic with a small, mostly religious corpus of texts; Berber dialects in North Africa without a written tradition; South Arabic in Yemen, a language closely related to Ethiopian; and finally Greek, which was used as a literary and official language in the provinces of the Byzantine empire. Of these languages, Greek disappeared completely, only to become important once more in the course of the translation movement that was connected with the *Bayt al-Ḥikma* in Baghdad. Coptic has remained in use as a liturgical language in the Coptic church, whereas both Aramaic and South Arabic are restricted to a few linguistic pockets, Aramaic in a few villages in Lebanon and the Soviet Union, South Arabic in the Mehri and Soqotri languages. Berber dialects are still spoken by a considerable part of the population of the Maghreb, according to a recent report by some 6,500,000 people on a total population of 29,000,000 (Gallagher 1968:134). Persian has been the most successful of the substratal languages: it was reinstated as the official language of Iran, although large minorities in the country use other languages.[11]

In considering the role of these substratal languages the first thing we notice is that they differed sufficiently from Arabic to allow for pidginization of the Arabic language at all.[12] Apparently, when source language and target language resemble each other too much, there is no need for pidginization. A Dutchman learning German without formal instruction, or a Norwegian learning Swedish, or a Czech learning Slovak, will not be tempted to pidginize the language he is learning. What will happen is that the speaker produces some kind of language mixture that will make him understood without forcing him to resort to simplifying strategies of the kind we are dealing with here. In most cases this means replacing lexical and morphological elements from his own language with elements from the language he is trying to speak.[13]

The substratal languages in the Arab empire being dissimilar to Arabic, the possibility sketched above was not available to the new speakers: they had to resort to facilitating strategies. In many areas there must have been a bilingual situation for a long time, with the substratal languages being used at home, and the Arabic language being used for public communication with people from other linguistic backgrounds. The linguistic homogeneity of the countryside and the segregation of Arabs and indigenous population in the agrarian settlements guaranteed the survival of the original languages for centuries. But in the cities, the polyglot composition of the population, and the need to communicate daily with other people in Arabic, the only common means of communication, were much less favourable conditions for the survival of Syriac and other local languages. What is more, mixed marriages became very common, so that even in the families Arabic was often the only means of communication. Whenever that happened, the children of the next generation learnt the pidginized variety as their mother tongue, thereby creolizing it.

We have no certain information about the actual number of mixed marriages in the early period of Islam. We have seen above that the soldiers in the first armies to be dispatched outside the peninsula took women from the local population as their wives, and in these families the children were no doubt brought up from the beginning in the new type of Arabic. There are also reports that many of the *ṣaḥābī*, the early companions of the prophet, had Christian wives, and that during the first century of the Hiğra there were many mixed marriages (Fattal 1958:130-131, quoting from Ṭabarī, *Ta'rīḫ* I, 2373). It is, of course, possible that the women in question belonged to the Christian Arab tribes which long before the coming of Islam had settled in the deserts of Syria and in Southern Iraq. Theoretically, it might be assumed that the Arabs would tend to marry within their own ethnic group. But no injunctions against marrying someone from another people are known, on the contrary, the *Qur'ān* expressly allows Muslim men to marry women from the *ahl al-Kitāb*, i.e. Christian and Jewish women, as long as these do not interfere with the religious duties of their husbands and with the Islamic education of their children (cf. Fattal 1958:129-37). The reverse — a marriage between a non-Muslim and a Muslim woman — is strictly forbidden, but nothing prevented the men from the conquered peoples to be converted and thereby obtain the right to marry a Muslim woman. This is exactly what is reported about Egypt, where mass conversions are said to have taken place after 755 for precisely this reason. As a result, so it is noted, the majority of the inhabitants of that country are now of mixed descent (Tritton 1930:36, quoting from Maqrīzī, *Ḫiṭaṭ* II, 500). It is, perhaps, significant that the permission to take a non-Muslim wife did not extend, at least not at the beginning, to women who professed Zoroastrianism, so that mixed Arab-Iranian marriages were rather rare during the reign of the Umayyads. Only after the 'Abbāsids had become the ruling dynasty do we find an increasing number of such marriages. The fact, however, that as late as 809 al-Ma'mūn's descent from an Iranian concubine was regarded as something remarkable shows that in some circles mixed marriages with Persian women were still frowned upon. We have seen above that at an early time the Arabic language of the invaders was superseded by Iranian as the new national language of the Iranian provinces.

Theoretically one could, of course, assume that the offspring of the mixed marriages learnt the mother tongue of their mothers as well as Arabic, the language of their fathers. The next generation might then have forgotten the substratal language, and only learnt Arabic. But this assumption does not take into account the fact that during these early decades the household language in these mixed families must have been the debased version of Arabic, and that there was no system of education capable of instructing so many children in a proper way. Consequently, these children were exposed only to the pidginized variety, just as the rest of the population, who had to learn Arabic, as it were, in the streets. Thus, it comes as no surprise that we hear almost right from the beginning of the period of the conquests complaints about the errors of speech (*laḥn*) that had crept into the speech of the new Muslims, and even threatened the purity of the language. The authorities tried in vain to turn the tide of what they called 'corruption' in speech by providing at least elementary education. However, in the first place it was impossible to reach more than the most important urban centres, and in the second place, even there it was impossible to reach more than the children from a relatively small elite. What was achieved by the grammarians, whose discipline was a direct result of the increasing uncertainty about the linguistic norms of the *'Arabiyya*, was the emergence of a linguistic community in which there were two levels of speech, the high variety of the Classical language, and the low variety of the creolized colloquial. Through the influence of the standardization of the grammarians and the enormous religious prestige the Arabic language had in the eyes of the new converts the low variety was constantly affected by a process of decreolization. This process caused the most stigmatized forms to disappear from the continuum of speech that existed within the community, even though the fundamental dichotomy between high and low level remained intact. Nothing much is known about the long-term effects of such a process of decreolization, but the few studies that have appeared confirm the fact that in principle decreolization may result in the disappearance of basilectal forms (cf. Escure 1981).

NOTES

1) On the legal position of the *d̠immī* see Fattal 1958; Noth 1975, and below, p. 75.

2) Cf. Donner (1981:222): "The army does not, then, appear to have been a collection of complete tribes or even of complete sections of tribes; it was, rather, a selection of people (mainly men) from various tribes who could effectively serve as part of a fairly well-organized army".

3) The linguistic situation in Persia at the time of the Islamic conquest is a complicated one. Between the period of the Achaemenids and the period of Sāsānian Iran a number of changes affected the language, which Lazard (1975:596) compares to the changes that took place between Latin and French. The development from Middle Persian to New Persian, on the other hand, was much less radical. According to the description of the linguistic situation in Iran given in the *Fihrist* (Lazard 1975:598ff.) there were, apart from Arabic, five languages being spoken, Syriac (*Suryānī*), Khuzestanian (?, *h̠ūzī*), the Parthian dialect of Media (*Pahlavī*, later the common designation for Middle Persian), the New Persian colloquial of Iran (*Darī* or *Parsī-i Darī*), and Middle Persian (*Parsī*, later called *Pahlavī*). Originally Parsī and Darī were two different registers of the same language, but gradually they grew apart, Darī being used primarily as colloquial, and Parsī as literary language.

4) Cf. the description given by Fück (1950:4-28) of the linguistic melting pot in the cities, as well as the general analysis of the Baṣrian society of the early centuries by Pellat (1953).

5) Cf. the 'linguisters' mentioned by LePage (1977:229-30) and the polyglots among the Indians of North America who first aided communication between the tribes, and then automatically became interpreters in the contacts with the white invaders (Drechsel 1976:66); other instances are mentioned by Valkhoff (1972).

6) Examples abound: Russenorsk, the Chinese-Russian jargon of Kjachta, the trade language of Welsh and Breton fishermen, etc.; cf. below, ch. VI.

7) Another controversial example of such a development is that of Afrikaans. Valkhoff (1972) in my view quite rightly maintains that the Dutch settlers in the Cape Colony — or rather their children — ended up by taking over the simplified version of Dutch that had been developed by the black population.

8) Or 'pre-pidgin', or 'pseudo-pidgin', or 'pre-pidgin continuum', cf. Meisel 1975; Pfaff 1981.

9) Cf. Meisel (1975:26): "Daraus resultiert die verstärkte Anpassung an das Deutsche, wobei ständig Möglichkeiten geboten sind, der Zielsprache näher zu kommen".

10) The approximative version is, of course, a caricature of the pidginized variety. The Englishmen using Tok Pisin thought they were doing the right thing by equating all Tok Pisin words with their English etyma, and by regarding every English word in principle as a suitable Tok Pisin word (Mühlhäusler 1981); this way of talking the language was called by 'native' speakers of the pidgin 'Tok Masta'. A similar approximative version of a pidginized variety is to be found in the collection of Chinese Pidgin English texts published by Hall (1944); these texts contain almost without exception utterances of Englishmen and Americans who had learned the pidgin as a second language, and they look sometimes very inauthentic.

11) Among these minority languages Arabic is the most important one in the province of Khuzestan, cf. Ingham 1973; 1976.

12) Possibly, this does not apply to the Aramaic dialects, some of which may have been similar to Arabic. In that case, one might assume that the coexistence and mutual interference of the languages of the conqueror and the conquered led to the emergence of a 'mixed' language.

13) A documented case of this phenomenon is the so-called Cocoliche used by Italians in Argentina. Italian immigrants in that country use in their contacts with the Spanish speaking inhabitants a curious, conventionally determined mixture of Spanish and Italian that does not exhibit any pidginizing features. This mixture is stable in the sense that it remains the same for every newcomer to the country, whereas it is unstable in the sense that each individual will gradually improve his speech in the direction of colloquial Spanish, as Whinnom (1971:97-102) explains. Possibly, the mutual intelligibility of Spanish and Italian explains the fact that undirected second language learning in this case only leads to massive interference of a temporary nature, and not to pidginization. Something similar happens with the Spanish-Portuguese dialects at the Brazilian border (Elizaincín 1976). It is perhaps superfluous to add that the same observation could be made about dialect speakers who at a later stage in their lives come into contact with the standard language: these speakers do not run the risk of being unintelligible when they use dialectal elements in their approximation of the standard language, and in their speech, interference will take the place of universal strategies of second language learning which are the rule rather than the exception in cases of undirected second language acquisition.

CHAPTER V

PIDGINIZATION AND CREOLIZATION IN ARABIC

5.1 In the preceding chapters I have attempted to demonstrate that in certain situations of language learning the learners are confronted with a limited input of linguistic material, so that they are forced to use certain strategies in order to either learn a second language or to reconstruct a first language. It was furthermore assumed that the application of these strategies leads to specific changes in the languages involved. The next step was an analysis of the context in which the Arabic language was learnt in the conquered territories. I concluded that such a language learning situation obtained in this case. Consequently, if these conclusions are accepted, one expects to find traces of similar changes in the modern Arabic dialects to those which are found in other creolized languages. In this chapter I shall adduce data from these dialects to illustrate the way in which the history of the Arabic language and the resulting structure of the modern dialects may be interpreted in the light of the theory sketched above. Obviously, these data in themselves can never be evidence of creolization (cf. also below, ch. VII, p. 139; 144) but they can be used as an illustration of the use of the approach chosen here.

A second preliminary point is that in this theory the Arabic dialects went through successive stages of development with different, sometimes contradictory, tendencies. All dialects, except the Bedouin dialects, originated as the result of a process of pidginization; all dialects then became mother tongues and, consequently, underwent the changes that accompany such a development. Most dialects remained within the sphere of influence of the Classical language and, as a result, they bear the traces of a decreolization that partly obliterated the product of the first two processes. This does not mean that it has become impossible to compare the end product with other languages that only went through one or two stages of a similar development, but only that there is no direct genealogical link between the target language and the resulting creole.

As a typical example I may cite the case of the Tok Pisin particle *bai* which as a prefix indicating aspect in the language of those who speak Tok

Pisin as their first language is not directly related with its English etymon *by and by*. During the first stage of the language most distinctions of tense and aspect had been lost as a result of the pidginization process, and lexical elements such as *baimbai* "soon, in the future" served as indicators of these lost distinctions. Their syntactic autonomy was evident: they were used optionally and did not have a fixed position in the sentence. In recent times, when the language became creolized, these lexical elements were reanalyzed as morphological elements, and they became, accordingly, part of the morphological inventory of the language, mostly in a shortened form. Thus, *baimbai* became an obligatory aspectual prefix *bai*, which indicates non-reality or future in creolized Tok Pisin. Similar instances in the history of Arabic have been mentioned in the preceding chapters and will be discussed below systematically.

It should be added that categories which disappear in the first stage of the process are lost forever, and cannot reappear in the subsequent stages. The use of the catchwords 'simplification' and 'expansion' to epitomize the processes of pidginization and creolization, respectively, may lead to confusion concerning the evidence to be found in languages that went through both stages. Obviously, a language which loses the morphological category of the dual is not likely to recreate a dual in subsequent stages, for the process of expansion (or rather grammaticalization) is always an expansion in terms of the available linguistic material. New rules are created that were not present in the input that is presented to the learner, involving the grammaticalization or reanalysis of lexical elements, for instance, but these rules operate on the material in that input. I do not believe that Rickford's doubts (1977) concerning the use of 'simplification' in Black English as evidence for prior creolization are warranted. In his view, Black English as a supposed creolized version of English ought to have expanded instead of simplified the target language. But there is no law that obliges the first language learners working on the pidginized variety to supplement all lost categories in the limited input. Besides, the opposition between 'simplification' and 'expansion' seems to be artificial: even at the pidginizing stage a lot of elaboration goes on, especially in those cases where a pidginized variety is used as a more or less permanent and stable means of communication between heterolingual groups. Many phenomena that are known from creolized varieties may be found in stable pidgins as well.

In connection with this last remark I should like to emphasize that the phenomena I shall discuss below are not linguistic laws, but tendencies —

correlating with strategies of language learning — which may or may not be operative in concrete cases. Given a tendency to regularize all paradigms, we expect the resulting language to exhibit a larger number of predictable forms — e.g., in the case of Arabic more sound plurals — but it would be unrealistic to expect the resulting language to consist only of predictable forms. Firstly, the influence of the normative literary language often acted as a counterforce, and secondly, many forms were protected by their relative frequency, their place within the system, or their analogous association with other forms. Finally, the situation in each area was different, and we may reasonably expect the difference in socio-linguistic make-up to be reflected by the degree to which the pidginized variety of the target language has been resistant to decreolization.

In his analysis of the Arabic creole (Ki-)Nubi, Heine (1982:17) enumerates the following characteristics of the process of pidginization (cf. also Heine 1973:227-33; Bollée 1977:104-111):

1. explicit linguistic transmission tends to become more implicit;
2. 'dispensable' linguistic items and rules tend to be eliminated;
3. inflectional/agglutinating constructions tend to be replaced be analytical/isolating ones;
4. marked forms tend to be replaced by unmarked ones;
5. context-sensitive rules tend to be replaced by context-free rules.

These features fall into two categories. The first feature is the reduction of the rate of redundancy: what is not necessary for effective communication disappears, both in the foreigner talk register and in the pidginized variety. This also applies to the second feature, the disappearance of 'dispensable' linguistic items. In learning a second language in an untutored situation and without socio-cultural inhibitions against incorrect speech, it is certainly more economical to reduce the number of categories to be learnt as much as possible. In practical terms: if it is possible to express a combination 'lexical item + grammatical morpheme' with two lexical items, for instance, instead of a dual *rağulāni* "two men" the combination *rağul iṯnāni*, this is preferred by the pidgin learner. This is what Heine's third feature states: synthetic constructions are replaced by analytical constructions. It is not always a simple replacement: the lexical elements used for the expression of grammatical meanings that had been expressed by lost morphological categories are often reanalyzed and subsequently grammaticalized.

The second category of features serves again a facilitating purpose for the second language learner: it is easier always to use the same form instead of having to concentrate on the correct distribution of two allomorphs, and having to bother with exceptions. Concrete examples are the exclusive use of the short form of adjectives in French creoles (Bollée 1977:35-37) and the generalization of the German weak verbs in Gastarbeiterdeutsch (*gehte*, *gedenkt*, instead of *ging*, *gedacht*, Meisel 1975:47). This category includes the regularization of exceptions and the tendency to impose paradigmatic unity or, in Heine's terms, the tendency to use the unmarked form and the context-free rule.

5.2 *Phonology*

Just like all known pidginized varieties (cf. Heine 1973:156-66; Bollée 1977:105-106) the Arabic dialects exhibit a simplification in the phonological inventory as compared with that of the Classical language. The most striking common development in this respect is the merger of the two phonemes /ḍ/ and /ḏ̣/ in virtually all dialects, one of the phenomena that have been adduced as evidence for the koine-theory (Ferguson 1959:630).[1]

In many dialects the interdentals as marked terms of the opposition dental/interdental disappear (Fischer & Jastrow 1980:50), just as the interdentals in most pidgins (Heine 1973:161-62). In the periphery many more marked phonemes disappear, especially those which may be regarded as specifically Arabic, i.e. not occurring in other languages, for example, /ʻ/, which merged with /ʼ/ or disappeared in Chad Arabic (Hagège 1973:21),[2] and partly merged with /ḥ/ in Anatolian Arabic (Jastrow 1973:18-19; 1978:43). Both /ḥ/ and /ʻ/ have disappeared in Nigerian Arabic (Kaye 1975:319).

In all dialects the vocalism differs from the Classical system. In the first place, the diphthongs /ay/ and /aw/ have disappeared and changed into /e/ and /o/, just as in almost all creole languages (Alleyne 1980:40; Heine 1973:160-61). In all dialects the position of the short /i/ and /u/, sometimes even of /a/, has been weakened in some, in extreme cases even in all contexts.[3] According to Ambros (1973-74:84-86) most dialects show a reduction of the opposition /a/ - /i/ - /u/ to /a/ - /i, u/, sometimes to /a, i/ - /u/ (for the Western dialects see Fischer & Jastrow 1980:249-59). In some dialects even these reduced oppositions disappear completely, for instance in the Algerian Arabic dialect of Djidjelli (but cf. Cohen 1965:7, 12) and in the Jewish Arabic of Algiers (Cohen 1912:161). Even with the long vowels the contrast is more limited than in Old Arabic (Ambros 1973-74:86, n.2). Ambros' analysis connects the disappearance of some vocalic oppositions with the situation in Old

Arabic where, according to his data, these oppositions had already begun to weaken. Such an analysis is certainly interesting, but it is no explanation of the actual loss: the question is precisely why and under which circumstances these potential weaknesses were actualized in the process of development of the dialects.

Another characteristic of the phonological inventory of the modern dialects is their use of new morpho-phonemic rules with regard to the phenomenon of velarization ('emphasis', *tafḫīm*). Without going into the problems that are connected with the synchronic analysis of this phenomenon,[4] I wish to draw the attention to similar developments in some creole dialects, in which nasalization is distributed in the same way as velarization in the Arabic dialects (cf. Valdman 1977a:170; 1977b:287). Perhaps, we are dealing here with what Samuels (1972:21ff.) calls "stylistically induced suprasegmentals", variations in the realization of phonemes that find their origin in different styles of pronunciation. In the case of the Arabic emphatic consonants an exaggerated and forceful pronunciation — such as is used in 'foreigner talk'? — could have led to a reanalysis of the phonetic context of these consonants, and in some cases even to phonemicization of new emphatic consonants.

5.3 *Morphology*

One of the most obvious characteristics of the pidginization of a language is the phenomenon that the rate of redundancy tends to be reduced drastically compared to the target language. This results in the loss of many morphological categories. Grammatical relations that are expressed in the target language with the help of morpho-syntactic elements are now expressed with the help of lexical elements. In the course of time, these lexical elements are reanalyzed, and through a process of grammaticalization they again become syntactic markers of grammatical relations used obligatorily. This transition from lexical to syntactic means may take place in the transition from pidginized variety to first language (creolization), but also in the pidginized variety itself, namely in those cases where a stable pidginized variety is used uninterruptedly by some generations of speakers.[5]

The chief example of morphological reduction of redundancy is, of course, the disappearance of the case-endings in the nominal declension in all Arabic dialects,[6] with the oblique ending as the sole remaining morpheme in the plural.[7] The disappearance of the case-endings coincided with the introduction of new analytical constructions to replace the older morpho-syntactic elements in their function as markers of grammatical relations. These new analytical expressions must have evolved from an earlier stage in the history of the dialects in which grammatical relations were expressed with the help of optional lexical elements. This evolution may be best explained with the example of the verbal markers.

One of the most spectacular phenomena in pidginized and creolized languages all over the world is the emergence of a new verbal system with special markers for mood, tense, and aspect.[8] The occurrence of three markers in a strict order and with certain combinations, is attested in a great number of languages which cannot be linked through common descent or common substratal influence by any stretch of the imagination. The exact status of the universal features of this system — as elaborated by Bickerton (1976; 1981:73-99) — is still a matter of debate (cf. Muysken 1981a and Bickerton's reaction, 1981:78ff.). The structural similarities in themselves, however, are not denied by anyone. I believe that Bickerton's method of trying to reconstruct the 'scenario' for the development of a particular verbal system is the most promising approach to the problem.

It seems that most, if not all, pidginized languages begin with a very simple system, consisting of an uninflected verb which can be modified with the help of adverbs in clause-external position to express temporal relations. Most pidgin languages possess — in Bickerton's terminology — an 'earlier' marker derived from an etymon with the meaning of "to finish", and a 'later' marker derived from an etymon with the meaning of "soon", "presently", "tomorrow", or something similar. A few examples are Tok Pisin *pinis* (Eng. *finish*) and *baimbai* (Eng. *by and by*); Hawaiian Creole English *pau* (Hawaiian *pau* "finished") and *baimbai*; Portuguese Creoles *caba* (Portuguese *acabar* "to finish") and *logo* (Portuguese *logo* "next, soon"); and an example from a non-European based pidgin, Sango *awɛ* "it is finished" and *fadé* "soon" (cf. Manessy 1977:147). When pidgin languages with these markers are being learnt as first languages by a new generation, the markers ordinarily do not develop into obligatory aspectual markers ('earlier' becoming the marker for past, anterior or completive, for instance, and 'later' the marker for future or irrealis), but a completely new system is developed. In this new system there are very often three markers: anterior, derived from a verb meaning "to be" (French Creoles *te*, English Creoles *bin*); durative or non-punctual; and irrealis, often derived from a verb meaning "to go" (French Creoles *va*, English Creoles *go*) or from auxiliaries (Jamaican Creole English *wi*, Negerhollands *sa*). Only in some cases did the 'earlier' marker remain to be used as an anterior marker, whereas the 'later' marker almost always disappeared. According to Bickerton (1981:78-82) this was to be expected, since the 'earlier' marker, being connected with a verbal etymon, stood a better chance of being included in the category auxiliary than the adverbial 'later' marker.

In those cases where the 'earlier' marker did remain, such as Indian French Creoles *fi(n)*, it often remained marginal, i.e. outside the category auxiliary, serving solely as a reinforcing element, or it was introduced into the category auxiliary, but without the possiblity of combination with other aspectual markers. Examples of these stages are found in Papiamentu, where the future marker *lo* and the anterior marker *ba* are syntactically clause-external. In Tok Pisin we find a system where the pidgin markers are retained even in the creolized variety: the markers *pinis* and *bai* (*baimbai*) are used as obligatory markers in the creole version (for *pinis* see Siegel 1981, for *baimbai* Sankoff & Laberge 1974). The data about the markers are taken from Bickerton (1981); according to him the difference between the development of the last mentioned system and the 'classical' creole systems is to be explained by their prolonged existence as pidgins before creolization, which stabilized their use as input for the new generation.[9]

It is not clear whether we have to posit one or two verbal bases for the original verbal system of the first pidginized varieties of Arabic. Apart from the modern Arabic pidgins, all Arabic dialects have two verbal stems, which may be regarded as reflexes of the Classical perfect and imperfect, the former being inflected for person with the help of suffixes, the latter with the help of prefixes. The only remaining verbal stem in Juba Arabic looks like a perfect, but may in fact be derived from an imperative. Moreover, modern creolized varieties of this pidgin — judging by the material presented by Mahmud (1979) — seem to develop a new form with prefixes through a process of reinterpretation of the prefixes in the standard language, first as aspectual markers, and then as new agreement markers (cf. below, ch. VI, p. 126). I believe, therefore, that the first pidginized varieties used only a zero verbal form — just as most pidginized languages all over the world — and that the agreement markers, both as suffixes to the zero verb, and as prefixes, are a later development. Obviously, empirical support for this hypothesis may be found in the development of Juba Arabic. The creolized speech in the South of the Sudan will enable us to determine, whether or not the scenario skecthed here briefly is realistic.

In the same context one may ask whether or not this earliest form of communication had something comparable to the 'earlier' and 'later' markers discussed above. The modern Arabic creole (Ki-)Nubi has a (non-obligatory) 'earlier' marker *kàlá(s)* (Classical *ẖalaṣa* "to finish", cf. Heine 1982:38), and even in the modern dialects we find traces of such a marker, for instance in Moroccan *temm* (Classical *tamma* "to be completed"), Chadian *ẖalaṣ* (Hagège 1973:49, 69-70) and perhaps Egyptian (Cairene) *ba'a* (< *baqiya* "to stay"), e.g., in *lēh ma-gibtiš il-kitāb ma'āk? nisīt ba'a* "why didn't you bring the book? I have quite forgotten" (El-Tonsi & Brustad 1981:4). Anatolian dialects have a marker for the perfective aspect (*kū, kūt, kət, kəl)* which is probably derived from a form of *kāna* "to be" (cf. Jastrow 1978:307-308). As for the 'later' marker, despite the fact that its adverbial character made it more liable to elision, we find nevertheless in some dialects verbal particles that are perhaps best explained as traces of adverbial 'later' markers, which survived the creolization of the pidginized variety, for instance Moroccan *ġa, ġadi* (Classical *ġadan* "tomorrow"?)[10], Tunisian *taw* (Classical *tawwan* "directly"?)[11]. Both particles are used semi-obligatorily within the auxiliary. Other dialects use a clause-external temporal adverb *daba* "now", which may be regarded as an adverb that dit not make the step to inclusion in the category auxiliary.[12] The Moroccan and Tunisian particles mentioned here are used as future markers, e.g. (Moroccan) *ma-ġa-nekteb-lek-š* "I won't write to you".

According to Diem (1978:130, n.4) the use of aspectual particles in the modern dialects is nothing new: Old Arabic already had particles such as *qad* (anterior) or *sawfa*, *sa-* (future). One could also point out that the verb *kāna* is used in Classical Arabic in combination with the imperfect to express a past durative or iterative (cf. on this construction Nebes 1982). But in Classical Arabic the verb *kāna* was always used at the head of the sentence regardless of the place of the main verb, and this no doubt contributed to its fossilization in Middle Arabic texts (Blau 1965:99-100). As for the particle *qad*, its behaviour in Middle Arabic texts shows that it was far from being a real verbal performative such as those which came into use in the dialects. In early Middle Arabic texts *qad* is often used without a fixed position, whereas the verbal particles are evidently stabilized forms of earlier adverbs or verbs (Blau 1965:65).

In most dialects the functions of future marker and anterior marker are taken over by new particles, just as in most creole languages. Often, the new future marker was derived from a verb with the meaning of "to go", for instance Egyptian *ḥa* < *rāyiḥ*, Syrian *raḥ*, *laḥ* with the same etymon. Other dialects use particles that are derived from the verb *mašā* "to go", for instance Jewish Arabic of Tunis (Cohen 1975:137)[13], or from the verb *sāra* "to go, to ride", for instance Standard Maltese *sejjer*, rural Maltese dialects *sa-* (Schabert 1976:131), or from Classical *ḥattā* "until", for instance in Anatolian Arabic *ta* (Jastrow 1978:302-303). In some cases the new future marker may have evolved from an earlier irrealis marker, whose original function was taken over partly by the imperfect without particles in its function as a modal, and partly by the new future marker itself. This explains cases such as Libyan *bbi-* from a verb *baġā* "to wish", which combines the meaning of irreality with that of future.[14] This might even explain the Syrian future marker *bi-* (Grotzfeld 1965:81-82), which is used as a volitional and may have evolved from the same verb *baġā*. A similar semantic development seems to have taken place in some dialects of Yemenite Arabic, which use *ša-* (< *šā'a* "to wish") for the volitional (Diem 1973:70, 98, 110, 126).

As for the anterior marker, virutally all dialects, even those which have retained traces of a 'later' marker, have developed a new anterior marker, derived from the verb *kāna* "to be" (cf. English Creoles *bin* < English *been*, French Creoles *te* < French *été*). In some dialects this marker is not inflected for person or number, for example in Anatolian Arabic (Jastrow 1969:37ff. 1978:308f.; Sasse 1971:157ff.), and in the 'Irāqī Arabic dialect of Kwayriš (Denz 1971:61-62, 101). Normally this is interpreted as a development towards erosion of the inflectional system, but I believe that it should rather be regarded as a reflection of an earlier situation in which all markers acted as verbal particles. At a later stage, the influence of the Classical language introduced the inflection of the verbal particle as a real verb. I know of only one dialect where apparently the anterior marker *kān* is almost unknown, the Jewish Arabic of Tunis (Cohen 1975:135). In Nigerian Arabic instead of *kān* the substantive *zamān* "time" is used, e.g., *zamān ana gā'it fī yarwa* "I used to live in Maiduguri", also as a past copula, e.g., *zamān hu ḫawwāf* "he was afraid", but more data are needed (Kaye 1975:319).

In the reconstruction of the verbal system during the stage of creolization the indication of irreality/future and anteriority was combined with another distinction, that of non-punctual (durative) action as against punctual action. In most creole languages the categories progressive and habitual are usually expressed by the same morpheme, but in this respect Arabic dialects deviate from the usual development, in that the categories progressive, habitual, future and modal (irrealis, volitional) are distributed in various ways. In all dialects there is minimally a marker for the progressive present, derived from a verb meaning "to sit", for example Rural Maltese *'aed* (Schabert 1976:131), Jewish Arabic of Tunis *qa-*, Egyptian *'ā'id bi-* alongside with simple *bi-* to indicate continuative action (Mitchell 1978:36), all derived from Classical *qa'ada* "to sit down", or from other verbs with similar meanings, for example Uzbekistan Arabic *wōqif* (Classical *wāqif*, active participle of *waqafa* "to stop, to stand up")[15], or from an intensive adjective *'ammāl*, for example Syrian *'am*. Semantically, this marker may be analyzed as non-punctual *tout court*, including the categories of general statements, habitual, and progressive, but a different categorization is possible, in which the first two of these functions are taken over, either by a different particle, or by the imperfect. The Syrian dialect is an example of the first possibility: *'am* is used for the present progressive, whereas the present habitual is expressed by *bi-*, one of the future markers. The second possibility is found, for instance, in Rural Maltese, where *'aed* indicated the present progressive, whereas the imperfect is used for the present habitual (Schabert 1976:130f.). This also occurs in 'Irāqī Arabic, where *da-* is used for the present progressive, and for some cases of habitual action, whereas the imperfect is used for habitual action in general.[16] In Moroccan and Egyptian, on the other hand, the progressive particle is used for habitual, progressive, and general aspect (*ka-* and *bi-*, respectively). A frequent consequence of this categorization is that the second form — the one with the meaning of habitual and general aspect — usurps the meaning of irrealis/modal, thus forcing the non-present or irrealis marker into the temporal meaning of future. In Syrian Arabic, for example, this results in a distinction between habitual and modal (volitional) *bi-* and purely temporal *raḥ*, *laḥ*. In 'Irāqī Arabic the imperfect also has the meaning of modal, which leaves only the temporal meaning for the future marker *raḥ*.

We have seen above that according to Bickerton (1977:58-60) one of the characteristics of 'early-creolized' creoles is the development of a specific aspectual system. One of the special features of this system is the combinability of the verbal particles in a fixed number of ways: anterior + non-punctual = ± past durative; irrealis + non-punctual = future progressive; anterior + irrealis = past irrealis; anterior + irrealis + non-punctual = durative past irrealis (Bickerton 1977:73ff.). It is impossible to compare here the combinations occurring in modern Arabic dialects with the universal system of creole languages of this type. It is obvious, though, that such an analysis would bring out many similarities between the two systems, for example the possibility that exists in almost all dialects of combining anterior *kān* with the progressive particle in order to express a past progressive. There are other combinations which occur only in some dialects, like Egyptian *ḥaykūn byiktib* (irrealis + non-punctual) "he will be writing", *kān ḥayi'mil* (anterior + irrealis) "he was going to do". For a detailed analysis of these combinations there is, however, not enough material at present.

The lack of material also makes it doubtful whether it is possible to set up classifications of Arabic dialects with respect to the changes in the verbal system they exhibit, as Czapkiewicz (1975) attempts to do. Any statistical analysis of dialectal data remains suspect, as long as the descriptions of the dialects are of questionable value, and as long as there are so many uncharted spots on the dialect map of the arabophone world. What does make Czapkiewicz's analysis interesting, however, is his identification of two tendencies in the development of the verbal system (1975:179-213): the reducing changes and the regenerating changes. About the regenerating changes Czapkiewicz observes that their role is either to renovate ancient forms, or to extend the system by creating new forms (1975:210), primarily with respect to the expression of verbal aspect. The chief means by which this is accomplished is the creation of analytical forms, which, in some dialects, show the beginning of synthetization, i.e. the incorporation in the verbal form (a process I have referred to above as 'grammaticalization'), in what Czapkiewicz calls a 'pulsatory course' (1975:211-12).

The breaking down of the temporal-aspectual system and the subsequent reconstruction of a new system is part of a general tendency in pidginization to dispose of those morphological elements that are dispensable, replacing them at a later stage through a reanalysis of the input by new markers which are grammaticalized versions of originally lexical elements. Some morphological distinctions, however, disappear completely. In the verbal system this tendency affects the dual (Ferguson 1959:620), the gender distinction in the 2nd person singular and plural, and in the 3rd person plural. The maximally symmetrical result, such as it is found, for example, in North African dialects looks as follows:

	sg	pl
1st ps	*n-*	*n- ... -ū*
2nd ps	*t-*	*t- ... -ū*
3rd ps	*y-*	*y- ... -ū*

The development of an *n-* prefix for both singular and plural 1st ps is only found in North Africa; it is not certain which of the two forms was developed first.[17]

Other features of verbal morphology that disappear completely or partially are:

1. The old distinction of three moods — indicative, subjunctive, jussive — is lost in the general process of the disappearance of the short endings. But just as in the nominal case-system it is not only the endings with short vowels that disappear, but other distinctive endings as well, e.g. *yaktubūna* > *yaktubū* "they are writing". For the far-reaching impact of this development on the syntactic structure of New Arabic, cf. below (p. 105).
2. Simplification of the vocalism of the verbal system, leading to a decrease in the number of possible morphological verbal classes. In most dialects the verbal type *faʿula* disappears, in some dialects only one of the three classes *faʿala*, *faʿila*, *faʿula* remains, in accordance with the principle that pidginization leads to a greater morphological regularity, by replacing marked members of an opposition with unmarked ones.
3. Disappearance of the internal passive, replaced by the Vth or the VIIth measure, which reduces the number of possible verbal forms enormously, and makes the expression of the passive much more analytical.[18]
4. A drastic reduction of the number of measures that are productive in the modern dialects, in particular of the IVth measure, whose Classical meaning of causativity was taken over by lexical periphrases, for instance, with the verb *ǧaʿala* "to make". The analysis of the verbal measures in the modern dialects (Fischer & Jastrow 1980:70-71) is complicated by the tendency in many dialect grammars to list as many forms as possible in order to connect them with the ten Classical measures, although in many cases the forms listed are obviously either lexical borrowings from the Classical languages, or fossilized items.[19]
5. Another example of the tendency to adopt greater morphological regularity is the simplification of the morphology of the so-called 'weak verbs'. In his enumeration of the features that are adduced to prove the common descent of the modern dialects Ferguson (1959:623; cf. Kaye 1976:148-49) gives a prominent place to the merger of the IIIw/y and the geminate verbs, e.g. *raddēt* instead of Classical *radadtu*, reanalyzed as a IInd measure of a IIIy verb.[20]

As a matter of fact, the old distinction between IIIw and IIIy verbs tends to disappear, so that only verbs of the type *ramā*, *yarmī* remain (Ferguson 1959:622-23; Kaye 1976:148). The number of analogical endings is enormous, e.g. the 3rd ps fem sg *baqāt* and the 3rd ps pl *baqāw* in Judaeo-Arabic.[21] In some dialects the endings of the strong verb are assimilated to those of the weak verbs, as in the case of Baġdādī *kitbaw* (3rd ps pl), and in the entire inflection of the strong verb in the Jewish dialect of Baghdad and in Daragözü, e.g. *təšrəbe* (< *-ay*; 2nd ps fem sg; Fischer & Jastrow 1980:154; Jastrow 1973:38-39) and *-aw* for all verbal classes in Uzbekistan Arabic (Fischer 1961: 247, n.6).

In the nominal system the reduction of the endings was much more drastic, whereas the inflectional morphology (formation of the plural) was on the whole better protected than that of the verbal system. All case-endings disappeared, being replaced in the singular by what might be termed the Classical pausal form, and in the plural by the generalized genitive/accusative endings *-īn*. The plural ending was reserved for the 'sound' plural, but in some dialects we find a tendency to let it take over other, originally broken, plurals as well.[22]

The controversy concerning the chronology of the loss of the case-endings has been discussed above. In this connection I should like to mention Corriente's concept of 'functional yield'. According to Corriente (1971) there is no structural difference between Old and New Arabic, because the inflectional and declensional endings had already lost their 'functional yield' in Old Arabic (i.e., in our terminology, Classical Arabic before the period of the conquests). He attempts to demonstrate this point with a statistical analysis of Old Arabic texts in which the endings are shown to be partially redundant, i.e. not necessary for the syntactic understanding of the text. But every linguistic system shows a certain amount of redundancy, and its reduction is precisely one of the characteristic features of pidginization (cf. Blau 1977: 4-7). Moreover, even granting that this phenomenon began indeed during the Ğāhiliyya, one still has to explain the use of the accusative/genitive ending for all masculine sound plural endings.

The loss of the case-endings during pidginization is so wide-spread that it is unnecessary to give any references (cf. out of many Heine 1973:151-53; Mühlhäusler 1976:84ff.; Bollée 1977:109). An example from Gastarbeiterdeutsch will bring us to the discussion of the posssessive construction in Arabic dialects: all speakers of pidginized varieties of Standard German use constructions such as *frau von chef* instead of Standard German *die Frau des Chefs* (Meisel 1975:37). In many accounts of the development of New Arabic the characteristics of this new type are epitomized with the emergence of the analytical genitive, the expression of the possessive relation by means of a genitive exponent instead of the Classical *status constructus*, in which case-endings, as well as a special form of the head noun express this relation. The actual shape of the genitive exponent varies from dialect to dialect area. The most commonly used exponents are (cf. Harning 1980; Fischer & Jastrow 1980:93-94):

gilit-dialects	*māl*
	(*gey*)
qəltu-dialects	*d̲ēl*, *d̲īl*
	līl
Syria, Palestine, Lebanon	*taba'*
	šīt, *šēt*
	mtā', *btā'*
	šuġl
	geyy
Cypriot Maronite Arabic	*tél*
	šáyt
Western Peninsula	*ḥagg*
	māl
Egypt	*bətā'*
	šuġl
	ihnīn
Tunisia, Libya	*mtā'* (*ntā'*, *tā'*)
	žna
Algeria	*ntā'* (*mtā'*)
	d-, *dyāl*
	eddi, *elli*
Morocco	*d-*, *dyal*
	nta'
Malta	*ta*
Sudan	*hūl*
	allīl
	bitā'
	ḥaqq
Chad	*hana*
Nigerian Arabic	*hana*, *hīl*, *hinē*, *hille*

The exponents are divided by Harning (1980:19) into two groups: in the first place there are those which are derived etymologically from substantives with the meaning of "possession"; in the second place there are those which are derived etymologically from relative or demonstrative elements. The list of genitive exponents makes one thing very clear: although the Arabic dialects are related, they cannot possibly stem from a common ancestor through a normal process of change, but they all exhibit the same tendency towards analytical structure.

The analysis of the system of the analytical genitive is made difficult by the fact that the existence of different levels of speech diminishes the usefulness of the published material. Almost all dialects have and use some form of genitive exponent, but if we take a look at the material used by Harning in her otherwise thorough and systematic treatment of this subject, we notice that in most cases she had to base herself on (traditional) folk stories, artificial dialogues, texts written with Arabic characters, etc. Her statistical conclusions, which do not take into account any difference in linguistic level in the texts, must, therefore, be regarded as non-significant, except insofar as the general results clearly indicate the high percentage of Classical influence in almost any sample of elicited material in the arabophone world.[23]

The general picture that emerges from Harning's survey is that the genitive exponents are most frequent in the Western dialects of Morocco and Algeria, where this construction even gained a new productivity after the replacement of the old exponent *btāʿ* with *d-*; that they are characteristic of sendentary dialects, whereas they are infrequent in rural, and practically absent in nomadic dialects[24]; and that they are almost exclusively used for relations that contain a concrete element. For the geographical factor I may perhaps with all due caution refer to Czapkiewicz's conclusion that the reducing changes in the verbal system become more important as one nears the Eastern or the Western periphery of the arabophone world: on the other hand, he does not find any correlation between frequency of regenerating changes and geography (1975:197, 211).

Harning concludes (1980:163) that the analytical genitive developed at a very early stage, and that this development was stabilized and brought to a stand-still after some time, so that the analytical genitive in most cases remained a mere stylistic alternative to the synthetic genitive. In my view, the stabilization of the analytical genitive was one of the results of an increasing influence of the Classical language. Within the context of the theory proposed here, I might refer to this as an effect of decreolization. It may well be the fact, as Harning notes, that the stabilization and the inability of the analytical genitive to expand into other semantic domains must be ascribed to the fact that many genitive exponents are derived from substantives with very concrete meanings, thus preventing the exponent from being used to express more abstract relations. It may be significant that the only really successful genitival exponent, Moroccan *d-*, is probably derived from a relative pronoun.

Harning's survey at least shows clearly that wherever the analytical and the synthetic genitives are competing construction, the analytical genitive tends to be used for concrete possession, or for qualifications (contents, material, etc.), whereas the synthetic genitive is always used — even in those dialects where the analytical genitive was highly successful — for the expression of abstract relations, such as periods of time, intimate relations of kinship, partitive relations, and for parts of the body.[25] This corresponds to an original situation in which almost only concrete possessive relations were eligible to be expressed with a substantive denoting "possession" or "property".

In all this it should be remembered that the material on which any analysis can be based at the present time is not always to be trusted: there is very seldom a distinction of levels of discourse[26], and there is no linguistic description of the continuum between dialect and Classical language. Consequently we know but very little about the way the individual speaker can move along the scale of the continuum. This is why Harning's attempt to correlate the use of the analytical genitive with stylistic parameters is insufficient: one cannot study the use of this construction with the help of semantic context alone, but the whole surrounding passage must be checked for the possibility of code switching — with the extra proviso that almost all informants will tend to use classicizing forms when questioned. This applies to the Bedouin dialects as well: there is always the possibility of sedentary influence, structural or incidental in their speech, and there will hardly be any group of nomads that have managed to stay outside the sphere of influence of sedentary civilization.

What does seem acceptable, however, is Harning's general conclusion that the nomadic dialects largely ignore the analytical genitive (1980:158), since it confirms the general picture of the Bedouin dialects as being the more conservative variety, in which New Arabic trends only appear as the result of sedentarization. The dialects of the *Sprachinsel* confirm this picture of the analytical genitive by not using synthetic constructions, except in fossilized forms (Harning 1980:160-61). Malta and Cypriot Maronite Arabic use a genitive exponent (*ta* and *tél*, respectively, < *matāʿ* "possession")[27], whereas Daragözü uses the preposition *lē*, even with nouns that indicate blood relationship, for instance *əbən lē ʿammi* "the son of my uncle" (Jastrow 1973:94). With possessive suffixes, however, the prepositional phrase is used only in the dual and (probably) in the sound plural in *-īn*, for instance *havāḷātna* "our friends" as against *santayn līlu* "his two years" (Jastrow 1973:95).

The situation in Uzbekistan Arabic is complicated: according to Fischer (1961:244) possessive relations are expressed either by the Classical *status constructus*, or by juxtaposition of possesor and possessed, the latter with pronominal suffix, for instance *amīr fulūsu* "the emir's money"[28]. It is not certain that the first construction mentioned by Fischer really is a reflection of the Classical construction: I believe there is good reason to regard this construction in Uzbekistan Arabic as a juxtaposition that developed from an earlier construction with a genitive exponent.[29] In African Arabic dialects we find for Chad Arabic a situation in which according to Roth (1979:142-43) the *status constructus* belongs to a more elevated style, whereas the dialect uses the genitive exponent *hana* (cf. Hagège 1973:40-41). As for the Arabic pidgins, they have lost this feature and express possessive relations by means of simple juxtaposition which, in the absence of any Classical influence, cannot be regarded as the reflection of a *status constructus*, but must be the result of an internal evolution, in my view one in which the original genitive particle was lost in the same way as in many English-based pidgins.

That originally the analytical genitive constituted the normal way of expressing possessive relations in the colloquial, before the onset of Classical influence, and ensuing decreolization, is also confirmed from an unexpected quarter, namely by Pedro de Alcalá's *Arte para ligera mente saber la lengua arauiga*, where we find as marker for the second case of the substantive declension (*mudaf*) *míta*, e.g. *míta dar* "of the house" (Corriente 1977:125). This implies that in 1505 for him the analytical genitive was the normal case, although in accordance with his sometimes classicizing style he occasionally uses synthetic genitives in what seem to be standard expressions that have become lexicalized or borrowings from Classical Arabic, e.g. *izm alláh* "the name of God" (*Arte* 41.19). Judaeo-Arabic makes use of various devices to express the possessive relation analytically: prepositions, *allaḏī li-* and, rarely, the exponent *matāʿ* (Blau 1965:82-83).

From the fact that in 'foreigner talk' registers of language which normally express their possessive relations in an analytical way — such as English — even possessive pronouns are replaced with analytical expressions, such as *of me* instead of *my*, we may infer that this phenomenon should be interpreted as a development towards a uniform and transparent expression of all possessive relations, in which an independent morpheme is used for the expression of possession.[30] In most pidgins, even when the target language does not have case-endings, a special exponent is developed, for example in Tok Pisin *haus bilong Jon* "John's house".[31] In some English-based creoles possession is indicated by means of a preposition, or by simple juxtaposition, e.g. (Jamaican) *mi sista buk*, *fi mi sista buk* "my sister's book", (Sranan) *disi brada fu mi* "my brother", but according to Alleyne (1980:101-103), who discusses these constructions, there is good reason to assume that the expression by means of juxtaposition was preceded by a stage in which the possessive relation was expressed by means of prepositions and that, therefore, the prepositional construction is older. This seems to confirm the conclusion given above concerning the possessive construction in Uzbekistan and in the modern Arabic pidgins, namely that their use of juxtaposition is a later development.

From the developments in the pronominal system I shall select three points that deserve to be discussed here briefly: the periphrasis of interrogative pronouns and adverbs: the changes within the deictic system, including the article; and the use of an indeclinable relative marker.

One of the most characteristic developments in pidginization is that of the interrogative pronouns and adverbs. When these are expressed in the target language by means of lexicalized froms that are semantically inexpressive, they are replaced by nominal periphrases with a much more concrete content. To quote a few examples from Tok Pisin (Bauer 1974:66-67): *wanem* (< *what name?*) "what?", *husat* (< *who's that?*) "who?", *wataim* (< *what time?*) "when?". This development is not limited to English-based creoles and pidgins, but it seems to be a universal of pidginization.[32] In French creoles we frequently find two sets of interrogative pronouns and adverbs, one of which represents the periphrastic development, whereas the other is derived from the normal French interrogative pronouns and adverbs. We find, for instance, in Seychellois French Creole both *kã* and *keler* (< *quelle heure?*) for "when?", and both *komã* and *ki maỹer* (< *quelle manière?*) for "how?".[33] Here, we can see the effect of decreolization at work again.

The replacement of the Classical interrogative pronouns and adverbs by nominal periphrases in the modern Arabic dialects has often been noted in studies about their origin and structure, but this phenomenon has never been connected with an explanation of the process that led to their origin. Fischer & Jastrow (1980:85-86) simply report the fact that most interrogative adverbs have been replaced by a periphrastic expression and, in particular, the fact that Classical *man* and *mā* have practically disappeared. When we compare the most important interrogative adverbs and pronouns in a few modern dialects, we find that in most cases some of the Classical forms have been replaced, and that in some cases there are parallel forms, one of them being a periphrastic expression, and the other the reflection of the Classical form (cf. the situation in French creoles described above). In other cases the reflection of the Classical form seems to be the only one available, although one wonders if the dictionaries accurately reflect the actual spoken language.

	Moroccan	Syrian	Egyptian	Uzbekistan Arabic (Fischer 1961)
when	*fuq-aš, waqt-aš*	*'ēmta*	*'imta*	*matā*
what	*aš, š-, šnu*	*šū, 'ēš*	*'ēh*	*ēš*
where	*fayn, fin*	*wēn, fēn*	*fēn*	*ēṣāb* (< *ayy ṣāb*)
who	*škun*	*mīn*	*mīn*	*mīn*
why	*'laš*	*lēš*	*lēh*	*lī, šinī*
how	*kif*	*kīf, šlōn*	*'izzāy, 'izzayy*	*ištūr* (< *ayyu šay'in ṭawr*)
how much	*šḥal*	*'addēš*	*'addī'ēh*	*kam*

	Lebanese (Bišmizzīn)	Maltese (St. Julian's)	Cypriot Arabic (Borg 1982)	Chad Arabic (Abbéché)
when	*'aymtīn, 'aymta*	*šhīn*	*mítan*	*mata, mitēn*
what	*'aš, 'ayš*	*ši-*	*ayš, aš*	*šinu*
where	*wayn*	*fæyn*	*ayn, an*	*wēn*
who	*mīn*	*mīn*	*men*	*yātu*
why	*layš, lay*	*ąlîš*	*kífta* (< *kayfa ḥattā*)	*le šinu, māla*
how	*kīf*	*kīf*	*áššik* (< *ayš šikl*)	*kikēf*
how much	*'iddayš, 'idday*	*kæmm*	*áška* (< *ayš qadr*)	*kam*

This small sample shows that although some dialects agree with each other in some forms, there is no total agreement for any form. This means that the problem of the expression of interrogative notions was solved in each dialect area differently.[34] Thus, the development of periphrastic expressions is as important for the explanation of the origin of the modern dialects as the development of the genitive exponent. Both phenomena rule out the possibility of a common descent for all dialects, and they demonstrate at the same time that all dialects went through a similar process of language change, though with different results.

Within the deictic system of languages that are pidginized several phenomena seem to be characteristic of the process which transforms the target language into a pidginized version. According to Heine (1973:207-210) all pidginized versions distinguish between two series of demonstratives, one for the category 'nearby' and one for the category 'far-off', as seen from the perspective of the speaker. When the target language has more distinctions in the demonstrative system, these tend to disappear. Heine's statement applies to pidginized languages in Africa, for instance Fanagalo and Kenya Pidgin Swahili, but many descriptions of other pidginized languages mention the same tendency (for French-based pidgins and creoles see Bollée 1977:37-41). As Classical Arabic already had two series of demonstratives, the modern dialects quite naturally exhibit the same choice in their demonstrative system.

Another trait of pidginization in the deictic system is the fact that pidginized versions of the target language often develop a definite article on the basis of a demonstrative which has lost its deictic force.[35] This demonstrative may either be used before or after the substantive. A postposed definite article derived from a Classical demonstrative is only found in (Ki-)Nubi, where *dé* is used both as a definite article and as a demonstrative, e.g. *júa dé* "the house, this house" (Heine 1982:31) with the same combination of functions as *-la* in some French creoles. In many Syrian-Lebanese dialects an element *hā-*, either derived from Classical *hāḏā* or from a general deictic element *hā-*, loses its deictic force when combined with the relative *illī* (> *halli*), and in some Palestinian dialects *hal* (< *hā-al-*) is equivalent to a definite article (Fischer 1959:50-52). A similar erosion of the deictic force of the Classical demonstrative may be seen in the use of the demonstrative to refer to something which is assumed to be worth knowing, although as yet only the speaker knows about it, approximately in the sense of the category that is called by Bickerton (1977:58) "existentially presupposed". Many examples of this use of *ha-* + article are given by Grotzfeld (1965:78-79 for Syrian Arabic; for Palestinian dialects see Fischer 1959:86), for instance *rkəbt bhalbāṣ* "I got into a, the, that bus [which happened to come by]", *ṣərt 'əṣrof 'ala halbēt* "I paid the expenses for our, the house". This semantic expansion may be related to the use of *da*, *di*, *dōl* in Egyptian Arabic at the beginning of a statement to assert the facts expressed by that sentence, e.g. *dal-bet bi'īd* "the house is far away" (Salib 1981:291), a phenomenon which contrasts with the normal postposition of the demonstratives in Egyptian.

A third phenomenon connected with the deictic system is the development of a new indefinite article in some Arabic dialects (Fischer & Jastrow 1980:88,97), either derived from the numeral "one" or of a word indicating "individual". A similar development is found in English-based creoles which have an indefinite article *wan* and in Haitian Creole which has an indefinite article *youn* (cf. Bickerton 1977:58). The Arabic dialects where such an article is found include Moroccan *waḥd* + article (Marçais 1977:163-65; other forms such as *fərd*, *ši*, are also mentioned), 'Irāqī *fat* (< *fard*; also in other *qəltu*-dialects, cf. Fischer 1961:242), Cypriot Maronite Arabic *éẖen*, *éẖte*.[36] In at least some varieties of Chad Arabic there is a tendency to omit the definite article and to use a postposed indefinite marker *wāḥid* serving as the marked term in the oppostion definite/indefinite (cf. Roth 1979:140-41).

In pidginized and creolized languages relative clauses are either introduced by a zero-element, or by a demonstrative element; there may be a difference in meaning between the two possibilities, in which case the zero-element is the one used for indeterminate antecedents (Heine 1973: 207-210). Most modern Arabic dialects use an indeclinable relative marker *illī*, one of Ferguson's features in his koine-theory (1959:630). The indeclinability of the relative marker *illī*[37] is one more instance of the disappearance of morphological distinction in New Arabic. More interesting is the fact that the use of the relative marker is extended beyond its Classical domain. In Classical Arabic the use of the relative marker *allaḏī* is impossible when the antecedent is indeterminate, but in Middle Arabic texts we find relatives used in sentences with an indeterminate antecedent.[38] We could regard this as an example of the tendency to express syntactic relations always with the same surface marker.

5.4 *Syntax*

Under this heading I wish to discuss very briefly four syntactic phenomena in modern Arabic dialects that may be regarded as typical of the development these dialects went through: the use of serial verbs; the restructuring of the agreement rules; the use of hypotactic verbs in asyndetic modal constructions; and the generalization of the word order SVO. Of these four phenomena only the first will be dealt with in any detail, the other three will only be mentioned in a few paragraphs.

In most Arabic dialects we find a phenomenon of verbal construction that bears a striking resemblance to what is called 'verbal serialization' in pidginized languages. I am referring here to a construction in which the verbal predicate consists of two verbal forms, both of which retain their own meaning, although one of them may lose its inflected character. In the literature on pidginization and creolization the term 'serialization' is used for several distinct phenomena, which have in common that they concern a series of verbs in juxtaposition that serves to express complex meanings which in the original language may be expressed by particles, purpose clauses, lexical items, etc.:

a. verb of motion + verb
The verb of motion may follow the main verb, as in Jamaican *kya im kom* "carry it come, i.e. bring it here", or *kya im go* "carry it go, i.e. take it away", or it may precede the main verb, as in Krio *i don lef fo go ep im brɔda* "he has left to (go) help his brother" (Alleyne 1980:90).[39]

b. verb + perfective complementizer
In most pidginized and creolized languages there is a special marker to indicate perfective aspect which has evolved from an 'earlier' marker in the first stage of pidginization (cf. Alleyne 1980:91-92; above, p. 84f.). In English-based creoles we find *don*, for instance in Jamaican *Mieri iit don* "Mary has eaten", or *pinis*, as in Tok Pisin.[40]

c. verb meaning "to say" as indirect complementizer
In many creoles a verb with the original meaning "to say, to talk" is combined asyndetically with the main verb, and eventually reanalyzed as a conjunction, for instance in Jamaican *mi bilib sɛ im a go kom* "I believe that he'll come", or in Sranan *konum kom bribi en wantron taki a no lei* "the king believed him at once (saying that) he didn't lie" (Alleyne 1980:94-95; Bickerton 1982:105-118).

d. verb meaning "to order, to make" + verb
This construction serves as an expression of causative meaning, for instance in Chabacano (Philippine Creole Spanish) *ase akordá* "to cause (someone) to remember", *manda ase akordá* "to let (someone) cause (someone) to remember" (Riego de Dios 1979:284-85).

e. verb + verb indicating case-relationship
The second verb can either function as an autonomous verb or

lose its verbal character and be reanalyzed as a preposition. Examples include the use of verbs with the meaning "to give" to indicate the indirect object, for instance in Sranan *Meri tek watra gi den plantjes* "Mary brought water give (i.e. for) the plants" (Bickerton 1982:128), or in Saramaccan *a táki en dá mi* "he told it give (i.e. to) me" (Alleyne 1980:94); and the use of verbs with the meaning "to take" to indicate the instrument, for instance in Sranan *Kofi teki a nefi koti a brede* "Kofi take the knife cut the bread (i.e. Kofi cut the bread with the knife)" (Bickerton 1982:124).[41]

Not all phenomena listed here will be accepted by all scholars as instances of serialization, and they are not equally relevant to the analysis of the structure of modern Arabic dialects. The link between all phenomena listed is that they consist of a series of juxtaposed verbs, and that they express complex notions.[42] In most descriptions of modern Arabic dialects constructions involving the use of asyndetically juxtaposed verbs with an independent meaning are analyzed as an asyndetic combination of two verbs that are derived from an earlier combination 'verb + conjunction + verb'. What I propose here is to analyze these constructions in the light of the serial constructions listed above. The construction involving perfective markers has been mentioned above (p. 85f.), as has the disappearance of the analytical causative (p. 90). I shall, therefore, limit myself here to a discussion of the constructions involving the use of verbs of motion as first members in a chain of verbs. There seem to be no equivalents in the Arabic dialects for the serial constructions mentioned above under c and e.

The asyndetic use of verbs of motion with main verbs has been noted in many dialects, but this construction has not always been recognized as deviant. Denz, for instance, regards the two verbs in 'Irāqī *gām kitab* as independent verbs, in meaning indistinguishable from *gām w-kitab*.[43] The verb *qāma* "to stand up" and other similar verbs of motion are mentioned for many other dialects, often as (semi-)auxiliaries with the meaning of an ingressive or a durative depending on the meaning of the main verb from which they are derived. Thus, we find in Egyptian Arabic (Mitchell 1978:87-88) verbal sequences with the imperative, such as *ẖúd íšrab* "take (and) drink!", *rū́ḥ 'ablu dilwá'ti* "go (and) see him now!", but also constructions with the verb *'ām* (< Classical *qāma*), for instance *'úmt^i nímt* "I fell asleep", *mišīt, 'ām ḥášni* "I went, (but) he stopped me", *'úmt ana 'ultī́lu(h)* "and then I said ...". In North African dialects several verbs can perform this role of 'auxiliaries' with an ingressive connotation, e.g. *qām*, *naḏ*, *q'ăd*, *bda*, *hda*, *ja*, *dāṛ*, *ṣāṛ*, *bġa*, or a durative connotation, e.g. *bqa*, *zād*, *ʿād*, *ʿāwəd* (Marçais 1977:76f.).[44] Roth (1979:55ff.) on the one hand distinguishes in Chad Arabic between semi-auxiliaries, which retain their independent meaning and may be inflected in both perfect and imperfect and, on the other hand, auxiliaries, which always have the same tense and have lost their independent meaning. The verb *gām* (< Classical *qāma*), for instance, may be used together with an imperfect in the sense of "to get up to do something, to start doing something". But the perfect of the verb has become stabilized as a temporal marker with the perfect, e.g. *gām katal* "then, he killed", *ad-dūd gām ḫalla* "then, the lion let her go". Similarly, Sieny (1978:148) calls the verb *rāḥ* in Ḥiǧāzī Arabic as a verb-modifier in expressions such as *rāḥ katab lana* "he went (and) wrote for us" a "semantically empty word", since the sentence "does not really mean that, but a simple statement that someone wrote, with a connotation of the speaker's irritation at the fact".

In none of these descriptions do we find an auxiliary without inflection. But in some dialects this is precisely what happens, for instance in the Lebanese dialect of Bišmizzīn (Jiha 1964:148-49). In this dialect there are a number of auxiliaries with an ingressive meaning, e.g. *ṣå̄r*, *'å̄m*, *rå̄ḥ*, *nizil*, *ṭiliʿ*, or a durative meaning, e.g. *bi'i*, *ḍall*, for instance *ṣå̄r yǟkul* "he started to eat", *ḍall yǟkul* "he continued eating". In these two sentences the main verbs are in the imperfect, but some of the verbs mentioned usually occur with a perfect (*ʿå̄d*) or with both tenses (*'å̄m*, *rå̄ḥ*). Jiha's most interesting remark about these verbs is that sometimes the auxiliaries do not agree with the main verb's subject, e.g. *'å̄m 'å̄lit* "then, she said", *ṣå̄r yǟklu* "they began to eat". In such cases the down-grading of the first member of the verbal chain has been completed or, rather, these phenomena demonstrate what serial verbs looked like in the older period, when the influence of the Classical languages had not yet completely classicized most dialects. Similar phenomena are reported about Syrian Arabic by Grotzfeld (1965:89): in this dialect *'ām* with a following perfect is used to indicate a "neu eintretendes, nicht andauerndes Geschehen in der Vergangenheit", e.g. *'ām waṣafli l-ḥakīm* "then, the doctor prescribed for me", *'əmt 'əltəllo* "then, I said to him". But Grotzfeld also mentions instances of uninflected *'ām*, which is used less frequently, e.g. *'ām 'əžətna sayyāra* "then, a car came towards us", *'ām 'aḫadu ʿaskari* "then, they took him as a soldier".[45] In view of the fact that this construction is in most descriptions regarded as a simple variant, it is possible that its existence in other dialects has become obscured through a tendency to regularize the described structure.

An uninflected verb of motion in postposition after the main verb occurs in Uzbekistan Arabic. In this dialect the verbs *ġadāk* and *ǧāk* are used, according to Fischer (1961:258) to indicate a "Richtung zum Sprecher oder vom Sprecher weg", e.g. *'al čūl ṭala' ġadāk* "he went out into the steppe", *'ašir dukkonāt arīzātin ǧābin ǧāk* "he brought the money from ten shops".[46]

In Middle Arabic one finds sentences in which a perfect explains a preceding perfect, e.g. *fa-qāmat al-imra'a .... qassamat* "and then, the woman divided". According to Blau (1965:93) this phenomenon is not very frequent, but he remarks that these perfects should not be interpreted as circumstantial clauses, but as being "preserved from an earlier stage ... in which asyndetical clauses were used in every syntactic environment". This phenomenon may be more important than Blau supposes for the Middle Arabic texts: for at least one text (Usāma ibn Munqiḏ's memoirs) Schen states (1972-73:90) that co-ordinate asyndeta are very frequent, e.g. *ǧā'a l-ġulām ... aḫaḏa* "the slave came (and) took", and he specifically mentions the use of *qāma*, *maḍā* as "semi-auxiliary verbs of motion".[47]

In most descriptions of this phenomenon its relevance for the transformation of Old Arabic into New Arabic is underestimated, either because the two verbs are regarded as an abbreviated syndetic construction, or because this construction is lumped together with the hypotactic combination of an imperfect verb with a modal expression (see below). Accordingly, the special connotation of this construction is either ignored or denied, and the absence of inflection in the first verb in some dialects is regarded as an idiosyncrasy.

One of the best-known features of the structure of New Arabic is the change in agreement rules, both in the noun phrase and in the verb phrase (Fischer & Jastrow 1980:47). In Classical Arabic a verb which precedes its subject agrees with it only in gender, not in number, whereas a verb which follows the subject agrees with it both in gender and in number. As we shall see below, the canonical word order in New Arabic changed from VSO to SVO and, accordingly, the verb in this position always agrees completely with its subject. In Middle Arabic we find instances of complete agreement even when the verb is in presubject position, most of them in cases where the subject is animate; in the case of inanimate subjects this phenomenon occurs sporadically (Blau 1965:80-81).

Obviously, the occurrence of complete agreement in Middle Arabic could be interpreted as an example of interference from the colloquial where verb and subject are always in the same number. According to Blau the complete agreement was brought about by the need to discriminate between subject and object in cases such as *ḍaraba l-walad ar-riǧāl* "the men hit the boy" or "the boy hit the men", where only the use of the plural in the verb can disambiguate the sentence. This explanation is not very convincing, however, because it only applies to a limited number of sentences. In most sentences word order is the only remedy against ambiguity concerning the identity of subject and object. It seems, therefore, preferable to regard the change from special agreement rules in Classical Arabic to a general rule of verb-subject agreement in New Arabic as an instance of regularization in sentence structure, by which the relation between verb and subject is always shown at the surface level. This tendency to reflect syntactic relations directly without interference from special surface rules which may obscure the relations is also found in many creole languages. Particularly striking is the reduction of grammatical agreement rules in the case of the pidginized versions of Bantu languages, which lose a considerable part of their complex system of class prefixes and concomitant agreement rules (Manessy 1977:139ff.).

The same phenomenon is at work in the agreement rules in the New Arabic noun phrase. Classical Arabic has a rule that prescribes feminine singular concord for adjectives predicated of inanimate plurals, regardless of the grammatical gender of the substantive, for instance *al-kutub al-ǧamīla* "the beautiful [fem. s.g] books [inanimate pl.]". Adjectival concord with dual nouns takes dual endings in Classical Arabic. In the modern dialects there is a tendency towards complete agreement between substantive and adjective, regardless of the (in)animateness of the substantive. This tendency is particularly strong in those dialects in which the influence of the Classical language is less perceptible. The plural concord in the adjective with dual nouns — in those dialects where dual nouns still occur — has been noted by Ferguson (1959:620-21; cf. Kaye 1976:142-44). Plural concord in the adjective with inanimate plurals is not a general feature of all modern dialects (cf. Fischer & Jastrow 1980:96), but it is found in most dialects as an alternative. In his discussion of Ferguson's remarks about the dual Blanc (1970:49) attributes the fluctuation between feminine singular and plural concord in the adjective to a new categorization of the plural into "enumerative" plurals which receive plural agreement, and "nonnumerative", i.e. collective plurals which receive feminine singular agreement. This distinction often coincides with that into animate and inanimate plurals. Modern Arabic dialects differ according to their acceptance of this distinction. In Chad Arabic, for instance, there is no such distinction at all, and agreement with a plural noun is always plural (Roth 1979:183). In Moroccan feminine singular agreement is found only in isolated idioms and stereotyped phrases (Harrell 1962:156-58). In Syrian Arabic inanimate plurals have plural agreement only when they are regarded as "separate, particular instances" (Cowell 1964:421). In 'Irāqī inanimate plurals only sometimes receive (broken) plural agreement (Erwin 1963:323). The case of Moroccan suggests a connection between feminine singular agreement and classicisms.

The disappearance of the endings in the imperfect verb led to the loss of the distinction of three moods (indicative, subjunctive, jussive or apocopated verb) which existed in Classical Arabic. In the Classical language hypotactic sentences were divided into modal sentences introduced by the conjunction *an* and connected with verbs expressing possibility, volition, obligation, etc., and affirmative sentences introduced by the conjunction *anna* and connected with verbs expressing information, perception, etc. The former class of hypotactic sentences contained a subjunctive verb, in the latter class of sentences the conjunction was followed by the accusative of the subject and the verb remained indicative. In the colloquials this distinction was lost and there remained only one hypotactic marker, *anna* (*ənno*) instead of Classical *an*, *anna*, and the topicalizing particle *inna* (cf. Blau 1965:85-86). In many cases, even the use of this all-purpose conjunction may be regarded as a classicism, instead of the usual asyndetic construction.

In some cases of pidginization there is a tendency to restructure hypotactic modal sentences. If the target language has a special subjunctive for such sentences, it disappears and is replaced with an infinitive or a simple verb, preceded by what Heine (1973:214-15) calls "Satzeinleitungswörter". The examples he quotes are from Fanagalo and Kenya Pidgin Swahili and involve expressions such as *mzuri* "advisable", *muhle* "necessary".[48] These expressions serve to specify the meaning of the verb and exemplify the tendency to express syntactic relations by a separate word instead of an inflectional ending. In some languages a fossilized modal verb is used in this function, for instance in Philippine Creole Spanish *pwéde* "be able", *kyére* "want", e.g. *ya pwéde yo mandá* "past-be able I send [I could send]" (Riego de Dios 1979:284). In other languages nominal expressions are used in this function, as in Vietnamese Pidgin French (Tây Bồi), where we find *il-faut*, *peut*, *veut* as fossilized verbal forms expressing "must", "can", "want", and as alternatives for the latter two *content* and *moyen*, for instance *monsieur content aller danser* "you want to go dance", *moyen manger* "[you] can eat" (Reinecke 1971:52-53). In the transition from Classical Arabic to modern dialects we find that in many cases nominal expressions develop to serve as introduction to hypotactic modal sentences which are joined asyndetically.[49] For the notion "must" we find, for instance, in Moroccan *ẖeṣṣ* (*ẖeṣṣni neẖdem l-yum* "I have to work today", Harrell 1962:185), in Egyptian *lāzim* (*lāzim arūḥ* "I have to go", Mitchell 1978:81), for "can", we find in Egyptian *mumkin*, *gāwiz* (Mitchell 1978:81), for "want" we find in many dialects expressions such as *bəddi*, etc. (< *bi-wuddī* "in my wish"). Another type of asyndetic hypotactic clauses concerns the use of the *y-* imperfect instead of a final clause with *li-*, e.g. *rāḥ yišrab* "he went to drink", which is to be distinguished from the verbal chain *rāḥ širib* "he went [and] drank", which we have seen above. With these remarks I only wish to suggest that there is a phenomenon worth further research.

The same qualification applies to my final remark in this chapter concerning a tendency in the transition from Classical Arabic to Arabic dialects towards the word order SVO instead of Classical VSO. According to Manessy (1977:141-42, cf. Heine 1978) this development is characteristic of pidginization. I shall not go into the complicated question of whether this development is a reflection of a tendency to express deep syntactic relations at the surface level. As most pidginized languages are derived from targets with word order SVO, we must turn to non-European based pidgins to exemplify this tendency. [50] In the Arabic dialects the change is obvious, although one often finds in collections of texts examples of sentences with the Classical order. I believe that these must be regarded as classicisms (cf. Diem 1974:42), but much more material will be needed before any conclusion can be reached concerning this point.[51] The evidence from Middle Arabic shows that the change in word order must be old (cf. Blau 1965:79-80; 1977:3, and n. 6).

NOTES

1) Exceptions are only found in the most conservative type of dialects, the dialects of the Bedouin in the Arabian peninsula, cf. Fischer & Jastrow 1980:39; for a discussion of the universality of this feature in the Arabic dialects see Kaye 1976:161.

2) Certain nomadic dialects are reported by Hagège to preserve the opposition between /ʿ/ and /ʾ/.

3) For a complete survey see Janssens (1972:65-124) who discusses the connection between vowel elision and stress.

4) Cf. Jastrow 1973:16-17; Sasse 1971:33ff.; Fischer & Jastrow 1980: 56-57.

5) As an example may be mentioned Tok Pisin, which has served people in New Guinea for some time as a second language. According to Mühlhäusler (1981:41, 43) redundant elements

were originally deleted from the predecessor of Tok Pisin, Samoan Plantation Pidgin. In this language, plurals of nouns are not indicated when the context is sufficient to indicate plurality; such markers as *plenti*, *ol*, *olgeta* may be used optionally (cf. also Bauer 1974:43ff.; for an analysis of the use of specifiers with the noun in Chinese Pidgin English, such as *-pisi* and *-fele* cf. ib. 124ff.). When the crude version of the pidgin graduated to a stable pidgin that was used by thousands of people, there was a marked development from optionality to a gradual increase in obligatory marking, reflected synchronically in the much greater frequency of obligatory markers in the speech of the younger people, some of whom already adopted the obligatory use of the plural markers, so that the optional use of a plural marker — mostly *ol* — is in their speech much less frequent than in the speech of the older generation.

6) On the retention of at least traces of the Classical *tanwīn* in Bedouin dialects, cf. above, ch. I, n. 14.

7) See, for instance, Fischer & Jastrow 1980:41; Blau 1965:78ff. On the loss of the case-endings as a universal feature of pidgins and creoles, cf. Bollée 1977:109.

8) See, for instance, Heine 1973:212-14; Bollée 1977:64-94; Manessy 1977:147; Valdman 1977b:292ff.; Bickerton 1976; Owens 1980.

9) This stabilization seems to be confirmed by the verbal system in Bahasa Indonesia, a pidginized variety which developed from Classical Malay through Pasar Malay (cf. Steinhauer 1980; Prentice 1978; Halim 1974). In Bahasa the verbal stem may be expanded by optional temporal adjuncts such as *sudah*, *telah* "already", *akan* (future), *sedang* (durative). In the Djakartan dialect of Indonesian, perhaps the largest conglomerate of first language speakers of Bahasa, these lexical elements appear to have evolved into obligatory verbal markers, e.g. *saya sudah menulis buku* "I've written a book" (often with the shorter form *dah*), *saya akan menulis buku* "I'll write a book" (often with a shorter form *kan*) (Maier, p.c.).

10) According to Marçais (1977:75) *ġadi* is a "forme participale" which may be inflected, *ġadi*, *ġadya*, *ġadyin*.

11) In Tunisian Arabic there is a temporal adverb *tawwa* "now" which is derived from the Classical *tawwan*, a local adverb with the probable meaning of "directly", cf. Fischer 1959:150-52; Marçais 1977:73.

12) For the origin of this particle (< *iḏā bi-* "behold"?) see Fischer 1959:152-56.

13) In combination with *tawwa* in sentences such as *māš ižyú tăwwä šə́b'ä šnīn ẖäyr* "there will come seven better years" (Cohen 1975:137).

14) Cf. Marçais (1977:73): "... pour marquer l'imminence, la possibilité (parfois la volonté, la finalité)".

15) This (inflected) form is used in postposition with an imperfect + *kun* to indicate the past progressive, e.g. *fi darb kun miği woquf* "he continued to go along the road" (cf. Fischer 1961:256); also in this function the participle *qā'id*. According to Jastrow (1978:300ff.) there are some Anatolian dialects in which the present progressive is not indicated formally; in most Anatolian *qəltu* dialects there is an uninflected progressive marker *ku-*, probably derived from the demonstrative copula "he is".

16) Cf. Erwin (1963:335-44) *tumṭur ihwāya hnā* "it rains here a lot", *da-tumṭur ihwāya hnā has-sana* "it rains here a lot this year", i.e. an action which "has recently become recurrent or habitual, or will be so only for a certain period of time".

17) On the question of priority in this analogical development see Blau (1965:58-59, 119-20) who asserts that the *n-* prefix for the singular is older, and that the *n-* ... *-ū* forms are neologisms, against the older proposal to explain the *n-* singular by a contraction of *'ana 'a-* (cf. Wansbrough 1967:309), but also Behnstedt's discovery (1978:69 and map 6) of *aktib/niktibū* dialects in the Egyptian delta, which demonstrates at least the possibility of the emergence of the plural form before the singular (cf. also Singer 1982:113, n. 39).

18) There is no trace in the Arabic dialects of the typical construction found in English and French creoles, where the transitive verb without an object is interpreted as a passive, cf. Bickerton 1981:71-72, e.g. Jamaican *dem plaan di tri* "they planted the tree", and *di tri plaan* "the tree was planted". But in (Ki-)Nubi this construction is at least partly productive, cf. below, ch. VI, p. 124f.

19) Cf. above, ch. II, n. 7. On the verbal measures in the modern dialects see Fischer & Jastrow 1980:70-71; cf. also Borg (1982:112) who comments on the verbal measures in Cypriot Arabic: "the lexically depleted state of these classes in KA [= Kormakiti Arabic], together with the semantic shifts reflected in many individual verbs, has given rise to large-scale lexicalization of historically derivational morphemes ...".

20) Ferguson 1959:623; cf. Kaye 1976:148-49. In Ancient South Palestinian texts geminate verbs are reanalyzed as IIw/y verbs, e.g. *halt* instead of *ḥallīt* for original *ḥalalt* (cf. Blau 1977:22).

21) Blau 1965:60f.; I do not believe that this is to be regarded as a mere "spelling device" as Corriente (1977:19) suggests for the 3rd ps fem sg.

22) In Uzbekistan Arabic, for example, *-īn* is used for all masculine animate plurals, e.g. *uẖwīn* "brothers", *zuğīn* "husbands", whereas the ending *-āt* may be used for all other plurals, *rāsāt* "heads", *uẖāt* "sisters", cf. Fischer 1961:243. In Cypriot Arabic *-āt* is used for a very large number of nouns, including masculine nouns, e.g. *'arisát* "grooms", and even for originally internal plurals of the pattern *fu'ūl*, which were reanalyzed as singulars and received a new plural ending, e.g. *ẖumát* < *luḥūm* "kinds of meat", *pturát* < *buḏūr* "seeds", cf. Borg 1982:180-82.

23) As a contrast Harning (1980:45) notes the "unexpectedly low frequency" of synthetic genitives in Daragözü Arabic, which is not so unexpected if one considers the nature of the material used by Jastrow in his description of this dialect, his methods in the field, and the fact that this dialect has for a long time been isolated from Classical influence. Likewise, the description of Cypriot Maronite Arabic, mentioned by Harning (1980:68) and drawn from Tsiapera (1969), is, not surprisingly, free of Classical influence: as Jastrow (1977) has shown, the author's knowledge of the Classical language was minimal. Finally, one should read Harning's own observations (1980:71) on the nature of the materials used by Reinhardt in his description of the Arabic dialect of Oman and Zanzibar (1894).

24) It may be noted here that according to Zavadovskij (1981:58) the analytical genitive is unknown in the Ḥassāniyya dialect of Mauretania; this confirms the nomadic character of this dialect, which is also one of the few dialects that still use an internal passive (ib. 35-36).

25) Contrast in the examples adduced by Harning (1980:89, n.3) between Egyptian *laḥmī* "my flesh" and *il-laḥm ibtā'ī* "my piece of flesh [which I have bought]".

26) Apart from socio-linguistic studies such as Diem (1974) and Forkel (1980) who analyze samples of radio-interviews, or Blanc (1960) who analyzes a sample of interdialectal conversation. The problem of distinguishing between more and less classicizing utterances is discussed by Palva (1969).

27) Or is *tél* related with *qəltu*-exponents such as *ḏēl*, cf. Borg 1982: 205; Jastrow 1978:125?

28) The comparison with topicalized possessors in other dialects, e.g. (Egyptian) *il-wazīr bēto fī baladna* "the vizir, his house is in our village", which is made by Fischer, is not quite appropriate: the Egyptian construction is only permitted at the beginning of the sentence, whereas the Uzbekistan construction occurs freely within the sentence, and is not likely to be indicated by a pause in intonation, as is the Egyptian.

29) Even if it is true that feminine nouns take the ending *-it* before the second noun (Fischer does not give examples; the only example I could find was *mart boy* "the bey's wife", Vinnikov 1957:453, l. 23), the fact remains that masculine sound plurals do not lose the ending *-īn* before the second noun, e.g. *adamīn amīr* "the emir's men" (Vinnikov 1957: 429, l. 20, cf. the alternative construction *adamīn il amīr*, ib. 430 pen., with the relative *il* acting as genitive exponent).

30) Ferguson 1975:6-7; cf. a similar development in Papia Kristang, a Portuguese Creole spoken in Malacca, where *Juan-să kaza* "John's house" is reported by Hancock (1975:219) alongside *yo-să kaza* "my house".

31) Bauer 1974:75-78; in creolized varieties of Tok Pisin there is a tendency to use a further eroded form *haus blo Jon*, cf. Siegel 1981:21.

32) Hall (1944:97) mentions independently developed forms in Chinese Pidgin English: *hwát θíng "what?", háw fæšen* "how?" (ib. 98), *hwát plḗs* "where?" (ib. 100). This development is not limited to English-based pidgins, but it seems to be a universal feature of pidginization. We find, for example, in Kenya Pidgin Swahili the following periphrastic forms (mentioned by Heine 1973:11; Manessy 1977:142; Bollée 1977:108): *saa gani* "which hour?, when?", *siku gani* "which day?, when?", *kitu gani* "which thing?, what?", *namna gani* "which kind?, what?", *sababu gani* "which reason?, why?".

33) Mentioned by Bollée (1977:108); she also mentions the corresponding forms in Haitian French Creole: *kã*, *kilè*, and *kumã*, *ki žã* (< *quel genre*). Given the independent development of the two languages, this demonstrates the universality of this phenomenon. The existence of doublets is probably due to influence of the target language, Continental French.

34) In some dialects the interrogative adverbs and pronouns have been borrowed, probably at a later date, from adstratal languages, for instance in Daragözü Arabic, which uses (probably Kurdish) words such as *čīčah̲ "when?"*, *čaqa* "how much?" (or, < *qadr*?), but the pronouns for "who?" (*məni*) and "what?" (*šṭaba*) appear to be Arabic, cf. Jastrow 1973:42-43; 1978:115-16. The (Ki-)Nubi interrogative adverbs and pronouns are, surprisingly, relatively Classical in appearance: *munú* "who?", *kéef*, *kefíin* "how?", *wén* "where?", *mitéen* "when?".

35) Heine (1973:208) mentions the case of the new article *lo* in Fanagalo, derived from the Zulu demonstrative *lowo*. Other instances are found in French creoles, for instance in Mauritian French Creole, where postposed *-la* frequently corresponds with the French definite article, and in Haitian Creole, where the same postposition is regarded in most descriptions as a definite article (Bollée 1977:39-40). Similarly, we find the generalized use of the Dutch demonstrative *die* as definite article in Afrikaans, where an extended form of this form, *hierdie* and *daardie*, is used as a new demonstrative. In the Romance languages, several Latin demonstratives evolved into a new definite article, in most languages derived from Latin *ille*, in Sardinian from Latin *iste*, whereas Rumanian uses forms which are derived from a postposed demonstrative *ille*.

36) Borg 1982:218, for instance, *ftáh̲ éhte táka* "open a window!", *pri t-áštri éh̲en h̲pír páyt* "I want to buy a big house". Borg discerns in the development of this indefinite article influence from Cypriot Greek, but in view of the fact that the same development has taken place elsewhere without the possibility of Greek influence, the assumption of interference does not seem to be necessary.

37) In some Middle Arabic texts *alladī* is used as a reflection of colloquial *illī*; in such cases it is indeclinable, cf. Blau 1965:53, 87, 109.

38) Blau 1965:91-92; Blau also mentions relative sentences with the relative marker *ayna* "where" (ib. 62).

39) Similar series occur in other creolized languages, e.g. in Papiamentu *sali kore yega e luga* "go-out run reach the-place, i.e. go quickly to that place", mentioned by Hancock (1975:222) with other examples from Portuguese creoles.

40) In French-based creoles we find derivates from the verb *finir* "to complete, finish", and in Portuguese creoles we find *kabá*, also as a borrowing in Sranan *mi papa dede kabá* "my father has already died", mentioned by Alleyne (1980:92).

41) According to Bickerton (1981:118-32) this kind of serialization is the only means available to mark case relations in a language stage when there are only nouns and verbs; when prepositions develop — often borrowed from the prestige language in a process of decreolization — these serial verbs are no longer necessary and tend to be reanalyzed: in the Sranan sentence quoted here the construction with *teki* will be analyzed by some speakers as a sentence, by some as a verbal part, and by some as a prepositional phrase.

42) Naro (ms. 13-14) opposes the view that the existence of similar constructions in several West African languages proves that this construction in pidginized languages was calqued on a substratal model. He asserts that there are no examples of natural languages developing serial verbs independently, although there are languages which abandon such verbs in favour of more complex verbs which incorporate the formerly serial verbs. This hypothesis, when proved, would constitute an important criterion for pidginization (cf. below, ch. VII, p. 142ff.).

43) This means that Denz denies the special connotation of suddenness inherent in this construction according to other descriptions of 'Irāqī Arabic (for instance, by Malaika 1963:79). Erwin (1963:346) mentions verbal strings with two imperfects, and only one instance of a verbal string with two perfects, namely *ǧā ḥiča wiyyāna* "he came (and) talked with us".

44) Cf. the description of auxiliaries in Moroccan Arabic by Harrell (1962:181ff.) where, however, hypotactic and paratactic constructions are mentioned together. A few examples from other dialects: Maltese *mur ħu l-kafè* "go take the coffee!" (Aquilina 1965:223), and in the rural dialect of St. Julian's *lha'na 'badna sitt hotît* "in the meantime we have caught six fishes", *lha'na domna sa s-sạtæyn* "until now it has taken us two hours" (Schabert 1976:133); Cypriot Arabic *ruẖt lakáyt yapáti ana* "I went (and) met my father" (Borg 1982:266.10), *rúẖu l-ⁱẖkáli lákuon* "go (and) find them in the fields" (ib. 268.6)

45) Cf. Bloch (1965:95) who mentions *'ām* as "Auftaktsverb" in the apodosis of conditional sentences, e.g. *mā kān yəskot 'əmt dabaḥto* "he didn't shut up, so I cut his throat".

46) Frequent examples of these verbs are found in the texts, e.g. *waḥt ṣalō ṭala' ġadāk* "in the morning he went out" (Vinnikov 1957:178.29), *lejl ṭala' ġadāk* "at night he went out" (ib. 178.30), and many others. Similarly in Chad Arabic the verbal forms *ǧa*, *fāt*, e.g., *gabbolo ǧo* "they returned", *maša fāt* "he left" (Roth 1979:58).

47) Another example is the frequent *daẖalū ṣallaw* "they entered (and) prayed" in the story of Bāsim the Blacksmith (Landberg 1888:2.21 and elsewhere).

48) The example Heine quotes from Kenya Pidgin Swahili is very instructive: in Swahili there are subjunctives for hypotactic modal clauses, e.g. *angoja hapa mpaka nifika* "he-wait-subj. here till I-arrive-subj."; in the pidginized form of the language this becomes *mzuri yeye nangoja hapa*

paka mimi nafika "advisable he wait-inf. here till I arrive-inf.", where the subjunctives are replaced with infinitives, the subject agents are expressed by separate personal pronouns, and the sentence is introduced by a "Satzeinleitungswort". Cf. the construction in (Ki-)Nubi Arabic *áána ááj(u) ásurubú* "I want to drink" (Heine 1982:38).

49) For an analysis of the hypotactic clauses in Damascene Arabic see Bloch 1965; he discusses the difference between clauses with and without *y-* imperfect (48-52), calling the former type "qualifiziert", because they follow expressions with a more or less modal meaning which qualify the hypotactic clause. But he puts together syndetic and asyndetic constructions (49, n. 1) because of the absence of a difference in meaning between these two constructions. This may be right from a synchronic point of view, but the material used should be checked for classicization, which may well be responsible for many of the syndetic constructions.

50) Although one could point at the lack of inversion in Gastarbeiterdeutsch, which maintains the order ... S ... V ... after adverbials or in question sentences, cf. Meisel (1975:41) and for Gastarbeiderhollands Werkgroep (1978:49).

51) A notable exception is Uzbekistan (and Afghanistan Arabic), where the object seems to be normally preposed (cf. Fischer 1961:242; Sīrat 1973:100). This results in the word order SOV, as in Turkish. The change of word order in Uzbekistan Arabic certainly merits further analysis because of the implications for the theory of universals (cf. Comrie 1981:80-97).

CHAPTER VI
MODERN ARABIC TRADE-LANGUAGES, PIDGINS, AND CREOLES

The subject of the preceding chapters has been the Arabic dialects as mother tongues of millions of speakers. In this chapter I shall discuss the use of Arabic as a second language, mainly for practical purposes, in multilingual communities in which Arabic is the only language for interlingual communication. In all known instances of this use the language has undergone a full process of pidginization, and in at least one case such a modern pidgin has become the mother tongue of a community. As far as we know, the use of Arabic as a pidginized trade-language is restricted nowadays to Africa, but there can hardly be any doubt that in the period immediately following the conquests a number of rudimentary trade-languages based on Arabic existed all over the empire in those regions where contact with the indigenous population had not yet led to their incorporation within the social, cultural, and linguistic structure of Muslim society. The existence of such pidginized varieties is acknowledged even by those who see in the modern dialects the result of a natural development of the language, for instance by Fück and Cohen.[1] Even long after the nativization of most pidginized versions of Arabic, simplified trade-languages based on Arabic must have been used along the frontiers, for example in the Eastern parts of the empire on both sides of the frontier with the Indo-Aryan and Turkic speaking peoples, and in Africa with the Berbers and the Bantu speaking tribes in and to the South of the Sahara.

It is hardly surprising that there are no traces left of such pidginized varieties, since they were soon superseded by creolized versions, which were based on them. They would, anyhow, almost certainly have contained exclusively Arabic elements, since the mixture of elements in such simplified trade-languages reflects the relative strength of the groups engaged in the creation of such languages. Only in cases where the groups have equal importance will the resulting trade-languages, indeed, be a mixture of two or more languages. It may even be a prerequisite for a language that has to function under such circumstances to allow a high degree of variability for the speakers of heterolingual groups, instead of favouring one above the other. An example of such a trade-language is Russenorsk, a Russian-Norwegian trade-language, which at the beginning of this century was being used by Russian and Norwegian traders. In this language there were for many items two alternatives depending on the choice of the speaker for one or the other of the target-languages (cf. Broch & Jahr ms.). In other cases the superiority of one of the two groups is reflected in the predominance of elements from their language, as is the case with the Kjachta pidgin that served as a Chinese-Russian trade-language along the trade-routes between the two countries in Siberia. This language contained almost exclusively Russian elements (cf. Neumann 1966). Obviously, such a limited means of communication may grow into a more elaborate pidginized version of one of the two target languages, but this happens only in those cases where the contact between the groups involved intensifies to a certain degree. If contact is broken off, the trade-language disappears completely, unless it can be used in contacts with newcomers, as was presumably the case with several Indian trade-languages in North America (cf. Drechsel 1976; 1981). On the other hand, if contacts grow so intense that one of the two groups is incorporated in the other, the pidgin is bound to become the mother tongue for a new generation, and in that case it is creolized.

Not in all instances of commercial contact with other peoples did the Arabic language become a means of communication for practical purposes. In some regions, its importance must have been more limited than in others. In East Africa, for example, the only noticeable effect of Arabic consists in the considerable number of loanwords in Swahili, which in its turn became the principal trade-language on the Eastern shores of the African continent, and, as a result, the first language for a growing number of people. One is tempted to speculate that the presence of a number of ʻUmānī settlers in Zanzibar gave rise to a trade-language or a pidginized version of Arabic, although already sources from the 10th century report that the Muslim community in Zanzibar used a local, Bantu-type language, *Zanǧī* (Miquel 1975:523), and our principal source for the Zanzibar dialect of Arabic (Reinhardt 1894) does not mention any differences between the Arabic of Oman and that of Zanzibar.[2] In commercial contacts with Western trade-centres around the Mediterranean there was no need for an Arabic-based trade-language, either, since from early times onwards merchants and seafarers in that part of the world had used the Italian- and Spanish-based *lingua franca* Sabir.[3]

Still, it is rather surprising that there is no mention at all of pidgins based on Arabic in any other part of the world, except in Africa. One wonders why, for instance, there did not arise an Arabic pidgin or trade-language in India, Malaysia, or Indonesia — provided, of course, our ignorance is not due to a lack of sources and to the ephemeral nature of trade-languages. The general picture that emerges is that of isolated communities of Muslims who did not have much success in spreading the use of Arabic, although they did succeed in converting the local population to Islam. Some of the colonies eventually even adopted the use of the local language (Miquel 1975:522-23). A possible answer could be that, when the first Arab (or Persian) traders, colonists, traders, invaders, or missionaries came to the East, they started to use a pidgin that must have already been widespread in the ports and harbours of the Indian Ocean and beyond, namely Malay, which in its pidginized varieties became the Eastern trade-language *par excellence*. Obviously, the Arabs could have learnt it through their frequent contacts with Indian seafarers and merchants and, accordingly, did not see fit to replace it with their own language. Malay continued to be used until it was replaced by an even more successful traders' pidgin, the Portuguese pidgin that was used, not only in the Mediterranean, but also in Asia and Africa (cf. Hancock 1975).

It is, perhaps, superfluous to add that in its role of religious language Arabic was not likely to be pidginized. In those countries where Arabic was recited as the language of the revealed Book, people either did not understand at all what it was they were reciting, or they received lessons of Arabic in its Classical form, in order to be able to read theological tracts and collections of religious traditions. In neither case was there any tendency to develop a colloquial variety of the language. At best there emerged a completely arabicized version of the indigenous written language, as in the case of the so-called kitap-Malay, as well as the kitap-Afrikaans that is used in theological literature written in a curious mixture of Arabic and Afrikaans by the so-called Cape-Malays in South Africa (cf. Kähler 1971:67).

In the preceding chapters I have attempted to adduce evidence for a theory that regards all modern dialects of Arabic as originally pidginized varieties of Classical Arabic, which were almost immediately creolized by children who were born of foreign mothers and Arab fathers or of foreign parents who belonged to different linguistic communities with only Arabic as a common language. Afterwards, these creoles were decreolized at a rate that was determined by the intensity of the contacts between the regions involved and the centre of the Islamic empire, as well as other factors, including the predominant religion of the community involved. In areas that were soon cut off from the empire, especially in those cases where the speakers were non-Muslims, who did not have the same attitude towards the *Qur'ān* as the Muslims, the local Arabic dialect could retain its pidginized and creolized features, since it did not undergo the normative influence of the Classical language which elsewhere filtered through via the recitation of the *Qur'ān*, and via its use as a prestige language.

It might be asked in what way the analysis of the Arabic pidgins and creoles used nowadays can contribute towards a deeper insight into the history of the Arabic language: after all, the modern pidgins represent a 'maximal' degree of 'corruption' and can hardly be compared with those varieties of Arabic that have levelled down to the Classical language. The only modern creolized variety, (Ki-)Nubi cannot have undergone any influence, either from any modern dialect, or from the Classical language, and remains, therefore, without any sign of decreolization. The only interesting development that might lead to predictions concerning the structure of the Arabic pidgins is the possibility that the Sudanese pidgin Juba Arabic might become a first language for a number of speakers and, as a result of advancing education, fall within the sphere of influence of Khartoum Arabic, or even Modern Standard Arabic. This will enable us to study the effects of decreolization at first hand. On the whole, however, I believe that the objection is justified, and that the modern pidgins and creoles which are based on Arabic cannot be used as evidence for or against the theses advanced here.

Nevertheless, I think that the modern pidgins can in a number of ways be very useful methodologically. In the first place they demonstrate convincingly — if such a demonstration is really needed — that it is possible for a larger number of speakers to break down the version of Arabic they are exposed to in an incredibly short time, thereby invalidating all objections that have been formulated against the 'corruption' of Arabic in the early period of Islam, for instance, by Zwettler (1978:137). They also demonstrate that breaking down a language or simplifying its morphological inventory has nothing whatsoever to do with a "capacity for linguistic abstraction and an ear for morphological subtleties", as Zwettler (1978:134) puts it, but it is a perfectly normal concomitant of a universal process of language learning in difficult linguistic situations.

In the second place, I should like to point out that the universal strategies that, in my view, are responsible for the transformation of a language in a process of pidginization and creolization do not lead to universally identical results. They only constitute methods of handling linguistic facts, the actual results being largely dependent on the input material involved. In this perspective, the transformation of any variety of Arabic into a pidgin or a creole is interesting, since it shows what the results of such a transformation may be in the particular language under investigation here.

Finally, it might turn out to be worthwhile to compare the difference between the modern pidgins and their target language, on the one hand, and the difference between the dialects of the *Sprachinsel* and Classical Arabic on the other. As the dialects of the *Sprachinsel* never, or only to a very limited degree, underwent the levelling influence of the Classical language,[4] they must be closer to the original type of Arabic creole than any other Arabic dialect and, consequently, more similar to the modern transformations of Arabic into pidgins and creoles. There are a few drawbacks to the drawing of such a comparison, however: we know very little about the isolated dialects of Arabic, and almost nothing about the modern Arabic pidgins and creoles, apart from the fact that they exist. What is more, in most cases we do not even know what the target language of these modern pidgins was. A comparison between the two groups of dialects will, therefore, have to remain a pious wish until more material becomes available. As a small contribution towards this, I shall present some details about the modern Arabic pidgins and creoles, as well as a few observations concerning their linguistic structure from a diachronic point of view, mainly on the basis of Heine's description of (Ki-)Nubi (1982).

In the literature mention is made of Arabic pidgins (and creoles) in the following countries: Sudan, Ethiopia, Uganda/Kenya, Nigeria, Chad:

a. *Sudan*

In the Southern provinces of Sudan a pidginized variety of Arabic — variably known as Mongallese, Juba Arabic, or Bimbashi Arabic — has been spoken since the Egyptian military campaigns at the end of the last century. This pidginized variety must have arisen in the military encampments, whence it was exported as a creolized variety under the name of (Ki-)Nubi (Reinecke a.o. 1975:707-709; Hancock 1971:518; 1977:389; Heine 1973:54; Nhial 1975; Bickerton 1976 Mahmud 1979; 1982)[5]. According to Bell (Bell & Hurreiz 1975:80) other pidginized varieties of Arabic are current in Equatoria Province (Southern Sudan). Recent developments in the South are mentioned by Mahmud (1979:171); he describes a situation in which many children are already speaking a creolized variety of Juba Arabic. Many people from neighbouring countries have come to live in the South and their children, too, have become speakers of a creolized variety.

b. *Ethiopia*
As a religious language Arabic plays an important role in Ethiopia — and in Somalia and Eritrea as well — but it is also used as a *lingua franca* among non-arobophones (Ferguson 1970:304-305) and even as a pidginized trade-language (Ferguson 1970:305).[6] Of the two traits mentioned by Ferguson as typical of the pidginized variety — the use of the 3rd ps masc sg for all persons of the verbs, and the use of the full form of the numerals 3-10 with singular nouns — the former is similar to one of the most characteristic developments in (Ki-)Nubi (cf. below, p. 120) and it is also found in some varieties of Chad Arabic, whereas the latter is, of course, present in many other dialects.

c. *Uganda/Kenya*
The Sudanese pidginized variety Juba Arabic became the mother tongue for a number of speakers (between 30,000 and 50,000) in Uganda and Kenya. This language is known as Nubian Arabic or (Ki-)Nubi (Reinecke a.o. 1975:707-709; Hancock 1977:390; Nhial 1975; Owens 1980; Heine 1982). As (Ki-)Nubi is the only modern Arabic creole, and at the same time the only variety that has been described in any detail, my remarks below will be primarily derived from the work by Heine (1982) on the language.

d. *Chad*
Apart from Chadian Colloquial Arabic,[7] Arabic is also used in this region in more or less pidginized varieties. Hagège (1973:9-10) mentions a pidgin Arabic ("arabe véhiculaire") that is used in contacts between arabophone and non-arabophone Chadians, as well as a variety that serves as a *lingua franca* between non-arabophone ethnic groups and that has even evolved in some cases into a first language, i.e. a creole. Something similar may, perhaps, be inferred from Roth's analysis of the linguistic situation (1979), but the information is not clear (cf. below, p. 120). The pidginized variety is probably the one mentioned under the name of Turku

(Reinecke a.o. 1975:707-709; Heine 1973:53-54; Kaye 1976:98) or Tourkol (Hancock 1977:388).[8]

e. *Nigeria*

Lethem (1920) is a description of what he calls Shuwa Arabic of Bornu (Nigeria); Kaye (1975:316) points out that this name is not used by speakers of Arabic themselves, who call their own language *kalām arab*; he, therefore, prefers to call the native variety Nigerian Arabic. According to Kaye, there are tens of thousands, maybe even hundreds of thousands of native speakers of Arabic in Nigeria, particularly in the North-eastern province of Bornu. Moreover, there are many speakers of Arabic as a second or a third language, and it is also used as an auxiliary trade jargon (Kaye 1982:ix). In the literature on pidgins two pidginized varieties of Arabic are mentioned for this area: one a pidgin Arabic used in Northern Nigeria in a Hausa-speaking environment (Hancock 1971:518), the other a pidgin called Galgalíya that is used by the Kalamáfi tribe in North-eastern Nigeria (Hancock 1971:518; 1977: 388). Kaye (1982:ix) reports that the name Galgalīye is used by non-Arabic speaking Nigerians as a general term for Arabic (probably < *gāl* "he said").

It is very likely that the names of Arabic dialects mentioned by Kampffmeyer (1899) for the Bornu and Brakna regions of modern Nigeria, Mali, and Mauretania in fact conceal pidginized varieties of Arabic. Similarly, the list of tribes mentioned by Zavadovskij (1981:12) of Ḥassāniyya-speakers in Senegal (Brākna), Gambia, Guinea, Mali (Kənta, Brābîš, Ahl Sīdi kəl Arawān, Gwānîn, etc.) and Niger almost certainly includes varieties of Arabic that are either trade-languages or pidginized/creolized varieties.[9] According to Kaye (1975:321, n. 10) there are many Arabic-speaking towns and villages in Cameroon. No doubt, further research on the spot — as already suggested by Kampffmeyer (1899:212) in the last century — would turn up many more pidgins and, possibly, creoles.

There is one persistent problem in the evaluation of those pidginized varieties of Arabic that are spoken in those countries in Africa where the Classical standard is still being used: the confusion between different levels of speech that is found in the descriptions of the local Arabic. In view of the prestige of the standard a typical reaction of the informants will always be to upgrade their speech, which is then used by the investigator as a representative sample of the colloquial. This problem is, of course, not unique to the study of the African Arabic-based pidgins: it is one of the major sources for inaccuracy in the description of many Arabic dialects.

To mention a typical example from the past, I should like to quote from Kampffmeyer's notes (1899) on the Bedouin dialects of Central Africa. In these notes he mentions the dialect of the Schua (Schoa) in Bornu (Nigeria), which, according to his sources, differed considerably from the neighbouring Maghrebi dialects. "während es in vielen Zügen die Reinheit und Gewandtheit der Sprache des Hidjās bewahrt habe, besonders in Beziehung auf die Endvokale in der Conjugatioñ" (1899:144, quoting from Barth 1857-59: II, 439). Kampffmeyer's most important source is a collection of vocabularies by Sigismund Koelle (1854), and the dialect with the alleged 'endings' is apparently that of the 'Ādirar tribe, in which fully inflected forms are said to be used, such as *ánfun* "nose", *fámun* "mouth" (1899:151), *gatáltu dīku* "I kill a fowl" (1899:61), *daáitu ábdan* "I call a slave", *ṣaráptulmāa* "I drink water" (ib.). But on closer inspection it turns out that Koelle's only informant for this dialect was someone who had studied the *Qur'ān* from his seventh to his sixteenth year (1899:147). Such an informant may be expected to have tried to cultivate his speech for the foreign traveller who wished to know more about his dialect. This would also explain the occurrence of typically hypercorrect forms, such as *tabáḥtu láḥamu* "I cook meat" (1899:161).[10]

This acceptance of classicizing forms from informants is not only found in 19th century writings, but even in modern publications. In her description of the Chad Arabic dialect of Abbéché, Roth (1979) bases her analysis mainly on information supplied by a *faqīh*, someone, that is, who may be expected to have a fairly good knowledge of Classical Arabic. One wonders, whether the analysis always accurately represents the basilectal variety of the Abbéché dialect. When Roth remarks (1979:3) that in this dialect the personal markers of the 2nd ps masc sg and the 1st ps sg of the perfect are often deleted, and that these endings are replaced by autonomous personal pronouns — *āna katab* "I wrote", *inta katab* "you wrote" — she may be referring to more than a mere optional variation in the Abbéché dialect. In fact, it might constitute a basilectal variety of Chad Arabic, similar to the zero verbal form of (Ki-)Nubi and Juba Arabic, which has become obscured by the more cultivated speech of Roth's principal informant. Educated informants tend to present a highly coloured and cultivated picture of the dialect they are expected to describe.[11]

When I now turn to the structure of the best-known of the Arabic pidgins and creoles, Nubi, the first thing that strikes us is the extreme erosion of the phonological inventory in this language, which has changed to such a degree that it has become almost irrecognizable as an Arabic dialect. This is the result, not only of the elision of word-final consonants, for instance *bée* < *bayt* "house", *rági* < *rağul*, *rāgil* "man", *sondú* < *ṣandūq* "box" (Heine 1982:18f.), but also of the loss of the opposition between non-emphatic and emphatic consonants, and the disappearance or merger of most velars and pharyngeals: /ḥ/ > /h/ or ø, for instance, *rúa* < *rāḥ* "to go"; /ḫ/, /ġ/ > /k/, for instance, *dákulu* < *daḫala* "to enter", *sakar* < *ṣaġīr* "small"; /ʻ/ > ø, for instance *wága* < *waqaʻa* "to fall down" (Heine 1982:18). In some cases the pharyngeal seems to have been reinterpreted as a vowel or as a lengthening of the preceding vowel, i.e., VḥK > V̄K, for instance, *áámeru* > *aḥmar* "red". This change may be connected with another tendency mentioned by Heine (1982:17-18), namely the drift towards bisyllabicity, which is very pronounced in Nubi. This makes it similar to many other creolized varieties all over the world (cf. Heine 1973:144-47).

A general trait in many pidginized and creolized varieties is the occurrence of wide-spread reinterpretation of morpheme boundaries (incorrect back-formations). In Nubi this phenomenon is found in many words that have been expanded with the article *al-* — otherwise lost in this language — thus making it in many cases a bisyllabic word, e.g. *láádum* < *al-ʻaẓm* "bone", *laájer* < *al-ḥağar* "stone", *lifíli* < *al-fīl* "elephant", *áánas* < *an-nās* "people", *ása* "now" < *as-sāʻa* "hour". A similar tendency towards agglutination of the French definite article in French creoles, for instance Seychellois *lamẽ* < *la main* "hand", *lisyẽ* < *le chien* "dog", is noted by Bollée (1977:31-34). She also mentions in this connection the tendency in creoles towards consonant initial words, and towards words with two syllables. The phenomenon of reinterpretation of morpheme boundaries is, of course, also known in other Arabic dialects, but there it is checked by the constant contact with the Classical language.

It is impossible to know if, morphologically, Nubi is more advanced than its immediate ancestor, Juba Arabic. Although we do have a good description of Nubi, there is only sporadic information about Juba Arabic. Besides, a well-established pidginized variety of a language undergoes a stage of expansion, too, and the distinction between simplified pidgin and expanded creole is useless in the analysis of pidginized and creolized varieties (cf. above, ch. III, p. 39). In both varieties, Nubi as well as Juba Arabic, the morphology is completely broken down compared to Classical Arabic, but for many syntactic relations new lexical elements have become grammaticalized and have established themselves as new grammatical morphemes with grammatical functions.

This applies, for instance, to the genitive exponent *tà-*, which in both dialects is obligatory, unlike its probable ancestor *matā*ʿ: both in Egyptian and in Sudanese Arabic it is possible to vary between the use of the genitive exponent and the Classical synthetic construction (Heine 1982: 31). This confirms the conclusion reached above (ch. V, p. 93f.) that the intrusion of the Classical construction in the possessive construction which we find in many modern dialects is the result of a process of decreolization. In general, we can say that the morphology of both Juba Arabic and Nubi, more than that of any other dialect which has become isolated from the main trend, has done away with almost every trace of Classical morphology, and in some cases has developed completely new means of expression that are not found elsewhere in the Arabic dialects.

In Nubi, for instance, the comparative may be expressed by means of the reflex of Classical *min*, for instance, *rági dé kebír min íta* "that man is older than you". But there is another way of expressing comparison, with the de-verbal particle *fútu* "to pass", "than", for instance, *úo kebír fút(u) áána* "he is bigger than me", *kél dé kebír fút(u) búra* "a dog is bigger than a cat" (Heine 1982:34).[12] This way of expressing the comparative is, of course, wide-spread in pidginized languages all over the world, for instance in Tok Pisin *mi bikpela winim yu* "I am bigger than you" (Bauer 1974:54-56), in Dahomey Pidgin English *he fine pass all woman* "she was finer than all other women", Haitian Creole *li lèd pase u* "she is uglier than you" (Hall 1966:82). Incidentally, this proves once again that the expression in the pidginized versions of English and French can hardly be the result of the influence of an alleged West African substratum.

A similar case is that of the development of pluralizers for collective nouns in Nubi, derived from Classical *nās* "people", for instance *nas-babá* "the group of fathers, fathers as a whole", *nas-yalá* "the group of children, children as a whole" (Heine 1982:29). With this development may be compared the use of *ban* (<*bande* "group, troop") as a pluralizer in Indian Ocean Creole French, which is mentioned by Bollée (1977:41-42; 106-107), for instance *mõ a ẽvit tu mõ ban zami* "I'll invite all my friends", *mõ amen zerb pur ban zanimo* "I bring grass for the animals".

In spite of the fact that the probable ancestor of Juba Arabic and Nubi, some form of Sudanese or Egyptian colloquial, must have had an aspectual prefix system, these two dialects had to develop themselves a new system by reinterpreting and expanding the old system. In Egyptian and Sudanese colloquial the aspectual prefixes are used with the inflected verbal forms and, in the case of the imperfect, together with the pronominal prefixes. When these disappeared, the aspectual prefixes disappeared, too, and a new system had to be built in the pidgin. In both languages there is only one verbal form that without aspectual prefixes indicates the simple past with action verbs. In Juba Arabic, this verbal form receives the following prefixes (Nhial 1975:82-83):

ána gá rówa fi súg	"I am going to the market"
ána bə rówa fi súg	"I shall go to the market"
ána kān rówa fi súg	"I had gone to the market"
ána kān gá rówa fi súg	"I was going to the market"

Mahmud (1979) mentions other combinations, in particular a future progressive *bi gi* and an irrealis, but does not discuss the anterior. It is difficult to compare the two accounts, since Mahmud describes a variable system. In Nubi we have (Heine 1982:38-39): anterior *káán*, irrealis *bi*, non-punctual *gí*, as well as a marker for the perfective aspect, *kàlá(s)* (cf. above, ch. V, p. 86). The following combinations are possible: future progressive *bi gí*, counterfactual *káán gí*, past progressive *káán bi*.

The designations of the aspects indicated by the aspectual prefixes have been borrowed from Bickerton's analysis of the aspectual system. As a matter of fact, Nubi aspects fit his system even better than those of Juba Arabic used in his comparative study (1976). But the resemblance between Nubi aspects and those in other creoles does not say very much: after all, there may be a lot of languages that express semantic distinctions in the verbal system in a similar way, particularly so, if these distinctions are indeed, as Bickerton claims, semantic primitives. The point is, however, that in a certain process of language acquisition the learners apparently always develop such a system: it is not the presence of the aspectual prefixes, but their development which counts. Therefore, it is useless to try, as Owens (1980) does, to find structural criteria that will define creolized languages. In my view, it is preferable to look at the strategies that operate in this process, and that are, eventually, responsible for certain changes in the languages involved — changes in the same direction, not necessarily identical changes, as the evidence from the languages used by Bickerton and Owens shows.

From the point of view of diachronic development it may be noted that there is some evidence that the verbal form without prefixes is derived from an original imperative. Nhial (1975:83) refers to some verbs in Juba Arabic which look very much like Classical imperatives: *ámsíku*(<*imsik*?) "to catch", *ásrebu*(<*išrab*?) "to drink". In Heine's Nubi vocabulary one finds among many others the following examples: *ábinu* "to build", *ísab* "to count", *ámulá* "to fill", *álbis* "to dress", *ágilíb* "to fry", *álibu* "to milk", *ásuma* "to hear", *ágder* "to be able", *ásurub(ú)* "to drink". This conjecture is strengthened by the fact that those verbs which are to be regarded as reflexes of Classical (or dialectal) verbs IIw/y, as expected, do not have the *a(a)*-prefix, e.g. *jíbu* "to bring", *num* "to sleep", and also the originally geminate verb *kútu* (< Classical *ḫaṭṭa*) "to put". In other pidgins, too, there have been attempts to explain the pidginized verbal system as a derivation from one verbal stem, the imperative, which after all, was most likely to have served as input for the new learners in the typically colonial context in which most pidgins developed.[13]

Something else is remarkable in the formation of Nubi verbal forms, namely their alternation between verbs which end in *-u* and verbs which do not have this ending. Obviously, much more data must be available before it is possible to reach a final conclusion on this question, but it would seem that in the majority of cases transitive verbs have the ending *-u*, whereas intransitive verbs do not. One possible explanation of this suffix would be to compare it with the suffix *-im* that is used as a transitivity marker in Tok Pisin in verbs such as *givim*, *hitim*, *kilim* (Bauer 1974: 87ff.)[14], and that is derived from the object form of the personal pronoun, *him*. In Nubi the suffix *-u* could be derived from the personal pronoun suffix of the 3rd ps masc sg, which in most dialects becomes *-u* after consonants and Ø after the vowel *a*. In accordance with this last rule we find in Nubi transitive verbs such as *gáta* "to cut", *ágara* "to read" without the *-u*. In some cases the presence of the suffix may have become obscured through the working of a phonological rule -Ku K- > -K K- (Heine 1982:26).[15]

An interesting example is furnished by the verbal pairs *kálas(u)/kálas* "to finish/be finished" and *kárabu/kárab* "to spoil/be spoilt" where the difference between the transitive and the intransitive verb is constituted precisely by the presence or absence of the suffix *-u*. These verbs are also interesting for another reason. They demonstrate a phenomenon that is well-known from other creolized languages: the possibility to use transitive verbs without an object as passive (cf. above, ch.V, n. 18). This possibility is also mentioned by Heine (1982:42) who says that there is a partly productive pattern of using transitive verbs as passives by moving the stressed high tone from the first to the last syllable of the verb, for example *úo séregú kalamóyo* "he stole a goat" and *kalamóyo dé seregú* "the goat was stolen". In her analysis of the Chad Arabic of Abbéché Roth (1979:40) mentions the occurrence of one single example of this phenomenon in her corpus, *al-ẖubza sirig* "the bread was stolen". But the details concerning this construction in Nubi are still unclear.

Both the derivation of the verbal form from an imperative and the use of the transitivizing suffix of the 3rd ps masc sg may perhaps be explained by referring to the socio-linguistic situation in which Juba Arabic arose and Nubi developed, namely that of the military settlements and encampments in Sudan. Juba Arabic was not nicknamed 'Bimbashi Arabic' for nothing, since it was primarily used between Arabic-speaking subaltern officers and non-arabophone recruits. It is not very difficult to imagine the kind of context in which verbal forms were first learnt by the new recruits in the Egyptian-trained armies, and it is quite possible that they were taken over in precisely those forms in which they were first heard by the learners.

The system of agreement rules in Juba Arabic and in Nubi provides us with a good example of the effect of decreolization, which influences the development of Juba Arabic, while being absent in Nubi. Apparently, Juba Arabic originally did not have number agreement between substantive and adjective, so that the normal way of expressing "we are all right" would be *anína kwés*. Nowadays, most Juba speakers use a plural ending with the adjectival predicate, saying *anína kwesín* (Nhial 1975:84). Doubtlessly, this use of the plural ending has spread as the result of the influence of the Classical Standard and of Sudanese Arabic. In Nubi, however, where neither the Classical Standard, nor any modern Arabic dialect play any role at all, normal agreement rules require a zero ending in the adjectival predicate (Nhial 1975:84).[16]

In general, one may expect decreolization to be an important factor in the development of Juba Arabic: the language policy of the Sudanese government in the Southern provinces must lead to a steadily increasing exposure to both Modern Standard and Khartoum Arabic, so that the pidginized version will either become part of a continuum or disappear because people will adopt the Khartoum dialect. This depends on the degree of success the government is able to attain in its policy. That the effects are already visible is demonstrated by the example given by Nhial. He also mentions, for instance, (1975:86-87) that Juba speakers have begun to use other prepositions besides the all-purpose ones *fi*, *fōg*, *warā*; some speakers occasionally use *ma* "with" and in the speech of educated speakers one even finds such prepositions as *tiḥit* "under" and *'ala* "on", which are clearly borrowed from

Khartoum Arabic. This phenomenon is unknown in Nubi, which only uses its inherited prepositions (Heine 1982:35-37) without having the possibility of borrowing from a standard language.

But the most striking example of the effects of decreolization on the structure of the basilect is provided by Mahmud's (1979) detailed analysis of variation in the aspectual system of Juba Arabic. Reference has been made above (ch. V, p. 85) to this analysis as a possible explanation of the development of two verbal forms in all modern Arabic dialects. Mahmud describes a stage in the life-cycle of this pidginized variety, in which on the one hand children start to to use it as a (creolized) mother tongue, and on the other hand, the influence of the dialect of Khartoum, and even the Modern Classical standard is spreading fast. Leaving aside the details of the aspectual system, I should like to draw attention here to one of the most remarkable developments in the speech of those who undergo this influence. Mahmud (1979:186-92) reports that in their speech some of the personal prefixes of the Sudanese Arabic imperfect, *ya*, *ta*, *na* (3rd, 2nd, 1st pl ps, respectively) are borrowed and used as aspectual markers alongside with and partly replacing the pidgin aspect markers, such as *gi*, *bi*. At a later stage, the use of these new markers evolves into what Mahmud calls an "embryonic agreement subsystem", until finally they shed their aspectual meaning and become part of a syntactic agreement system that is virtually identical with the one used in the acrolectal variety, the dialect of Khartoum. An example quoted by Mahmud (1979:187) illustrates very well the free alternation within the speech of one speaker between the original aspect marker *bi* and the borrowed markers *ya* and *ta*: *ma ya kutu-balu fi lstadi*, *ta kutu-balu bes je del ali fi sekondari*, *ma bi kutu-balu fi giraya bitau* "[the students] don't care to study, they care only like those who are in secondary school, they don't care for their studies". Obviously, such a system with a high degree of free alternation represents only a transient stage for the speech community. Whether or not this also applies to the speech of an individual speaker, is of course a question which can only be answered with the help of a longitudinal investigation.

The importance of Mahmud's analysis can hardly be exaggerated. It shows the effect of decreolization in a pidginized/creolized variety of Arabic over a few decades. Without unduly extrapolating one can, I think, safely say that the effect of such a process over some centuries can indeed account for a major levelling towards a standard language, such as I have assumed to have taken place in the history of the Arabic dialects. Thus, the Juba aspectual system and its movement towards the Sudanese standard may be one of the most rewarding subjects of research for diachronic linguistics in the years to come.

NOTES

1) Cf. Fück 1950:5; Cohen 1970:108; for a similar acknowledgement in the case of the Romance languages see Hall 1974:76.

2) According to Meillet & Cohen (1952: I, 138) an Arabic *sabir* was used in Madagascar; no further details are known.

3) Cf. Kahane, Kahane & Tietze 1958; Whinnom's theory about the descendance of all known pidgins and creoles from this source has been mentioned above, ch. III, p. 50.

4) But cf. Borg (1982:23, 180), who mentions the use of internal plurals in the Cypriot Arabic dialect of the elderly people, in particular with words from the learned vocabulary; this suggests at least some degree of contact with the Classical standard.

5) Bickerton (1976) used Juba Arabic as one of the languages for his analysis of the aspectual system in creolized languages (not available to me).

6) Drewes (1976:175f.) denies that Arabic is used as a *lingua franca* in Ethiopia. According to Andrzejewski (in Whiteley 1974:66) many Somali traders use colloquial Arabic in their contacts with Arab traders in Kenya, and sometimes also in trading with Ethiopia.

7) Apparently, Chadian Arabic is a dialect that was bedouinized at one time or has evolved from a Bedouin dialect (cf. Kaye 1976:91-98).

8) It is not clear whether it is also identical with the variety mentioned under the name Tekrur (Hancock 1971:518) which is reportedly spoken as a *lingua franca* to the East of Lake Chad and in the Bodélé region. Some of these names may derive from the French designation 'Toucouleurs'. The situation is complicated by the fact that there are Peul-(Ful-)speaking groups in the Senegalese Foûta which are called Toucouleurs, Tokoror, Tekarir or Tekrour (Meillet & Cohen 1952: II, 837). The Shuwa Arabic that is mentioned in the sources (cf. Kaye 1976:96-98, quoting from Lethem 1920) is identified by Hancock (1977:388) with Tourkol; it is probably the Nigerian designation for the variety spoken by those people for whom Arabic is a mother tongue.

9) Cf. Meillet & Cohen (1952: I, 140): "[Ḥassanīyya] sert de langue de relation à de nombreux musulmans". This may also apply to the Peul (Ful) of Darfur who are said to have adopted Arabic as their language, according to Meillet & Cohen (1952: II, 387, n. 1).

10) The informant in question studied in another region, Bēṛān, and his expertise in the dialect of this region was also used by Koelle. Interestingly enough, the forms quoted for this dialect (for which he is the only informant) are much more colloquial, cf. *ráaitu* vs. Beran *ṣíft* (i.e. *šíft*), or *tálābtu* vs. Beran *tálapt*.

11) The theory of decreolization is clearly connected with the current discussion in Arabic socio-linguistics about the question of the maximal domain of classicization. According to Palva (1969) lexical borrowing and phonological modification are the principal means used by speakers of Arabic to upgrade their speech-level, but subsequent research has shown that in many cases grammatical features are borrowed as prestige features (for instance, Killean's unpublished dis-

sertation which is quoted by Schmidt 1977:14). Diem (1974:41) mentions the fact that dialect speakers sometimes use imperfects without the verbal particle *bi-* in Egypt through interference of the Classical language. The awareness of prestigious and of stigmatized features — often showing itself through the use of hypercorrect forms — is, indeed, one of the most important characteristics of the continuum situation in the arabophone countries that has to be accounted for in any description of that situation.

12) The verb *fāt* in Chad Arabic seems to be used in a similar way, but the facts are not entirely clear, e.g., *ğarēnā futnā ko* "we ran quicker than you" (Hagège 1973:53) and *mūsa bufūtna kullina fī ilim* "Mūsa surpasses us all in knowledge" (Roth 1979:133); this last example looks like a blend of Classical Arabic and dialect.

13) Forms such as Tok Pisin *hitim* "to hit" in which the verbal stem is combined with a transitivizing suffix might perhaps be explained as derivations from the English imperative, rather than as an abstraction of the English verbal stem, or as infinitives. The verbs in the Russian-Chinese trade-language of Kjachta look very much like the imperatives of Russian verbs, e.g. *potorguj* "to trade" from the Russian verb *(po)torgovat'* (cf. Neumann 1966:242).

14) Such a suffix possibly also occurs in Russenorsk, cf. Neumann 1956:228.

15) A similar suggestion has been made by Roth (1979:64-68, cf. Kaye 1976:126-28, n. 82) for the mysterious *a-* suffix in mostly transitive verbal forms in the Chad Arabic of Abbéché.

16) But see Heine (1982:33), who states that the plural suffix is not always used and that there is considerable fluctuation in its use, for example *lakáta úe-dé asás* "this house is nice", *lakáta dól-dé asas-ín* "these houses are nice", *lajerá milán* "many stones", *aanási jedid-ín* (ib. 50) "new people", *juá milán* (ib. 51). "many houses".

CHAPTER VII
CONCLUSIONS AND PROSPECTS

In the preceding chapters I have attempted to advance a theory to account for the origin of the Arabic dialects, their differences, their similarities, and their divergence from the Classical language. My primary hypothesis was that an untutored process of second language learning brings about a number of changes in the target language aimed at in the process of learning. These changes, it was argued, are similar everywhere, irrespective of either the target language or the source language, with regard to their direction, though not with regard to the end result. I then went on to adduce evidence that in the case of the Arabic language such a process did take place on a massive scale, and that the changes the language underwent in the process were indeed similar to those that took place in other languages which had undergone the same kind of process. I concluded that the resemblance was not accidental and, accordingly, attributed the changes from the Classical language to the process of second language learning. Referring to the similar processes elsewhere I proposed to use the term 'pidginization' for the primary changes in Arabic, and the term 'creolization' for the changes that took place in the subsequent stage of nativization of the resulting language variety. I also asserted that the creolized variety was strongly influenced by the Classical norm and, consequently, affected by a constant proces of levelling towards that norm. The degree of influence differed, however, according to the degree of isolation from the centre of Arab-Islamic culture.

As we have seen, the methodological problem was how to detect and to prove that a process of pidginization/creolization had taken place, while asserting simultaneously that the traces of the process had partly been obliterated by the subsequent levelling towards the Classical language. In this connection I have stated above that in my view the problem of knowing what a pidgin is, or the question of whether or not language x is a pidgin, must be rephrased into: did language x in the course of its history ever undergo a process of pidginization/creolization, which brought with it specific changes, and are there changes in the history of the language which may be interpreted in this light? Even so, there remains the problem of detecting the traces of such a proces when subsequent developments have interfered with its results. We have seen that this problem is not unique, and that it has, in fact, confronted linguists studying other languages than Arabic for which the claim of pidginization/creolization has been made, to mention but a few examples, in the case of English, French, Afrikaans, Marathi, and Black English.

The case of Afrikaans is very instructive: as Todd (1974:89) observes, Valkhoff's claim that Afrikaans represents a pidginized/creolized version of Dutch can only be made because we know something about the history of the two languages — and even so, the historical data are not conclusive. The thesis of creolization in the case of Afrikaans has been attacked from many sides (cfr. for an early polemic Bosman 1932). It is hardly ever the case — if at all — that the features present in a language are so inherently and specifically characteristic of pidginization/creolization that they can prove in themselves that the language in question has gone through a stage of such a process. Features that have been mentioned in this connection are, for instance, the presence of reduplicated forms, the phenomenon of verbal serialization, the development of an aspectual system that operates with verbal preformatives. But, in fact, it is very uncertain that it is possible at all to speak of inherent features of the process. Moreover, our problem is that there is no control group of 'normal' languages, since every language may very well hide a pidgin skeleton in the cupboard of its history which invalidates any reference to phenomena that are said to be decisive signs of pidginization/creolization.

What I wish to do here is to examine whether the theory expounded above may be useful for other languages as well. I have started with certain features in the modern Arabic dialects which were absent in the Classical language. Because of the similarity between these features and phenomena in languages that are commonly known as pidgins and creoles I started to look for correlating similarities in the history of these languages and in Arabic, and I concluded that the two factors, history and structural change must be connected: 'history' being equated with the complex of factors that determined the adoption of Arabic as a mother tongue by the population of the conquered territories, and 'structural change' with the restructuring of the morphological system, the reduction of redundancy, and other characteristic features of the modern Arabic dialects *vis-à-vis* the Classical language. I also attempted to find out which mechanisms are held responsible for these particular changes under these particular circumstances by specialists in the field of pidgins and creoles, and I discussed the assumption of a set of universal strategies which operate in situations of language learning under handicapped circumstances.

It remains to investigate here how far this argument works the other way round: how far may it be used as a prediction concerning the analyses of the features of a language? In more concrete terms, when we find that a language has gone through a turbulent period of conquests and subsequent language switching on the part of the subdued peoples, does the thesis correctly predict the presence of specific changes in its structure? In other words, does a comparison between the former state of that language before the period of language learning, and its later state, show the same kind of evolution with the same kind of tendencies as, for instance, in the case of Arabic? Fortunately, we have a candidate for such a comparison in the same region, namely Turkish. Although much in the history of the Turkish language is still unclear, one thing is certain: it has become the first language of a large number of speakers throughout Anatolia and the former Byzantine empire, who originally spoke Greek. Assimilation may have been slow in some parts of the Turkish empire, particularly in the case of those who clung to their Christian beliefs (cf. Vryonis 1972), but we may assume that the inhabitants of Istanbul (formerly Byzantium), for example, took over the language of their masters quickly in order to be able to coexist with them and go about doing their jobs under the new circumstances.

The variety of Turkish these people were exposed to — the colloquial of the conquerors — is not easy to determine, but recent research, as discussed by Hazai (1978: 42ff.) seems to point not to an independent development of Osmanic Turkish in Anatolia, but to the continuation of a standard language that had already developed in Central Asia. This language became the basis for the Turkish literary language, but the situation is complicated by the fact that there were actually two literary languages: the so-called High-Osmanic language, a highly iranicized and arabicized variety of Turkish, abounding in Persian and Arabic words, and even grammatical constructions, and the continuation of the original literary language that was used, for instance, for less formal poetry than the High Osmanic court poetry. It was this 'informal' literary language which, at the beginning of the twentieth century, constituted the point of departure for Atatürk's language reform, which aimed at the reinstalment of a 'pure' Turkish language. Alongside these two literary languages there must from the beginning have been a colloquial language. It is hardly surprising that we know very little about the colloquial language of the early centuries of Turkish domination in the Near East, but we are not completely at a loss for information about its structure. Just as in the history of the Arabic language we have the Middle Arabic texts — i.e. texts written by people who were relatively free from the influence of the Classical Standard, often in other scripts than the Arabic (cf. above, ch. I, p. 7f.) — we have for Turkish the so-called *Transkriptionsdenkmäler* — i.e. Turkish texts in other scripts, often by non-native speakers (cf. Hazai 1978: 32 ff.), as well as grammars written by non-native speakers (cf. Hazai 1978: 123f.).

The varieties of Turkish that we find in these texts range from extremely simplified to almost literary Turkish. It seems that thus far, no one has yet thought of describing and analyzing them in terms of the limited command of Turkish that is to be expected in view of the fact that so many millions of people in the former Byzantine empire had to change their linguistic habits -perhaps not overnight, but certainly within a few decades in most parts without the advantages of an efficient educational system.[1]

What I wish to suggest here is that the presence of unexplained divergences, in these and similar texts, from the Turkish language as we know it from the literary sources at our disposal might make much more sense when we try to see them in the light of the proces of second language learning that must have taken place in the early centuries of the Turkish conquests. This process has led to significant changes in the structure of the Turkish colloquial.[2] The question of the periodization is as complicated in Turkish as it is in Arabic. It is *a priori* not very likely that the *Transkriptionsdenkmäler* mentioned above reflect a genuine colloquial, and they cannot be used as a means to establish a chronology of the changes. Just like the Middle Arabic texts, they represent a speech variety that was much less influenced by the literary standard of the High Osmanic language than other written sources, but all the same the authors no doubt avoided the more conspicuous vulgarisms. Consequently, one should not use them as a *terminus a quo* for specific changes in the structure of Turkish.

These considerations lead me to believe that a new approach to the history of Turkish on the basis of an increased attention for the role of the new speakers of that language after the Osmanic conquests might turn out to be a welcome contribution towards a better understanding of the development of the language and the structural changes it underwent.[3] These remarks are only intended as a suggestion for further research along the lines proposed here, in which attention is given not to the development of individual forms and constructions of a language, but to its development as a whole. In my view, the analysis of the history of written languages sometimes becomes obscured by an atomistic approach and, in particular, by a failure to take into account the fact that written texts, whatever their cultural or social provenance, are always influenced by the literary language. There are no doubt other cases to which this method may be applied — one thinks of Chinese, for example, or the English language in Ireland (cf. Ó Muirithe 1977) — but the important thing is to remember that such examples cannot serve as corroboration of the theory concerning the history of Arabic and its pidginization in the period after the conquests. Using them as evidence would engage us in a circular argument. The same proviso applies to the next two examples I should like to discuss, that of Ivrit and the history of the Romance languages.

The history of Hebrew and its artificial introduction as a spoken language in Israel is a special case. Because of the special ties connecting the immigrants with the Hebrew language, and because of the deliberate and planned language learning policy adopted by the Israeli government from the beginning, the Hebrew language escaped pidginization on a large scale, although we do find many simplifications and characteristic tendencies in the modern spoken form of the language, such as, for example, the use of an analytical genitive construction with the relative *šel-* instead of the *status constructus* of Classical Hebrew, the use of the active participle for the present tense, the word order SVO instead of VSO. The presence of typological features in itself is not so important — as a matter of fact, some of these tendencies may have originated in earlier processes of change the language underwent — but something else is: the nativization of the language by the first *sabras* was carried out on an unnatural input, so that their situation of language learning could be called a handicapped one. A certain amount of creolization is, therefore, to be expected, but in the absence of material on the changes Ivrit underwent, one cannot draw any conclusions. One thing is obvious, though: the limited input did not contain all registers of speech that were necessary for the formal functioning of the language in everyday life, and this constituted one of the first contributions of the new speakers to their mother tongue.[4]

The development from Latin to the Romance language constitutes *a priori* perhaps the most promising parallel to the history of Arabic. There is an unmistakable similarity between the process by which Arabic 'became' the modern dialects, and the process by which Latin 'became' the Romance languages. In the Roman empire the popular variety of Latin that was spoken by the Roman soldiers who conquered the provinces constituted the primary input for anyone who wished to speak the language of the new masters. This popular variety is often identified with Vulgar Latin, the name that is usually given to written testimonies which range from inscriptions to texts written by illiterate authors. These testimonies with their varying divergences from Classical Latin are often believed to be a true reflection of the colloquial and thus, their language was regarded as the true ancestor of the Romance languages. It seems that we are dealing here with the same fallacy as in the case of the Arabic language during the Ǧāhiliyya: in my view, there is no reason to doubt that Romans, whatever their social class, spoke essentially the same language before the great conquests started. As for the Vulgar Latin texts, they belong to the same category as Middle Arabic texts and Turkish *Transkriptionsdenkmäler*: as written texts they were intended to some degree as an imitation of the standard language, and thus, they can never be used for a chronology of change.

As soon as the inhabitants of the provinces started to learn Latin without formal training in everyday intercourse with the Roman soldiers and settlers, they pidginized the language. After a while, when a system of education found its way into the provinces, the Classical language became a model for those who had the opportunity to go to school. For others outside the intellectual minority who did not have this opportunity the Classical language still acted as a target and a stimulus to decreolization, in much the same way as the inhabitants of the Arab empire reacted to the introduction of a system of schools after the conquests. The ordinary legionary, more often than not a provincial from some other part of the empire, who finally settled down in the province took over the regional variety of the corrupted language that was pidgnized Latin and so, local varieties were even adopted by first language speakers of Latin. But most of the colonists were not native speakers of Latin anyway, the official policy of the authorities being to stimulate the settlement of soldiers as far away as possible from their home-country. When the ties between Rome and the provinces were loosened or severed, the local varieties developed into the Romance language as we know them. In this view, the Romance languages are actually creolized varieties of Classical Latin. In the case of the Romance languages the standardizing influence of Classical Latin came rather late to many areas and this prevented full decreolization.

This theory is, of course, not novel or revolutionary in any way but, at the same time, it is far from being commonly accepted. A common way of looking at the development of the Romance languages is to acknowledge the existence of contact languages during and shortly after the conquests, when the conquered peoples addressed their new masters in broken Latin. But these are believed to have been replaced soon by an approximation of Classical Latin when the provinces received an educational system.[5] In this view, the origin of the Romance languages must be put at a much later date, starting with the disintegration of the Roman empire during the 4th and 5th centuries. Only a few romanists would subscribe to the thesis advanced by Křepinský (1958:1), who maintains that the characteristic changes took place right at the beginning of the conquests: "... les langues romanes sont nées lorsque les indigènes dans les provinces ont essayé de parler la langue de leurs vainqueurs". The separation between the Romance colloquials and Latin as language of culture and religion that took place as a result of the Germanic invasions led to a socio-linguistic situation in the 9th and 10th centuries that can best be compared with the situation of those communities where a creole coexists with an original target acting as language of prestige in a classic diglossia.[6]

Generally speaking, there is a tendency to deny that major simplification of the language has taken place in the speech of the conquered peoples. They may have started to speak varieties of Latin that might be termed 'pidgins', so it is claimed, but later they abandoned this stage and learned 'normal' Latin. Many romanists ascribe the differences between Latin and the Romance languages not to a complete restructuring of the language, but to normal language change. Hall (1974:76), for example, says: "All the Romance developments ... could have taken place in the course of normal slow linguistic change over the centuries, without the sudden sharp break and the drastic restructuring which is by definition involved in pidginisation" (cf. Schlieben-Lange 1977: 91). We must keep in mind, however, that the evidence for the slow development is derived from written sources, which do not reflect the chronology of the changes in a reliable way.

But a major objection to this view of the development of the Romance language is that nobody learns his first language at school. Schools exist in order to teach children a 'high' variety that sometimes acts as a superposed variety for a 'vulgar' mother tongue. But it is simply inconceivable that the inhabitants of the provinces at any time during the Roman domination should have spoken a variety of Classical Latin at home and, consequently, I do not follow the current opinion that Classical Latin at the time of the Germanic invasions disintegrated into the Romance languages because of the disintegration of the empire. In the isolated parts of the provinces, people retained their original languages for a long time, for instance, Gallic in France, Dacian in Rumania, Basque in Spain, etc. But in the cities, there must have been a *lingua franca* based on he first contact languages that originated directly after the conquests. This *lingua franca* became the mother tongue of many children because intermarriage — for instance, between native women and soldiers from other parts of the empire — necessitated the use of the *lingua franca* as a means of communication even at home, and thus brought about the acquisition of this *lingua franca* as a first language by the offspring. The foundation of schools at a later stage only changed this sitution inasmuch as a diglottic relationship developed between Latin and the colloquials. Obviously, the influence of Classical Latin varied according to the degree of schooling and the point in the development of the colloquials at which schools were introduced, as well as the point at which contact with Rome was broken off again. These factors determined the degree of decreolization the colloquial had to go through.[7] This is not to say that the socio-cultural circumstances determined the structure of the language, but they determined the part of the linguistic scale that survived (cf. above, ch. III, p. 53ff.).

In view of these considerations I cannot go along with Jespersen's opinion (1922) that, generally speaking, the inhabitants of the provinces at some stage in the history of the language mastered Classical Latin as completely as the inhabitants of Rome themselves. It remains imperative to distinguish carefully between the language of the ordinary people who learnt Latin, first in the streets, and later as a first language at home, and the language of the intellectuals, who learnt Classical language as a second language at school to such a degree that they could replace their home-learnt patois by a fair approximation of the Roman standard. There were, no doubt, many intellectuals who even became near-native in their command of the Classical Standard, but they remained a minority compared to the masses who had no chances of going to school. While the popular variety grew into a full-fledged language, the Classical language became the international means of communication for scholars and intellectuals — a living language as long as the ties with Rome remained intact, a fossilized book language when the living standard had disappeared. The two varieties were carefully kept apart, and our only testimonies for the popular variety are the mistakes in Classical texts written by those who wished to imitate the popular language for stylistic reasons, or those who did not master the standard completely. I have stated above that this situation is not dissimilar to that obtaining in the field of Arabic studies, where the corpus of texts in Middle Arabic constitutes one of the major sources for the history of the popular language.

A different view of the status of Latin as a spoken language in the Romance countries is taken by Wright in a recent publication (1982). In his view, Classical Latin as we know it — contrary to what has been assumed here — was never a spoken variety in the period after the fall of the Roman empire (476 A.D.), and probably not even before that date.[8] He asserts that all documents written in Classical Latin after the fall of the empire provide us with evidence not of the fact that there was some spoken norm of Classical Latin, but of the fact that everywhere there was a spoken vernacular in use that had superseded the Classical language, and that was the only variety in spoken communication. Only with the Carolingian reform did there arise an artificially imposed spoken norm on the basis of the Classical language that had nothing to do with any preceding living language, but was a pure and simple invention of the reformers. For our purpose, this thesis, important though it may be for the development of the Romance languages, is not of primary interest. The important point is that in Wright's thesis the Romance language had developed at an early date, even though he does not adhere to a thesis of radical change right at the beginning of the conquests, as Křepinský does. In many cases he seems to accept a gradual development of typically Romance features.[9]

The most important aspect of the position of the Classical language in the period after the conquests is its possible role in the process of decreolization: did the Classical language have any opportunity at all to exercise influence on the development of the Romance vernaculars? According to Wright, it did not, since the Classical language was spoken by no one. The existence of so-called *cultismos*, i.e. words that did not undergo the 'normal' development, but were borrowed from the Classical language through a *formation savante*, must be explained, therefore, in another way. Wright does so (1982: 1-44) by rejecting the current view of language change as an automatic process that takes place indiscriminately and by adopting, instead, a diffusionist model, in which words do not change at the same rate and in the same period. As I have repeatedly stated above, I regard *cultismos* as words that went through a change and were changed back afterwards as the result of the growing influence of the target language, or as words that were borrowed directly from the target language. Thus, it is not a question of some speakers "resist[ing] phonetic changes that were generally affecting the rest of the community, for a thousand years or more" (Wright 1982: 44), but of some speakers letting themselves be influenced by the prestigious target language.[10]

Contrary to Wright's conclusions, I hold that right from the beginning there was a parallelism between the situation in the Roman empire and the situation in the Arab empire. In both cases there was a formal register which while it cannot be regarded as actual spoken speech, did nevertheless exercise a real influence upon the everyday vernacular because of its use as prestigious variety on formal occasions and in writing. The norms of the standard were kept alive not only for a select group of educated people, but also, through them and through the use of the standard language for religious purposes for the rest of the population. Some of the changes the vernacular had undergone were reversed, and in some cases this led to the disappearance of the stigmatized vernacular form from the scale of the linguistic continuum. Obviously, the influence of the decreolizing factor differed not only geographically, but also linguistically: the rate of reversal and the extent to which the basilectal forms disappeared differed according to the linguistic level, phonology being one of the last levels to be affected, morphology and syntax being affected first.[11] The standardization of the popular varieties in the case of the Romance languages and their promotion to the status of national language is, of course, a different story.

It has not been my intention to produce in any way a theory about the origin of the Romance languages, but I only wish to argue that there is a methodological similarity between the cases of the Arabic dialects and the Romance languages. In both cases the argumentation must consist of two parts: a historical part, in which the context of the contact between a language and a group of new speakers is traced, and a comparative part, in which universals of linguistic change are pinpointed in the development of the languages involved. I should like to stress that in my view it is not necessary to work out an exact typology of historical contexts — as demanded by Schlieben-Lange (1977) — in order to be able to compare different developments: as long as we know which mechanism we wish to hold responsible for the change it is enough to know that the circumstances which trigger the mechanism in question — in our case the taking over of the language by a large part of the population, in a relatively short period of time, without any formal help in the form of an educational system — were present.

In this connection it should also be pointed out once more that the universals of linguistic change that are supposed to have been brought about by the process of undirected language learning cannot be used as a test for pidginization. There are degrees of pidginization, depending among other things on the amount of levelling to which the pidginized/creolized varieties are subjected. Diem is quite right in mentioning (1978:131-32), for instance, the case of the Aramaic/Syriac dialects as a counter-example to the development of the Arabic dialects, and he is probably right in attributing the considerable divergence between the various Aramaic dialects at an early date to the effect of the Arab conquests which broke up the homogeneity of the area in which Aramaic was spoken and prevented the exchange of linguistic innovations between these dialects. But this comparison only serves to emphasize the importance of the standard language acting as a target in the process of decreolization.

As a contrasting example to the case of the Romance languages, one might think of the history of the Slavonic languages. Apparently, the tribes which introduced these languages in Europe simply continued to speak their own languages without forcing them onto others, with the exception of Bulgarian, which — not surprisingly — exhibits many of the features we have found to be characteristic of pidginization/creolization, for instance, the development of a definite article in postposition[12], the use of an analytical genitive construction instead of the Old Slavonic case-endings, the development of a highly idiosyncratic aspectual system, the loss of the entire declensional system. It is tempting to think that this idiosyncratic behaviour of Bulgarian *vis-à-vis* the other Slavonic languages is connected with the fact that the Bulgarian language was taken over by other tribes, and that the radical changes in Bulgarian are the result of a process of pidginization/creolization. This is not to say that the other Slavonic languages did not undergo any changes. Czech, for instance, lost its aorist and its dual in historical times, just as English and Dutch lost their case system, English at an early date, Dutch in the course of the last few centuries. But then, tendencies similar to those claimed to be characteristic of the process of pidginization may also be found in a non-pidginizing context. It is, however, the combined occurrence of these features, as well as the shortness of the period of time in which the changes take place — immediately connected with the process of language acquisition — which characterize the processes of language change discussed here.

There have been other approaches to the problem of 'detecting' pidginization in cases that do not belong to the traditionally acknowledged pidgin languages. Southworth (1971) investigates the possibility of explaining the divergence between Marathi — an Indo-Aryan language spoken in an area that is contiguous to the Dravidian-speaking provinces of India — and the other Indo-Aryan languages of India by positing an early pidginization process in the history of Marathi. In the case of this language, the problem is the length of time in which the changes may have taken place. If it is true that in the long run 'normal' development produces the same results as pidginization, one might ask whether it is still possible, in the absence of documentation, to detect the traces of a process of pidginization/creolization in the present structure of the language. Southworth holds that after the introduction of the Aryan languages into India around 1500 B.C. the prestigious position of the speakers of these languages brought about a linguistic continuum in which the ability to produce an approximation of the language of the invaders determined the social position of the speaker. Thus, local varieties ranged from near-native command of the colloquial form of Sanskrit to deep pidgin. Creolization followed whenever groups of users did not have any other language in common, or when they had to abandon their own language for military or economic reasons.

One of the sources Southworth uses are texts in Old Marathi; these reflect a social variation in that the speech of the uneducated bears a greater resemblance to the Dravidian languages than the sanskritized speech of the educated does. A special problem is that the evidence for the speech of the uneducated is derived from texts in which the interference of educated speech was, of course, rather strong — again, a situation reminiscent of the problems connected with the use of Middle Arabic texts, Turkish *Transkriptionsdenkmäler*, and texts in Vulgar Latin. Southworth's method consists in looking for evidence in the structure of Marathi, or rather, in the changes in that language *vis-à-vis* Sanskrit. But, as he himself points out (1971:260-61), neither changes in the phonological inventory, nor the restructuring that must have taken place in the course of the development of Marathi are in themselves relevant, since similar changes took place elsewhere as well and, what is more, we do not know whether the restructuring process was a gradual or a sudden one. His next step is to look for evidence of Dravidian influence in those features that are characteristic of Marathi as against Proto-Indo-Aryan or Sanskrit.

One of the examples quoted by Southworth (1971:263-64) seems to have implications for more than the history of Marathi alone. According to Southworth, the old Sanskrit case-system was lost in the subsequent Indo-Aryan languages, in which it was replaced by a number of periphrastic constructions consisting of passive participles acting as postpositions. Examples mentioned by him include the following: instead of the Sanskrit genitive the periphrastic construction *rāmāya kṛtaḥ* "made for Ram" was used, which became in Prakrit *rāmā kiya* and subsequently in Modern Hindi *rām kā* "Ram's"; instead of the Sanskrit dative the periphrastic construction *rāmāya ditaḥ* "given to Ram" was used, which became in Prakrit *rāmā diya*, and in Modern Panjabi *rām dā* "Ram's". The interesting point about this phenomenon is that it is displayed by all modern Indo-Aryan languages, but they all use different exponents as replacement devices for the old cases. I do not think it is necessary to invoke Dravidian influence in this change, since the phenomenon, as well as the typical pattern of identical changes with different results, is known from other areas, for instance, from the Arabic dialects (cf. above, ch. II, p. 18; V, p. 92f.).

It appears that Southworth's main argument for prior creolization in Marathi is the fact that Marathi resembles the structure of Dravidian more than the rest of the Indo-Aryan languages do. Further arguments concern the comparatively large phonological random variation, and the low vocabulary retention, although it is not altogether clear against which language these features are to be measured. He assumes that at first the local non-Aryan language competed with a Prakrit dialect — a colloquial version of Sanskrit — or a Prakrit pidgin. In the end, the latter won, with the result that a creolized version of the local Prakrit became the colloquial language, which then developed into Marathi. The problem with this procedure is that substratal influence cannot be taken as a decisive argument for or against creolization. In fact, Southworth mentions the possibility of including the rest of the Indo-Aryan languages into his schema, but he rejects it in order to retain the distinction between borrowing and creolization.

This means that his theory restricts the meaning of the term 'pidginization' (1971:270-71): "The hypothesis proposed here assumes that pidginization took place throughout the Indo-Aryan area, but that its long-range linguistic effects were tempered or reinforced by other social factors (caste structure, diglossia, and Sanskritization); these factors have led, at the extreme end of the spectrum, to a result which is similar to the classic modern cases of pidginization known from the Caribbean and the Pacific". The view I have taken here relies much less on the evidence of the substratal language(s), and emphasizes, instead, the universality of the changes a language undergoes when being learnt in an undirected process of acquisition. This means that I should like to know first how far the similarity of the processes of change in the Indo-Aryan languages is related to the social factors mentioned by Southworth, in order to find out if the occurrence of the features discussed by him correlates with an influx of new speakers, rather than with similar features in the substratal languages (cf. also Gumperz & Wilson 1971).

Another approach to the problem of detecting prior creolization is that of Naro (ms., 1978). Naro's main assumption is that, given the fact that pidgins originate in an 'unnatural' language learning process, the creoles that are based on these pidgins may be expected to contain 'unnatural' rules in their grammar. Whether or not this assumption is correct is a matter of empirical research. In this view, there must be correspondences between the creole and the target language (in his terminology the 'base') which, though systematic, do not follow the universal constraints that are associated with linguistic changes. Obviously, this kind of evidence can never be the only evidence for the creole 'character' of a language, since that would result in a circular argument, attributing all rules which violate the alleged universal constraints to creolization, so that the universality of the constraints remains intact. Naro offers two examples of the 'unnaturalness' of such rules. In the first place, he points out that in some pidgins/creoles (Portuguese Creole of Cabo Verde and Vietnamese Pidgin French or Tây Bồi) there seem to be changes that are best stated with rules in terms of negative context, contrary to the constraint against such rules.

A second example concerns the phenomenon of verbal serialization which is known both from 'natural' and from pidginized languages. The difference is that these constructions tend to develop into more complex morphological structures. This occurs in some Bantu languages, for example (Naro ms., p. 14), whereas pidginized languages go through the whole process the other way round. Naro himself assumes that such 'unnatural' changes are the result of substratal influence disturbing the normal process of pidginization. Grammatical interference from the substratal language with the evolving pidgin is severely restricted by the condition of acceptance on the part of the native speakers of the target language, so that utterances resulting from substratal influence can only work their way into the system if they are not too deviant in terms of the target system.[13] An example of a deviant form that could be included in the pidgin structure because of its superficial resemblance to a construction in the target language is that of the transitivizing suffix *-im* in Tok Pisin, as in *ju hitim Jon* "you hit John", which could very well be interpreted by a native speaker of English as *you hit him, [that is] John*".

This means that many of the features which are commonly regarded as evidence for substratal influence, because they seemed to be too radical to be a restructuring of a European language, very well fit into a general schema of language change as the result of a language learning process under difficult und unusual circumstances. A special aspect of Naro's theory is that he regards the language learning process by the new speakers as part of a conscious effort on the part of the native speakers of the base (i.e. target) language to teach their language to the new speakers (cf. Naro 1978). Now, while this may have been the case in the situation studied by Naro — the training of Africans as interpreters by the Portuguese — and possibly in some other cases as well, one can hardly assume such a conscious effort in all instances of pidginization — if only because in many cases the target language was removed after the first period of contact.

It might seem strange that in spite of the fact that in the case of Pidgin Portuguese there was a (supposed) process of conscious language learning, whereas in other instances there was a process of undirected language learning, there still was a strong similarity between the results of both processes. This could, however, be explained by assuming that in both cases the use of a foreigner talk register played an important rule in providing a model for the language of the new speakers. Obviously, if Naro is right, and if the Portuguese addressed their African trainees in broken Portuguese, it is not surprising that the result resembles other pidgins where such conscious training did not take place. According to Naro, the unnatural developments that may be used as signs or evidence of pidginization/creolization are the result of substratal influence in those parts of the linguistic system that were not immune to that influence. This might, indeed, be a good diagnostic instrument, but unfortunately, as Naro himself points out, such instances of substratal influence are very rare because of the low prestige of these languages. This means that although the idea in itself may be correct, its actual usefulness in the detection of traces of creolization turns out to be rather limited.

A much discussed case of alleged prior creolization is that of American Black English. Rickford (1977) claims that prior to any conclusion concerning the status of Black English, socio-historical research ought to provide an answer to the question of whether or not the circumstances in the period in question were favourable to creolization, i.e. in his terminology, to the extension in use and range of communicative and expressive functions of a pidginized variety of a language (1977:192). In this view, nativization is not a necessary condition of the process. Detecting prior creolization thus becomes a question of finding out how far linguistic criteria permit us to say that a pidgin was expanded and complicated in order to serve in new functions, provided the socio-historical conditions make it probable that such a process took place.

The criteria enumerated by Rickford — simplification, admixture (i.e. substratal influence), divergence from other dialects, similarity to other creoles — seem to beg the question of what actually sets creolization apart from other linguistic changes. Rickford himself points out that it is difficult to determine exactly what should be regarded as simplification, but in my view the difficulty is more fundamental than that. Any comparison between a candidate for creole status and an 'ordinary' language will remain an equation with two unknown factors, as long as we do not have a theory about the nature of the process by which languages are pidginized/creolized. This leaves the way open for the kind of objections that we find, for instance, in Woolford's discussion (1981) of the system of complementizers in Tok Pisin (cf. above, ch. III, n. 12). She points out that similar changes are also found in 'other' languages, the 'otherness' of those languages having been conceded by the adherents of creole status from the beginning. Thus, the only two conclusions that can be reached are either the fatuous one that all languages are creoles, or the equally unsatisfactory one that there are no creoles at all. This dilemma may perhaps be avoided, provided we do not concentrate on the question of whether or not a language is a pidgin/creole, but on the question of whether or not it has ever undergone a process of pidginization/creolization. Similarity to other pidgins/creoles — other languages that are commonly called 'pidgins' or 'creoles' — can at best be used as confirmation of a conclusion reached by other means, namely that the language in question was taken over by new speakers in an irregular, unnatural way, in short, through a process of undirected language acquisition or from an unnatural input. This notwithstanding the fact that the comparison sometimes helps to re-evaluate the synchronic data of the language in question, or to put them in their proper light — as we have seen in the case of some of the changes in Arabic.

Not even the very reasonable formulation which justifies the use of the criterion of similarity with other creoles in terms of 'clear cases' can do away with the fact that such 'clear cases' are essentially no more than a *petitio principii*.[14] Moreover, attempts to find parallels for pidgin features in other languages — for instance, Rickford's attempt (1977:206-208) to find a parallel for the stressed auxiliary *bín* of American Black English — are doomed to failure, because such a comparison should not be carried out with a view to find etymologically related morphemes in other languages, but in terms of a parallel development that may result in quite different linguistic expressions in other languages.

There is one important point raised by Rickford that deserves to be mentioned in this context, namely the question of decreolization and its role in the development of a language that has been pidginized/creolized. In particular, we must know whether or not decreolization can go so far as to totally suppress the creolizing variety in favour of the standard language. It is obvious that decreolization is a process that affects not the linguistic system as such, but the speech community. The members of that community, or rather, some of its members, learn to level their speech towards the standard language with its attributes of social prestige and cultural superiority. It is conceivable that in the course of time more and more members of the community will expand their speech span along the continuum that ranges from basilect to acrolect. One can even imagine a situation in which a new generation starts speaking the language they learn at school in contexts in which up to then the low, creolized variety has been used, thus eventually replacing it completely by the standard language. Obviously, this means the end of the creole in question. On the other hand, factors such as group cohesion and language solidarity will in many cases prevent the children from totally abandoning their mother tongue. The emerging picture is that of a community in which the centripetal attraction of the standard typically affects the speech of the higher and middle-class members, whereas the interference in the speech pattern of the lower classes will be largely dependent on the infiltration of schooling within the community.[15]

If we accept the view that pidginization is the rule in untutored language learning, and that creolization is nothing more than the nativization of a limited input, it follows that most languages at one time or another have gone through a stage of pidginization and creolization, for almost every language has acquired from time to time an influx of new speakers. When the changes resulting from such an influx were allowed to affect the speech of the whole community, this meant a sudden leap in the development of the language in question, which was broken down and then reconstructed. The strategies applied by the new speakers to the linguistic material at their disposal resulted in a system that was more analytical, less redundant and, above all, limited in functions and range of stylistic variation. Further developments depended largely on the position of the target language and the substratal language(s). When the target language was permanently there to stay in the area where the pidgin variety was spoken, levelling became almost inevitable because of the prestige of the target language. Whether or not the pidginized variety became creolized depended on the socio-linguistic make-up of the community: in a multilingual community, creolization almost immediately followed on the establishment of a pidginized variety that could act as an interlingual means of communication. In a monolingual community the original language could hold out much more successfully against the influence of the new language. When the target language disappeared from the scene, the same alternatives applied, with the difference that there was no levelling towards a standard, so that the existing tendencies remained in force.

Creolization implies the elaboration of a linguistic system that is by definition a limited one. Examples of this elaboration are numerous, but they are particularly striking in the domain of the morphology of the limited system. The elaboration shows itself not so much in the expansion of the system, but in a grammaticalization of the analytical expressions and the lexical periphrases of syntactic relations and morphological categories. An example of this tendency at work at this very moment is that of the independent adverb *baimbai* in Tok Pisin: in the speech of the younger generation who speak the language as their mother tongue this adverb is becoming an obligatory aspectual prefix *bai-* (Sankoff & Laberge 1974; cf. above, ch. V, p. 79ff.). An example from the past is that of the future in the Romance languages, where independent verbs became enclitic auxiliaries and ended as suffixes, *venire habeo* becoming French *je viendrai*, Spanish *vendré*, etc.[16] Generally speaking, we find at this stage a transition from lexical to syntactic elements, e.g. again in Tok Pisin the development of a plural marker *ol* (Mühlhäusler 1981:47) and of a complementizer *olsem* (Woolford 1981). Obviously, this process is repeatable, as we can see in the case of the Arabic pidgins and creoles which developed in modern times.

In an article entitled "The linguistic cycle" Hodge (1970) suggested that all languages go through a constant modification of their morphological inventory, changing from synthetic to analytical, from analytical again to synthetic, and so forth. Hodge bases his suggestion on data from the history of Egyptian, whose documented history is exceptionally long: it ranges from the oldest inscriptions in Old Egyptian to the last products of literary activity in Coptic. In its rudimentary form Hodge's suggestion does not explain very much but, provided the 'linguistic cycle' is not regarded as an inescapable natural law, or as an inherent feature of language as an organism, but as a correlate of the socio-linguistic history of the community which uses the language in question, it fits in with what has been said in the preceding paragraphs. Instead of 'synthetic' and 'analytical' we could perhaps also use the terms 'grammaticalized' and 'lexicalized' to describe what takes place in a language that becomes the second language for a large group of speakers in an untutored language learning situation and is subsequently adopted as a first language by a new generation. As we have seen, grammatical distinctions and syntactic relations tend to be indicated in the first stage by separate words; in the second stage these separate lexical items become grammaticalized again, so that the morphological inventory regains its former complexity, though on a completely different lexical base. In subsequent stages, the resulting language may become pidginized again, and the language in question may indeed give the appearance of going through a regular cycle, without any connection with the external history of the linguistic community.

Another way of formulating the role of creolization in the history of many languages is indicated by Bailey (1973:99): "The view already expressed earlier is that natural changes caused by children acquiring a language — unmarking, generalization — will never create a new system. This is created by heterosystematic mixture. Thus, every legitimate node (every node representing a new system on a socalled family tree) must have two or more parents." According to this view, whenever a major change is observed in the history of a language, there is an *a priori* case for what Bailey calls "heterosystematic mixture", and what I should like to regard in terms of the language learning process involved.

It is quite possible that we will find phenomena that are comparable to those discussed in the preceding chapters in normal linguistic transmission, too. Languages without a history of conquest or invasion may also lose their endings, to mention only one feature.[17] But it should not surprise us to find analogies between pidginization and second language learning in general, or between creolization and first language learning in general: as far as pidginization is concerned, there are bound to be resemblances between the learning of a second language in an undirected context and learning it in an official educational environment; and as far as creolization is concerned, we may expect similarities between the acquisition of a mother tongue in normal and in handicapped situations.

In the chapters above I have attempted to give a consistent view of the factors that have determined the growth and development of the modern Arabic dialects. In doing this I have tried to connect the phenomena in

Arabic with analogous developments in other languages. Many questions have been left open, the most obvious being the specification of notions such as ‘universal strategies of second language learning’, ‘compensatory strategies’, etc. I am perfectly aware that in using these notions freely without further specification, I have treated them as independent entities with some kind of axiomatic existence. Obviously, further research is needed to clarify these and similar issues.

It is comforting to know that in simply leaving open so many issues I am following the example of the Arab grammarians. In discussing the possibility of giving explanations in linguistics, the Arab grammarian Ibn Ǧinnī (d. 392/1002) tells us that there has to be a limit to the ‘causes’ a grammarian can legitimately investigate for any given grammatical phenomenon. One can find out the cause (*‘illa*) of a grammatical process, and even, on a higher level, explain this cause — one might call this the ‘cause of the cause’ (*‘illat al-‘illa*). But to try and find for every cause a higher explanation would only lead to a reasoning *ad infinitum*, and to confusion in speech, rather than to a profounder insight into the workings of language (*H̱aṣā’iṣ* I, 173-74).

NOTES

1) To mention one example, the texts written by the Croatian Bartolomaeus Georgievits (16th century) which are discussed by Hazai (1978:32f.): the significant divergence from Turkish standard in these texts has given rise to a discussion between Németh (1968), who maintains that the characteristic features of the language of these texts mark it as being merely a regional variety of Turkish identical with the one we find nowadays in Western Balkanic Turkish dialects, and, on the other hand, Kißling (1968), who maintains that these texts exhibit a “barbarisches Türkisch auf serbokroatischer Grundlage” (1968:127); cf. also Hazai (1974). Another text that is mentioned in this context is *Colloquia familiaria turcico-latina* (1672) by Jakab Nagy de Harsány, cf. Hazai (1973). The possibility that we are dealing here with a variety of Turkish that has been simplified in the course of an incomplete process of language learning is not mentioned in these discussions.

2) Cf. Hazai (1978:64), who mentions a “Vereinfachung der morphologischen Struktur” that took place in the second half of the 15th century; specific changes mentioned by him are the emergence of the *iyor* present tense and the *acak* future tense (1978:58); cf. also his general remark about this period (1978:64): “Die mittelosmanische Periode kann in erster Linie durch die allmähliche Auflösung der alten phonologischen und morphologischen Struktur charakterisiert werden, die ihre volle Ausprägung oder Vollendung in den Jahrzehnten der Wende des 18. zum 19. Jahrhundert gefunden haben mag”, but cf. the remarks about the difficulty of establishing a chronology of the changes on the basis of written texts, below in this chapter.

3) A case in point might be the dialect of the so-called Karamanlides, turkophone Greek-Orthodox Christians who lived in Anatolia in the 19th century (cf. Vryonis 1971:452-63). There

is a remarkable contradiction in the evaluation of their Turkish: compare the statement of a modern author who asserts that their speech is purer than that of the Muslim Turks (Cami Baykurt, quoted by Vryonis 1971:456) with that of the 17th century traveller Evliya Çelebi, who regards the speech of the turkophone Christians as erroneous (Vryonis 1971:456). These contradictory statements can perhaps be reconciled by pointing out that what made this dialect seem 'erroneous' in the eyes of a 17th century Turkish intellectual — its divergence from the prevailing High Osmanic standard — made it pure and attractive Turkish in the eyes of a modern intellectual who strove after the purification of the Turkish literary language from all Persian and Arabic loans. The dialect of the Karamanlides would thus be a good example of a creolized variety of Turkish that was decreolized much later and to a lesser degree than the other colloquials because of the social and cultural isolation of the Christians in Anatolia. Obviously, these speculations go far beyond the scope of our discussion.

4) Cf. Kornblueth & Aynor (1974); on language planning in Israel see Fellmann (1974). It would be interesting to see if the few cases of native Esperanto — cf. above, ch. III, n. 4 — warrant the conclusion that an unnatural, but tutored input leads to the development of modifications in the domain of styles and registers.

5) Cf. Jespersen 1922; Hall 1974:76; Schlieben-Lange 1977:86; also Valkhoff (1960:243): "... but soon after these early years of romanization the comparison [between Romance and Creole languages] ceases to be valid, because the schools where Classical Latin was to be taught, were founded and a general reaction started against the centrifugal tendencies of Vulgar Latin".

6) Ferguson (1959a) used Haiti as one of his four examples of diglossia; cf. Schlieben-Lange 1977:88ff.

7) Maurer (1962) emphasizes the importance of the sharp distinction between the Eastern Romania — i.e. in particular Rumania (Dacia) — and the rest of the Romania, resulting from the early isolation of Dacia from the Roman empire.

8) Cf. his remarks about Quintilian (1982:56).

9) For instance, his discussion about the assimilation of *adfluo* > *affluo* (1982:79-80) situated by him after the 5th century. The grammarians tell us that the correct pronunciation of the word is in an unassimilated form; they describe the pronunciation of the living language, and since there is, in Wright's thesis, only room for one living language, the Romance vernacular, it must be the pronunciation of the vernacular.

10) The assumption that the grammarians were solely concerned about orthography, teaching people to write *solem* where they said [solẽ] or [sole], is invalidated by the fact that they speak in the same context about the correct use of the declensional endings in speech. Why should the grammarians be willing to admit that people say [sole], but should write *solem*, and at the same time make up a completely fictional speech variety — spoken Classical Latin — with declensional endings and everything else?

11) For decreolization in Papiamentu see Baum 1976; for decreolization in Belize see Escure 1981; for decreolization (classicization) in modern Arabic see above ch. VI, n. 11. Classicization may involve the modification of the entire system, as exemplified by one of the texts transcribed by Diem (1974:78-80). About the use of context forms in pause — a very frequent hypercorrection — in Moroccan Arabic and Egyptian (Radio) Arabic see Forkel (1980:62-63) and Harrell (1960:37), respectively.

12) The development of this article has been ascribed to areal linguistic influence, cf. Bynon 1977:246ff.

13) Cf. Naro (ms., p. 19): "If an utterance is not interpretable to a speaker of the base language he will most likely reject it and it will probably not therefore become a permanent part of the pidgin or subsequent creole".

14) Cf. Rickford (1977:198): "If a certain set of clear cases are agreed upon by everyone to constitute pidgins and creoles in terms of the standard theoretical parameters, and these cases display certain characteristic linguistic features, the other cases that also display these characteristics can be assumed to belong to the same type of class, unless evidence to the contrary is shown".

15) See the case-study by Escure (1981) on decreolization in Belizean Creole English, which seems to confirm this picture. Note also her conclusion (1981:37) that decreolization affects grammatical rather than phonological features in the continuum.

16) Cf. the discussion concerning English auxiliaries by Bynon (1977:159-64).

17) One must, of course, always allow for the possibility that such a loss of endings took place at a much earlier date in the colloquial than is normally assumed: very often a change in the colloquial is not reflected in the literary language for a long time because of the normative power of the written standard. But our sources for the historical development of a language are always written texts with an unavoidable carry-over of standard forms.

REFERENCES

Algee, J.T. 1960. "Korean Bamboo English". *AmSp* 35.117-23.

Alleyne, Mervyn C. 1980. *Comparative Afro-American: An historical-comparative study of English-based Afro-American dialects of the New World*. Ann Arbor: Karoma.

Ambros, Arne. 1973-74. "Die morphologische Funktion des Systems der Vokalqualitäten im Althocharabischen". *WZKM* 65-66.77-150.

Anawati, Georges C. 1975. "Factors and effects of arabization and islamization in Medieval Egypt and Syria". *Islam and Cultural Change in the Middle Ages*, ed. by Speros Vryonis, Jr., 17-41. Wiesbaden: O. Harrassowitz. (= *Fourth Giorgio Levi Della Vida Biennial Conference*.)

Anwar, Mohamed Sami. 1981. "The legitimate fathers of speech errors". *HL* 8.249-65.

Aquilina, Joseph. 1970. *Papers in Maltese Linguistics*. Valletta: Royal Univ. of Malta.

Badawī, as-Sa'īd Muḥammad. 1973. *Mustawayāt al-'Arabiyya al-mu'āṣira fī Miṣr* [Levels of Contemporary Arabic in Egypt]. Cairo: Dār al-Ma'ārif.

Bailey, Charles-James N. 1973. *Variation and Linguistic Theory*. Arlington: Center for Applied Linguistics.

Barth, Heinrich. 1857-59. *Reisen und Entdeckungen in Nord- und Central-Afrika....* 5 vols. Gotha.

Bauer, Anton. 1974. *Das melanesische und chinesische Pidginenglisch: Linguistische Kriterien und Probleme*. Regensburg: H. Carl.

Baum, Paul. 1976. "The question of decreolization in Papiamentu phonology". *IJSL* 7.83-93.

Beck, Edmund. 1945. "Der 'u̱tmānische Kodex in der Koranlesung des zweiten Jahrhunderts". *Orientalia* N.S. 14.355-73.

-----. 1946. "'Arabiyya, Sunna und 'Āmma in der Koranlesung des zweiten Jahrhunderts". *Orientalia* N.S. 15.180-224.

Behnstedt, Peter. 1978. "Zur Dialektgeographie des Nildeltas". *ZAL* 1.64-92.

Bell, Herman, and as-Sayyid Ḥāmid Hurreiz [= Ḥurrayz], eds. 1975. *Direc-*

tions in Sudanese Linguistics and Folklore. Khartoum: Univ. of Khartoum Press.

Bickerton, Derek. 1975. *Dynamics of a Creole System*. Cambridge: Cambridge Univ. Press.

-----. 1976. *Creole Tense-Aspect Systems and Universal Grammar*. Turkeyan (Guyana): Univ. of Guyana.

-----. 1977. "Pidginization and creolization: Language acquisition and language universals". In: Valdman 1977:49-69.

-----. 1977a. "Putting back the clock in variation studies". *Lg* 53.353-60.

-----. 1981. *Roots of Language*. Ann Arbor: Karoma.

-----, and Carol Odo. 1976. *Change and Variation in Hawaiian English: General phonology and pidgin syntax*. Honolulu: Univ. of Hawaii Press.

Birkeland, Harris. 1952. *Growth and Structure of the Egyptian Arabic Dialect*. Oslo: Dybwad.

Bishai, Wilson B. 1960. "Notes on the Coptic substratum in Egyptian Arabic". *JAOS* 80.225-29.

-----. 1961. "Nature and extent of Coptic phonological influence on Egyptian Arabic". *JSS* 6.175-82.

-----. 1962. "Coptic grammatical influence on Egyptian Arabic". *JAOS* 82.285-89.

Blanc, Haim. 1960. "Stylistic variation in spoken Arabic: A sample of interdialectal educated conversation". In: Ferguson 1960:79-161.

-----. 1964. *Communal Dialects in Baghdad*. Cambridge MA: Harvard Univ. Press.

-----. 1969. "The fronting of Semitic G and the qāl-gāl dialect split in Arabic". *Proceedings of the International Conference on Semitic Studies Jerusalem 1965*, 7-37. Leiden: E.J. Brill.

-----. 1970. "Dual and pseudo-dual in the Arabic dialects". *Lg* 46.42-57.

-----. 1971. "Arabic". *Current Trends in Linguistics*, VII, ed. by Thomas E. Sebeok, 501-509. The Hague: Mouton.

Blau, Joshua. 1961. "The importance of Middle Arabic dialects for the history of Arabic". *Studies in Islamic History and Civilization*, 206-220. Jerusalem

-----. 1965. *The Emergence and Linguistic Background of Judeo-Arabic: A study of the origins of Middle Arabic*. London: Oxford Univ. Press. (2nd ed., Jerusalem: Ben Zwi, 1981.)

-----. 1966-67. *A Grammar of Christian Arabic, Based Mainly on South-Palestinian Texts from the First Millennium*. 3 vols. Louvain: Imprimerie Orientaliste.

-----. 1972-73. "On the problem of the synthetic character of Classical Arabic as against Judeo-Arabic (Middle Arabic)". *JQR* 63.29-38.

-----. 1977. *The Beginnings of the Arabic Diglossia: A study of the origins of Neo-Arabic*. Malibu: Undena. (= *AfrLing*, 4:4.)

-----. 1981. "The state of research in the field of the linguistic study of Middle Arabic". *Ar* 28.187-203.

-----. 1981a. Addenda to the 2nd ed. of Blau 1965, 213-49.

-----. 1982. "Das frühe Neuarabisch in mittelarabischen Texten". *GAP* I, 83-95.

Bloch, Ariel A. 1965. *Die Hypotaxe im Damaszenisch-Arabischen, mit Vergleichen zur Hypotaxe im Klassisch-Arabischen*. Wiesbaden: F. Steiner. (= *AKM* 35:4.)

Bodemann, Michal Y., and Robin Ostow. 1975. "Lingua Franca und Pseudo-Pidgin in der Bundesrepublik: Fremdarbeiter und Einheimische im Sprachzusammenhang". *LiLi* 18.122-46.

Bohas, Georges. 1979. *Contributions à l'étude de la méthode des grammairiens arabes en morphologie et phonologie d'après des grammairiens 'tardifs'*. Thèse d'état, Univ. de Paris III inédite. (Lille: Univ. de Lille III, 1982.)

Bollée, Annegret. 1977. *Zur Entstehung der französischen Kreolendialekte im Indischen Ozean*. Genève: Droz.

-----. 1977a. "Remarques sur la genèse des parlers créoles de l'Océan Indien". In: Meisel 1977:137-49.

Borg, Alexander. 1982. *Cypriot Arabic: A historical and comparative investigation into the phonology and morphology of the Arabic vernacular spoken by the Maronites of Kormakiti village in the Kyrenia district of Northwestern Cyprus*. Habilitation, Univ. of Erlangen.

Boris, Gilbert. 1958. *Lexique du parler arabe des Marazig*. Paris: Klincksieck. (= *Etudes Arabes et Islamiques, Etudes et Documents*, 1.)

Bosman, Daniël Brink. 1923. *Oor die ontstaan van Afrikaans*. Amsterdam: Swets & Zeitlinger.

Broch, Ingvild, and Ernst Håkon Jahr. ms. *Russenorsk: A new look at the Russo-Norwegian pidgin in Northern Norway*. Tromsø: Univ. of Tromsø. [Published in Norwegian as *Russenorsk: Et pidginspråk i Norge*. Oslo: Novus, 1981 (= *Tromsø-Studier i Språkvitenskap*, 3.).]

Browning, Robert. 1969. *Medieval and Modern Greek*. London: Hutchinson.

Butler, Alfred J. 1978. *The Arab Conquest of Egypt and the Last Thirty Years of the Roman Dominion*. 2nd ed., ed. by P.M. Fraser, with a critical

bibliography. Oxford: Clarendon Press.
Bynon, Theodora. 1977. *Historical Linguistics*. Cambridge: Cambridge Univ. Press.
Carter, Michael G. 1968. *A Study of Sībawaihi's Principles of Grammatical Analysis*. Diss., Univ. of Oxford.
Chaudenson, Robert. 1977. "Towards a reconstruction of the social matrix of Creole languages". In: Valdman 1977:259-76.
Clark, Herbert, and Evelyn Clark. 1977. *Psychology and Language: An introduction to psycholinguistics*. New York: Harcourt Brace Jovanovich.
Clyne, M.G. 1979. "German and English working pidgins". In: Mühlhäusler 1979:135-50.
Cohen, David. 1963. *Le dialecte arabe ḥassānīya de Mauritanie*. Paris: Klincksieck. (= *Etudes Arabes et Islamiques. Etudes et Documents*, 5.)
-----. 1965. "Le système des voyelles brèves dans les dialectes maghrébins". *Communications et Rapports du 1er Congrès International de Dialectologie Générale*, III, 7-14. Leuven.
-----. 1970. "Koinè, langues communes et dialectes arabes". In: David Cohen, *Etudes de linguistique sémitique et arabe*, 105-125. The Hague & Paris: Mouton.
-----. 1975. *Le parler arabe des Juifs de Tunis*. Tome II. *Etude linguistique*. The Hague & Paris: Mouton. (= *Janua Linguarum, Series practica*, 161.)
Cohen, Marcel. 1912. *Le parler arabe des Juifs d'Alger*. Paris: H. Champion.
Comrie, Bernard. 1981. *Language Universals and Linguistic Typology: Syntax and morphology*. Oxford: B. Blackwell.
Corne, Chris. 1977. *Seychelles Creole Grammar: Elements for Indian Ocean Proto-Creole Reconstruction*. Tübingen: J. Narr.
Corriente, Federico C. 1971-72. "On the functional yield of some synthetic devices in Arabic and Semitic morphology". *JQR* 62.20-50.
-----. 1975. "Marginalia on Arabic diglossia and evidence thereof in the Kitāb al-Aġānī". *JSS* 20.38-61.
-----. 1976. "From Old-Arabic to Classical Arabic through the pre-Islamic koine: Some notes on the native grammarians' sources, attitudes and goals". *JSS* 21.62-98.
-----. 1977. *A Grammatical Sketch of the Spanish Arabic Dialect Bundle*. Madrid: Instituto Hispano-Árabe de Cultura.
Cowell, Mark W. 1964. *A Reference Grammar of Syrian Arabic (based on the dialect of Damascus)*. Washington D.C.: Georgetown Univ. Press.
Crone, Patricia, and Michael Cook. 1977. *Hagarism: The making of the*

Islamic world. Cambridge: Cambridge Univ. Press.
Czapkiewicz, Andrzej. 1975. *The Verb in Modern Arabic Dialects as an Exponent of the Development Processes Occurring in them*. Wrocław: Wydawnictwo Polskiej Akademii Nauk.
Csiszár, Ernő. ms. *Observoj pri infanaĝa dulingveco*. Várpalota.
Danner, Victor. 1975. "Arabic literature in Iran". *CHI* IV, 566-94.
DeCamp, David. 1971. "Toward a generative analysis of a post-creole speech continuum". In: Hymes 1971:349-70.
-----. and Ian F. Hancock, eds. 1974. *Pidgins and Creoles: Current trends and prospects*. Washington D.C.: Georgetown Univ. Press.
Declerck, Christian R.A. 1969. "Lingva evoluo ĉe denaska dulingvulo". *GP* 11/12.4-16.
Dennett, Daniel C. 1950. *Conversion and the Poll Tax in Early Islam*. Cambridge MA: Harvard Univ. Press.
Denz, Adolf. 1971. *Die Verbalsyntax des neuarabischen Dialektes von Kwayriš (Irak) mit einer einleitenden allgemeinen Tempus- und Aspektlehre*. Wiesbaden: F. Steiner. (= *AKM* 40:1.)
Diem, Werner. 1973. "Die nabatäischen Inschriften und die Frage der Kasusflexion im Altarabischen". *ZDMG* 123.227-37.
-----. 1973a. *Skizzen jemenitischer Dialekte*. Beirut & Wiesbaden: F. Steiner. (= *Beiruter Texte und Studien*, 13.)
-----. 1974. *Hochsprache und Dialekt: Untersuchungen zur heutigen arabischen Schriftsprache*. Wiesbaden: F. Steiner. (= *AKM* 41:1.)
-----. 1978. "Divergenz und Konvergenz im Arabischen". *Ar* 25.128-47.
-----. 1979. "Studien zur Frage des Substrats im Arabischen". *Islam* 56.12-80.
-----. 1979a. "Untersuchungen zur frühen Geschichte der arabischen Orthographie. I. Die Schreibung der Vokale". *Orientalia* N.S. 48.207-257.
-----. 1981. "Untersuchungen zur frühen Geschichte der arabischen Orthographie. III. Endungen und Endschreibungen". *Orientalia* N.S. 50.332-83.
Dittmar, Norbert. 1973. *Soziolinguistik: Exemplarische und kritische Darstellung ihrer Theorie, Empirie und Anwendung*. Frankfurt a. Main: Athenäum. (= *Fischer Athenäum Taschenbücher*, 2013.)
Donner, Fred McGraw. 1981. *The Early Islamic Conquests*. Princeton: Princeton Univ. Press.
Drechsel, Emanuel J. 1976. "'Ha, now me stomany that!': A summary of pidginization and creolization of North American Indian languages". *IJSL* 7.63-81.
-----. 1981. "A preliminary sociolinguistic comparison of four indigenous

pidgin languages of North America (with notes towards a sociolinguistic typology in American Indian linguistics)". *AL* 23.93-112.

Drewes, Abraham J. 1976. *Classical Arabic in Central Ethiopia*. Leiden: E.J. Brill. (= *Oosters Genootschap in Nederland*, 7.) [pages numbered 169-98.]

Elizaincín, Adolfo. 1976. "The emergence of bilingual dialects on the Brazilian-Uruguayan border". *IJSL* 9.123-34.

El-Tonsi, Abbas and Kristen Brustad. 1981. *An Advanced Reader in Egyptian Colloquial Arabic*. Part One. Cairo: American Univ. Center for Arabic Studies.

Enderwitz, Susanne. 1979. *Gesellschaftlicher Rang und ethnische Legitimation: Der arabische Schriftsteller Abū ʻUṯmān al-Ǧāḥiẓ (gest. 868) über die Afrikaner, Perser und Araber in der islamischen Gesellschaft*. Freiburg: K. Schwarz. (*Islamkundliche Untersuchungen*, 53.)

Erwin, Wallace M. 1963. *A Short Reference Grammar of Iraqi Arabic*. Washington D.C.: Georgetown Univ. Press.

Escure, Geneviève. 1981. "Decreolization in a creole continuum: Belize". In: Highfield & Valdman 1981:7-26.

Fattal, Antoine. 1958. *Le statut légal des non-Musulmans en pays d'Islam*. Beyrouth: Imprimerie Catholique. (= *Recherches publiées sous la direction de l'Institut des Lettres Orientales de Beyrouth*, 10.)

Feagin, Crawford. 1976. *Variation and Change in Alabama English: A sociolinguistic study of the White community*. Washington D.C.: Georgetown Univ. Press.

Fellman, Jack. 1974. "The Academy of the Hebrew language: Its history, structure and function". *IJSL* 1.95-103.

Ferguson, Charles A. 1959. "The Arabic koine". *Lg* 25.616-30.

-----. 1959a. "Diglossia". *Word* 15.325-40.

-----, ed. 1960. *Contributions to Arabic Linguistics*. Cambridge MA: Harvard Univ. Press.

-----. 1968. "Myths about Arabic". *Readings in the Sociology of Language*, ed. by Joshua A. Fishman, 375-81. The Hague & Paris: Mouton.

-----. 1970. "The role of Arabic in Ethiopia: A sociolinguistic perspective". *Georgetown Univ. Monographs, Series on Language and Linguistics* 23.355-68. (Repr., Charles A. Ferguson, *Language Structure and Language Use*, 292-312. Stanford: Stanford Univ. Press, 1971.)

-----. 1971. "Absence of copula and the notion of simplicity: A study of normal speech, baby talk, foreigner talk, and pidgins". In: Charles A. Ferguson, *Language Structure and Language Use*, 277-92. Stanford: Stan-

ford Univ. Press.
-----. 1975. "Toward a characterization of English foreigner talk". *AL* 17.1-14.
-----. 1981. "'Foreigner talk' as the name of a simplified register". *IJSL* 28.9-18.
-----, and Charles E. DeBose. 1977. "Simplified registers, broken language, and pidginization". In: Valdman 1977:70-98.
Fischer, August. 1905. "Arab. [ayš]". *ZDMG* 59.807-818.
Fischer, Wolfdietrich. 1959. *Die demonstrativen Bildungen der neuarabischen Dialekte: Ein Beitrag zur historischen Grammatik des Arabischen*. The Hague: Mouton.
-----. 1961. "Die Sprache der arabischen Sprachinsel in Uzbekistan". *Islam* 36.232-63.
-----. 1982. "Frühe Zeugnisse des Neuarabischen". *GAP* I, 83-95.
-----, and Otto Jastrow, eds. 1980. *Handbuch der arabischen Dialekte*. Wiesbaden: O. Harrassowitz.
Fishman, Joshua A., a.o., eds. 1968. *Language Problems of Developing Nations*. New York: J. Wiley.
Fleisch, Henri Robert. 1961. *Traité de philologie arabe*. I. *Préliminaires, phonétique, morphologie nominale*. Beyrouth: Imprimerie Catholique.
-----. 1964. "Arabe Classique et Arabe dialectal". *TJ* 12.23-64. (Repr., Henri Fleisch, *Etudes d'Arabe dialectal*, 3-43. Beyrouth: Imprimerie Catholique, 1974.)
-----. 1979. *Traité de philologie arabe*. II. *Pronoms, morphologie verbale, particules*. Beyrouth: Imprimerie Catholique.
Flügel, Gustav. 1862. *Die grammatischen Schulen der Araber*. Erste Abtheilung. *Die Schulen von Baṣra und Kūfa und die gemischte Schule*. Leipzig: F.A. Brockhaus. [Alles erschienene.]
Forkel, Fritz. 1980. *Die sprachliche Situation im heutigen Marokko: Eine soziolinguistische Untersuchung*. Diss., Univ. of Hamburg.
Fück, Johann. 1950. *Arabiya: Untersuchungen zur arabischen Sprach- und Stilgeschichte*. Berlin: Akademie-Verlag. [French transl. by Claude Denizeau, *'Arabīya: Recherches sur l'histoire de la langue et du style arabe*. Paris: M. Didier, 1955.]
Gallagher, Charles F. 1968. "North-African problems and prospects: Language and identity". In: Fishman 1968:129-50.
Garbell, Irene. 1958. "Remarks on the historical phonology of an East Mediterranean Arabic dialect". *Word* 14.303-337.
Gilbert, Glenn G., ed. 1971. *The German Language in America*. Austin:

Univ. of Texas Press.

Givón, Talmy. 1979. "Prolegomena to any sane creology". In: Hancock a.o. 1979:3-35.

Goodman, Morris F. 1964. *A Comparative Study of Creole French Dialects*. The Hague: Mouton.

Granda, Germán de. 1976. "A sociohistorical approach to the problem of Portuguese Creole in West Africa". *IJSL* 7.11-22.

-----. 1978. *Estudios lingüísticos, hispánicos, afrohispánicos y criollos*. Madrid: Gredos.

Grotzfeld, Heinz. 1965. *Syrisch-arabische Grammatik (Dialekt von Damaskus)*. Wiesbaden: O. Harrassowitz. (= *Porta Linguarum Orientalium*, N.S., 8.)

Gumperz, John, and Robert Wilson. 1971. "Convergence and creolization: A case from the Indo-Aryan/Dravidian border in India". In: Hymes 1971: 151-67.

Haddad, Robert M. 1970. *Syrian Christians in Muslim Society: An interpretation*. Princeton: Princeton Univ. Press.

Hagège, Claude. 1973. *Profil d'un parler arabe du Tchad*. Paris: P. Geuthner.

Halim, Amran. 1974. "The vernacular languages in relation to the standardization of Bahasa Indonesia". *PCSAL* 297-303.

Hall, Robert A. Jr. 1944. "Chinese Pidgin English grammar and texts". *JAOS* 64.95-113.

-----. 1974. *External History of the Romance Languages*. New York: Elsevier.

Hancock, Ian F. 1971. "A survey of the pidgins and creoles of the world". In: Hymes 1971:509-523.

-----. 1975. "Malacca Creole Portuguese: Asian, African or European?". *AL* 17.211-36.

-----. 1977. "Repertory of Pidgin and Creole languages". In: Valdman 1977: 362-91.

-----. a.o., eds. 1979. *Readings in Creole Linguistics*. Ghent: E. Story-Scientia.

Harning, Kerstin Eksell. 1980. *The Analytical Genitive in the Modern Arabic Dialects*. Göteborg: Acta Universitatis Gothoburgensis. (= *Orientalia Gothoburgensia*, 5.)

Harrell, Richard Slade. 1960. "A linguistic analysis of Egyptian Radio Arabic". In: Ferguson 1960:3-77.

-----. 1962. *A Short Reference Grammar of Moroccan Arabic*. Washington D.C.: Georgetown Univ. Press.

Hazai, György. 1973. *Das Osmanisch-Türkische im 17. Jahrhundert: Untersuchungen an den Transkriptionstexten von Jakab Nagy de Harsány*. The Hague: Mouton.

-----. 1974. "Zum balkanischen Hintergrund der türkischen Texte von Bartholomaeus Georgievits". *SSASH* 20.71-106.

-----. 1978. *Kurze Einführung in das Studium der türkischen Sprachen*. Wiesbaden: O. Harrassowitz.

Heidelberger Forschungsprojekt "Pidgin-Deutsch". 1975. "Zur Sprache ausländischer Arbeiter: Syntaktische Analysen und Aspekte des kommunikativen Verhaltens". *LiLi* 18.78-121.

-----. 1975a. *Sprache und Kommunikation ausländischer Arbeiter: Analysen, Berichte, Materialien*. Kronberg/TS: Scriptor. (= *Monographien Linguistik und Kommunikationswissenschaft*, 20.)

Heine, Bernd. 1973. Pidgin-Sprachen im Bantu-Bereich. Berlin: D. Reimer. (= *Kölner Beiträge zur Afrikanistik*, 3.)

-----. 1978. *A Typology of African Languages Based on the Order of Meaningful Elements*. Berlin: D. Reimer.

-----. 1979. "Some linguistic characteristics of African-based pidgins". In: Hancock a.o. 1979:89-98.

-----. 1982. *The Nubi-Language of Kibera: An Arabic Creole*. Berlin: D. Reimer. (= *Language and Dialect Atlas of Kenya*, 3.)

Heinrichs, Wolfhart. 1982. Review of Zwettler 1978. *JNES* 41.63-67.

Highfield, Arnold, and Albert Valdman, eds. 1981. *Historicity and Variation in Creole Studies*. Ann Arbor: Karoma.

Hodge, Carleton T. 1970. "The linguistic cycle". *LS* 13.1-7.

Holes, Clive. 1983. "Baḥraini dialects: Sectarian differences and the sedentary/nomadic split". *ZAL* 10.7-38.

Holm, John. 1981. "Sociolinguistic history and the creolist". In: Highfield & Valdman 1981: 27-39.

Hymes, Dell, ed. 1971. *Pidginization and Creolization of Languages*. Cambridge: Cambridge Univ. Press.

Ingham, Bruce. 1973. "Urban and rural Arabic in Khuzistan". *BSOAS* 36.533-53.

-----. 1976. "Regional and social factors in the dialect geography of Southern Iraq and Khuzistan". *BSOAS* 39.62-82.

-----. 1982. *North east Arabian Dialects*. London: Kegan Paul International. (= *Library of Arabic Linguistics*, 3.)

Janssens, Gerard. 1972. *Stress in Arabic and Word Structure in the Modern*

Arabic Dialects. Leuven: Peeters. (= *Orientalia Gandensia*, 5.)

Jastrow, Otto. 1969. "Die arabischen Dialekte des Vilayets Mardin (Südosttürkei)". *ZDMG* Suppl. I, 2.683-88.

-----. 1973. *Daragözü: Eine arabische Mundart der Kozluk-Sason-Gruppe (Südostanatolien)*. Nürnberg: H. Carl.

-----. 1977. "Gedanken zum zypriotischen Arabisch". *ZDMG* 127.258-86.

-----. 1978. *Die Mesopotamisch-Arabischen Qəltu-Dialekte*. I. *Phonologie und Morphologie*. Wiesbaden: F. Steiner.

Jespersen, Otto. 1922. *Language*. London: Allen & Unwin.

Jiha, Michel. 1964. *Der arabische Dialekt von Bišmizzīn: Volkstümliche Texte aus einem libanesischen Dorf mit Grundzügen der Laut- und Formenlehre*. Wiesbaden: F. Steiner. (= *Beiruter Texte und Studien*, 1.)

Johnstone, T.M. 1967. *Eastern Arabian Dialect Studies*. London: Oxford Univ. Press. (= *London Oriental Series*, 17.)

Kahane, Henry, and Renée Kahane. 1979. "Decline and survival of Western prestige languages". *Lg* 55.183-98.

-----, Renée Kahane, and A. Tietze. 1958. *The Lingua Franca in the Levant*. Urbana: Univ. of Illinois Press.

Kähler, Hans. 1971. *Studien über die Kultur, die Sprache und die Arabisch-Afrikaanse Literatur der Kap-Malaien*. Berlin: D. Reimer.

Kampffmeyer, Georg. 1899. "Materialien zum Studium der arabischen Beduinendialekte Innerafrikas". *MSOS* 2.143-221.

Kay, Paul, and Gillian Sankoff. 1974. "A language-universals approach to pidgins and creoles". In: De Camp & Hancock 1974:61-72.

Kaye, Alan S. 1975. "Nigerian Arabic and diachronic linguistics". *Proceedings of the 9th Annual Mid-Western American Linguistic Conference*, ed. by H. Sharifi, 314-22. Omaha: Univ. of Nebraska Press.

-----. 1976. *Chadian and Sudanese Arabic in the Light of Comparative Arabic Dialectology*. The Hague: Mouton. (= *Janua Linguarum, Series Practica*, 236.)

-----. 1982. *A Dictionary of Nigerian Arabic*. Malibu: Undena. (= *Bibliotheca Afroasiatica*, 1.)

Kieffer, Charles M. 1980. "L'arabe et les arabophones de Bactriane (Afghanistan). I. Situation ethnique et linguistique". *WI* 20.178-96.

Kißling, H.J. 1968. "Bemerkungen zu einigen Transkriptionstexten". *ZB* 6.119-27.

Koelle, Sigismund W. 1854. *Polyglotta Africana*. London: Church Missionary House.

Koopman, Hilda, and Claire Lefebvre. 1981. "Haitian Creole Pu". In: Muysken 1981: 201-221.

Kontzi, Reinhold, ed. 1978. *Zur Entstehung der romanischen Sprachen*. Darmstadt: Wissenschaftliche Buchgesellschaft. (= *Wege der Forschung*, 162.)

Kornblueth, Ilana, and Sarah Aynor. 1974. "A study of the longevity of Hebrew slang". *IJSL* 1.15-37.

Křepinský, Maximilian. 1958. "Romanica II: La naissance des langues romanes et l'existence d'une période de leur évolution commune (latin vulgaire, période romane)". *RČSAV* SV 13.1-55. [Abbreviated version in Kontzi 1978: 301-365.]

Kuhn, Walter. 1934. *Deutsche Sprachinselforschung: Geschichte, Aufgaben, Verfahren*. Plauen i. Vogtl.: G. Wolff. (= *Ostdeutsche Forschungen*, 2.)

Labov, William. 1971. "The notion of 'system' in Creole languages". In: Hymes 1971:447-72.

Landberg, Carlo. 1888. *Bâsim le Forgeron et Harun er-Rachid: Texte arabe en dialecte d'Egypte et de Syrie, publié d'après les manuscrits de Leyde, de Gotha, et du Caire*. Leiden: E.J. Brill.

Lanly, André. 1970. *Le français de l'Afrique du Nord: Etude linguistique*. Paris & Montréal: Bordas. (= *Collection Etudes Supérieures*, 64.)

Lass, Roger. 1980. *On Explaining Linguistic Change*. Cambridge: Cambridge Univ. Press.

Lazard, G. 1975. "The rise of the new Persian language". *CHI* IV, 566-94.

LePage, Robert. 1977. "Processes of pidginization and creolization". In: Valdman 1977:222-55.

Lethem, G.L. 1920. *Colloquial Arabic: Shuwa dialect of Bornu, Nigeria, and of the Region of Lake Chad*. London: Crown Agents for the Colonies.

Liem, Nguyen Dang. 1979. "Cases and verbs in Pidgin French (Tây Bồi) in Vietnam". In: Mühlhäusler 1979:217-46.

Lombard, A. 1974. "Un rapprochement nouveau: L'histoire du maltais peut-elle nous aider à mieux comprendre celle du roumain?". *RRL* 19.3-22.

Mahmud, Ushari Ahmad [= 'Ušārī Aḥmad Maḥmūd]. 1979. *Variation and Change in the Aspectual System of Juba Arabic*. Unpublished Ph.D. Georgetown Univ.

-----. 1982. "Tadrīs al-lahğa al-fuṣḥā lil-mutaḥaddiṯīn bi-l-'Arabiyya al-hağīn fī ğanūb as-Sūdān [Teaching Classical Arabic to speakers of Pidgin-Arabic in Southern Sudan]". *AJLS* 1.92-102.

Malaika, Nisar. 1963. *Grundzüge der Grammatik des arabischen Dialektes von Bagdad*. Wiesbaden: O. Harrassowitz.

Manessy, Gabriel. 1977. "Processes of pidginization in African languages". In: Valdman 1977:129-54.

-----. 1981. "Expansion fonctionnelle et évolution". In: Highfield & Valdman 1981:79-90.

Mantran, Robert. 1979. *L'expansion musulmane (VIIe-XIe siècles)*. 2ème ed. Paris: Presses Universitaires de France. (= *Nouvelle Clio*, 20.)

Marçais, Philip. 1977. *Esquisse grammaticale de l'Arabe maghrébin*. Paris: A. Maisonneuve. (= *Langues d'Amérique et d'Orient*.)

Marçais, William. 1961. "Comment l'Afrique du Nord a été arabisée". In: William Marçais, *Articles et Conférences*, 171-92. Paris: Adrien-Maisonneuve.

Marrou, Henri-Irénée. 1948. *Histoire de l'éducation dans l'Antiquité*. 7ème ed. Paris: Editions du Deuil. (Repr., 1965.)

Maurer, Theodoro Henrique Jr. 1962. *O problema do Latim Vulgar*. Rio de Janeiro: Livraria Acadêmica. (= *Biblioteca Brasileira de Filologia*, 17.)

Meillet, Antoine, and Marcel Cohen, eds. 1952. *Les langues du monde*. Nouvelle édition. 2 vols. Paris: H. Champion.

Meisel, Jürgen M. 1975. "Ausländerdeutsch und Deutsch ausländischer Arbeiter: Zur möglichen Entstehung eines Pidgin in der BRD". *LiLi* 18.9-53.

-----, ed. 1977. *Langues en contact — Pidgins — Creoles — Languages in contact*. Tübingen: G. Narr.

Miquel, André. 1975. *La géographie humaine du monde musulman jusqu'au milieu du 11e siècle: Géographie arabe et représentation du monde: la terre et l'étranger*. Paris & La Haye: Mouton. (= *Civilisation et Sociétés*, 37.)

Mitchell, T.F. 1978. *An Introduction to Egyptian Colloquial Arabic*. Oxford: Clarendon Press.

Molan, Peter D. 1978. *Medieval Western Arabic: Reconstructing elements of the dialects of al-Andalus, Sicily, and North-Africa from the laḥn al-'āmma literature*. Ph.D. microfilm, Univ. of California, Berkeley.

Morgan, Raleigh. 1981 Jr. "Guadeloupean Creole pronouns: A study of expansion in morphosyntactic structure". In: Highfield & Valdman 1981:91-103.

Mosel, Ulrike. 1980. *Tolai and Tok Pisin: The influence of the substratum on the development of New Guinea Pidgin*. Canberra: Australian National Univ. (= *PL* Series B, 73.)

Mühlhäusler, Peter. 1974. *Pidginization and Simplification of Language*.

Canberra: Australian National Univ. (= *PL* Series B, 26.)
-----, ed. 1979. *Papers in Pidgin and Creole Linguistics*. No. 2. Canberra: Australian National Univ. (= *PL* Series A, 57.)
-----. 1981. "The development of the category of number in Tok Pisin". In: Muysken 1981:35-84.
-----. 1981a. "Foreigner Talk: Tok Masta in New Guinea". *IJSL* 28.93-113.
Muysken, Pieter, ed. 1981. *Generative Studies on Creole Languages*. Dordrecht: Foris Publications. (= *Studies in Generative Grammar*, 6.)
-----. 1981a. "Creole tense/mood/aspect systems: The unmarked case?". In: Muysken 1981:181-99.
-----. 1981b. "Halfway between Quechua and Spanish: The case for relexification". In: Highfield & Valdman 1981:52-78.
Naro, Anthony J. 1978. "A study on the origins of pidginization". *Lg* 54.314-47.
-----. 1979. Review of Valdman 1977. *Lg* 55.886-93.
-----. ms. *Pidginization, creolization, and natural change*. Rio de Janeiro.
Nebes, Norbert. 1982. *Funktionsanalyse von 'kāna yafʿalu': Ein Beitrag zur Verbalsyntax des Althocharabischen mit besonderer Berücksichtigung der Tempus- und Aspektproblematik*. Hildesheim: G. Olms. (= *Studien zur Sprachwissenschaft*, 1.)
Németh, J. 1968. "Die türkische Sprache des Bartholomaeus Georgievits". *ALH* 18.263-71.
Neumann, Günter. 1966. "Zur chinesisch-russischen Behelfssprache von Kjachta". *Sprache* 12.237-51
Newton, Brian. 1964. "An Arabic-Greek dialect". *PLCN* 5.43-52. [= Suppl. to *Word* 20:3.]
Nhial, Abdon Agaw Jok. 1975. "Ki-Nubi and Juba Arabic: A comparative study". In: Bell & Hurreiz 1975:81-93.
Nöldeke, Theodor. 1904. "Das klassische Arabisch und die arabischen Dialekte". In: Theodor Nöldeke, *Beiträge zur semitischen Sprachwissenschaft*, 1-14. Straßburg: K.J. Trübner.
-----, and Friedrich Schwally. 1961. *Geschichte des Qorans*. 2. Aufl. by Gotthelf Bergsträßer and Otto Pretzl. Hildesheim: G. Olms.
Noth, Albrecht. 1975. "Zur Stellung der Nicht-Muslime im islamischen Recht". *BOS* 27:4.
Ó Muirithe, Diarmaid, ed. 1977. *The English Language in Ireland*. Dublin & Cork: Mercier Press.
Owens, Jonathan. 1980. "Monogenesis, the universal and the particular in creole studies". *AL* 22.97-117.

Palva, Heikki. 1969. *Notes on Classicization in Modern Colloquial Arabic*. Helsinki: Snellmanink. (= *SO* 40:3.)

-----. 1969a. *Balgāwi Arabic. 2. Texts in the Dialect of the yigūlgroup*. Helsinki: Snellmanink. (= *SO* 40:2.)

Peeters, Paul. 1950. *Le tréfonds oriental de l'hagiographie byzantine*. Bruxelles: Société des Bollandistes.

Pellat, Charles. 1953. *Le milieu basrien et la formation de Ǧāḥiẓ*. Paris: Maisonneuve.

Pfaff, Carol W. 1981. "Sociolinguistic problems of immigrants: Foreign workers and their children in Germany (a review article)". *LSoc* 10.155-88.

Platt, John T. 1975. "The Singapore English speech continuum and its basilect 'Singlish' as a 'creoloid'". *AL* 17.363-74.

Poliak, A.N. 1938. "L'arabisation de l'Orient sémitique". *REI* 12.35-63.

Prentice, David J. 1978. "'The best chosen language'". *Hemispherus* 22:3.18-23; 22:4.28-33.

Rabin, Chaim. 1951. *Ancient West-Arabian*. London: Taylor's Foreign Press.

-----. 1955. "The beginnings of Classical Arabic". *SI* 4.19-37.

Reinecke, John E. 1971. "Tây Bồi: Notes on the Pidgin French of Vietnam". In: Hymes 1971:47-56.

-----, a.o., eds. 1975. *Bibliography of Pidgin and Creole Languages*. Honolulu: Univ. of Hawaii Press.

Reinhardt, Carl. 1894. *Ein arabischer Dialekt gesprochen in 'Oman und Zanzibar*. Stuttgart. (Repr., Amsterdam: Philo Press.)

Rickford, John R. 1977. "The question of prior creolization in Black English". In: Valdman 1977:190-221.

Riego de Dios, Maria Isabelito O. 1979. "The Cotabato Chabacano (Ct) verb". In: Mühlhäusler 1979:275-90.

Roth, Arlette. 1979. *Esquisse grammatical du parler arabe d'Abbéché (Tchad)*. Paris: Geuthner. (= *Atlas Linguistique du Monde Arabe, Matériaux*, 4.)

Rundgren, Frithiof. 1976. "Über den griechischen Einfluß auf die arabische Nationalgrammatik". *AUU* 2.119-44.

Salib, Maurice. 1981. *Spoken Arabic of Cairo*. Cairo: American Univ. of Cairo Press.

Samarin, William. 1979. "Simplification, pidginization and language change". In: Hancock a.o. 1979:55-68.

Samuels, Michael L. 1972. *Linguistic Evolution with Special Reference to English*. Cambridge: Cambridge Univ. Press. (= *Cambridge Studies in Linguistics*, 5.)

Sankoff, Gillian, and Susan Laberge. 1974. "On the acquisition of native speakers by a language". In: DeCamp & Hancock 1974:61-72.

Sasse, Hans-Jürgen. 1971. *Linguistische Analyse des arabischen Dialekts der Mḥallamīye in der Provinz Mardin (Südosttürkei)*. Diss., Univ. of München.

Schabert, Peter. 1976. *Laut- und Formenlehre des Maltesischen anhand zweier Mundarten*. Erlangen: Palm & Enke. (= *Erlanger Studien*, 16.)

Schen, I. 1972-73. "Usāma ibn Munqidh's memoirs: Some further light on Muslim Middle Arabic". *JSS* 17.218-36; 18.64-97.

Schippers, Arie. 1980. Review of Zwettler 1978. *BiOr* 37.366-71.

Schlieben-Lange, Brigitte. 1977. "L'origine des langues romanes: Un cas de créolisation?". In: Valdman 1977:81-101.

Schmeck, Helmut. 1955. *Aufgaben und Methoden der modernen vulgärlateinischen Forschung*. Heidelberg: C. Winter.

Schmidt, Richard W. 1977. "Arabic sociolinguistics: A selected bibliography". *SN* 8.10-17.

Schumann, John. 1978. *The Pidginisation Process: A model for second language acquisition*. Rowley MA: Newbury House.

Semaan, Khalil I. 1968. *Linguistics in the Middle Ages: Phonetic studies in early Islam*. Leiden: E.J. Brill.

Seuren, Pieter A.M. 1981. "Tense and aspect in Sranan". *Linguistics* 19.1043-1076.

-----. 1982. "Internal variability in competence". *LB* 77.1-31.

Shaban, M.A. 1970. *The 'Abbāsid Revolution*. Cambridge: Cambridge Univ. Press.

Siegel, Jeff. 1981. "Developments in written Tok Pisin". *AL* 23.20-35.

Sieny, Mahmoud Esma'il [Maḥmūd Ismā'īl Ṣīnī]. 1978. *The Syntax of Urban Hijazi Arabic (Sa'udi Arabia)*. London: Longman.

Silverstein, Michael. 1972. "Chinook Jargon: Language contact and the problem of multi-level generative systems". *Lg* 48.378-405, 596-625.

Singer, Hans-Rudolf. 1958. "Grundzüge der Morphologie des arabischen Dialektes von Tetuan". *ZDMG* 108.229-65.

-----. 1982. "Der neuarabische Sprachraum". *GAP* I, 96-109.

Sīrat, Abdul-Sattār. 1973. "Notes on the Arabic dialect spoken in the Balkh Region of Afghanistan (annotated by Ebbe Egede Knudsen)". *AO* 35.89-101.

Slobin, Dan Isaac. 1973. "Cognitive prerequisites for the development of grammar". *Studies of Child Language Development*, ed. by Charles A.

Ferguson and Dan Isaac Slobin, 175-208. New York: Holl, Rinehart & Winston.

Snow, Catherine E., Roos van Eden, and Pieter Muysken. 1981. "The interactional origins of Foreigner Talk: Municipal employees and foreign workers". *IJSL* 28.81-91.

Sokolova, Bojka. 1983. *Die albanische Mundart von Mandrica*. Wiesbaden: O. Harrassowitz. (= *Balkanologische Veröffentlichungen*, 6.)

Southworth, Franklin C. 1971. "Detecting prior creolization: An analysis of the historical origins of Marathi". In: Hymes 1971:151-67.

Spitaler, Anton. 1953. Review of Fück 1950. *BiOr* 10.144-50.

Spuler, Bertold. 1952. *Iran in früh-Islamischer Zeit: Politik, Kultur, Verwaltung und öffentliches Leben zwischen der arabischen und der seldschukischen Eroberung*. Wiesbaden: F. Steiner.

Steinhauer, Hein. 1980. "On the history of Indonesian". *SSGL* 1.349-75.

Sutcliffe, David. 1982. *British Black English*. Oxford: B. Blackwell.

Todd, Loreto. 1974. *Pidgins and Creoles*. London & Boston: Routledge & Kegan Paul.

-----. 1982. *Cameroon*. Heidelberg: J. Groos. (= *Varieties of English Around the World*, T 1.)

Togeby, Knud. 1957. "Désorganisation et réorganisation dans l'histoire des langues romanes". *Miscelánea Homenaje a André Martinet. Estructuralismo e Historia*, ed. by Diego Catalán, I, 277-87. Canarias: Universidad de la Laguna. [Also in Kontzi 1978:292-300.]

Tritton, A.S. 1930. *The Caliphs and their Non-Muslim Subjects: A critical study of the Covenant of 'Umar*. London: F. Cass. (Repr., 1970, = *Islam and the Muslim World*, 14.)

Tsereteli, George V. 1956. *Arabskie dialekty Srednej Azii*. I. *Buxarskij Arabskij Dialekt*. Tbilisi: Izdatel'stvo Akademii Nauk Gruzinskoj SSR.

Tsiapera, Mária. 1969. *A Descriptive Analysis of Cypriot Maronite Arabic*. The Hague: Mouton. (= *Janua Linguarum, Series Practica*, 66.)

Traugott, Elizabeth Closs. 1977. "Pidginization, creolization, and language change". In: Valdman 1977:70-98.

Turner, G.W. 1966. *The English Language in Australia and New Zealand*. London: Longmans.

Turner, Lorenzo Dow. 1949. *Africanisms in the Gullah Dialect*. Chicago: Univ. of Chicago Press.

Valdman, Albert. 1968. "Language standardization in a diglossia situation". In: Fishman 1968:313-26.

-----, ed. 1977. *Pidgin and Creole Linguistics*. Bloomington & London: Indiana Univ. Press.

-----. 1977a. "Creolization: Elaboration in the development of Creole French dialects". In: Valdman 1977:155-89.

-----. 1977b. "On the structure and origin of Creole French". *Studies in Romance Linguistics*, ed. by Peter Michio Hagiwara, 278-301. Rowley MA: Newbury House.

-----. 1978. Le *Créole: Structure, statut et origine*. Paris: Klincksieck.

-----. 1981. "Sociolinguistic aspects of Foreigner Talk". *IJSL* 28.41-52.

Valiska, Juraj. 1980. *Nemecké nárečíe Dobšínej: Príspevok k výskumu zanikania nárečí enkláv*. Rimavská Sobota: Gemerská Vlastivedná Spoločnost'.

Valkhoff, Marius F. 1960. "Contributions to the study of Creole". *AS* 19.230-44.

-----. 1966. *Studies in Portuguese and Creole, with special reference to South Africa*. Johannesburg: Witwatersrand Univ. Press.

-----. 1972. *New Light on Afrikaans and 'Malayo-Portuguese'*. Louvain: Imprimerie Orientaliste.

Versteegh, Cornelis H.M. 1977. *Greek Elements in Arabic Linguistic Thinking*. Leiden: E.J. Brill. (= *Studies in Semitic Languages and Linguistics*, 7.)

-----. 1980. "The origin of the term 'qiyās' in Arabic grammar". *ZAL* 4.7-30.

-----. 1982. "Structural change and pidginization in the history of the Arabic language". *Proceedings of the 5th Conference of Historical Linguistics*, ed. by Anders Ahlqvist, 362-73. Amsterdam: J. Benjamins.

-----. 1982a. "Progress and change in the history of Arabic grammar". *Linguistics in the Netherlands 1982*, ed. by Saskia Daalder and Marinel Gerritsen, 39-50. Amsterdam: North-Holland.

-----. forthcoming. "Arab grammatical studies before Sībawayh". *Proceedings of the 2nd International Conference on the History of the Language Sciences*, ed. by Sylvain Auroux.

-----. forthcoming a. "Arabic grammar and corruption of speech". *al-Abḥāth* 1984.

-----. forthcoming b. "The origin of the Romance languages and the Arabic dialects". *Proceedings of the 11th Conference of the Union Européenne des Arabisants et Islamisants*, ed. by Adel Sidarus.

Vinnikov, I.N. 1957. "Obrazcy fol'klora Bucharskich Arabov". *ArOr* 25.175-89, 426-51.

Vitale, Anthony J. 1980. "Kisetla: Linguistic and sociolinguistic aspects of

a Pidgin Swahili of Kenya". *AL* 22.47-65.
Vollers, Karl. 1906. *Volkssprache und Schriftsprache im alten Arabien*. Straßburg: K.J. Trübner. (Repr., 1981.)
Vryonis, Speros Jr. 1971. *The Decline of Medieval Hellenism in Asia Minor and the Process of Islamization from the Eleventh Through the Fifteenth Century*. Berkeley: Univ. of California Press.
Wald, Benji. 1981. "Swahili Pre-Pidgin, Pidgin and Depidginization in coastal Kenya: A systematic discontinuity in non-first varieties of Swahili". In: Highfield & Valdman 1981:7-26.
Wansbrough, John. 1967. "A Judaeo-Arabic document from Sicily". *BSOAS* 30.305-313.
-----. 1977. *Quranic Studies: Sources and methods of scriptural interpretation*. London: Oxford Univ. Press.
Wartburg, Walther von. 1967. *La fragmentation linguistique de la Romania*. Paris: Klincksieck. (= *Bibliothèque Française et Romane*, Série A *Manuels et Etudes Linguistiques*, 13.)
Washabaugh, William. 1977. "Constraining variation in decreolization". *Lg* 53.329-52.
-----. 1981. "Pursuing Creole roots". In: Muysken 1981:85-102.
-----, and Fred Eckman. 1980. Review of Schumann 1978. *Lg* 56.453-56.
Watt, William Montgomery. 1956. *Muhammad at Medina*. Oxford: Clarendon Press.
Webster, G. 1960. "Korean Bamboo English once more". *AmSp* 35.261-65.
Wehr, Hans. 1952. Review of Fück 1950. *ZDMG* 102.179-86.
Weinreich. Uriel. 1953. *Languages in Contact: Findings and problems*. The Hague: Mouton.
Werkgroep Taal Buitenlandse Werknemers. 1978. *Nederlands tegen Buitenlanders*. Amsterdam: Universiteit van Amsterdam. (= *Publikaties van het Instituut voor Algemene Taalwetenschap*, 18.)
Whinnom, Keith. 1956. *Spanish Contact Vernaculars in the Philippine Islands*. Hong Kong: Univ. of Hong Kong Press.
-----. 1971. "Linguistic hybridization and the 'special case' of pidgins and creoles". In: Hymes 1971:91-115.
-----. 1977. "Lingua Franca: Historical problems". In: Valdman 1977: 295-310.
Whiteley, Wilfred H., ed. 1974. *Language in Kenya*. Nairobi: Oxford Univ. Press.
Wise, Hilary. 1975. *A Transformational Grammar of Spoken Egyptian*

Arabic. Oxford: B. Blackwell. (= *Publications of the Philological Society*, 26.)

Woolford, Ellen. 1979. "Variation and change in the i 'predicate marker' of New Guinea Tok Pisin". In: Mühlhäusler 1979:37-49.

-----. 1981. "The developing complementizer system of Tok Pisin". In: Muysken 1981:125-39.

Wright, Roger. 1982. *Late Latin and Early Romance in Spain and Carolingian France*. Liverpool: F. Cairns. (= *ARCA Classical and Medieval Texts, Papers and Monographs*, 8.)

Wurm, Stephen A. 1968. "Papua-New Guinea nationhood: The problem of a national language". In: Fishman 1968:345-63.

Zarrinkūb, 'Abd al-Ḥusain. 1975. "The Arab conquest of Iran and its aftermath". *CHI* IV, 1-56.

Zavadovskij, Ju.N. 1981. *Mavritanskij dialekt Arabskogo jazyka (Chassanija)*. Moscow: Nauka. (= *Jazyki Narodov Azii i Afriki*.)

Zwettler, Michael. 1978. *The Oral Tradition of Classical Arabic Poetry: Its character and implications*. Columbus: Ohio State Univ. Press.

LIST OF ABBREVIATIONS

Afrling	*Afroasiatic Linguistics*. Malibu.
AJLS	*Arab Journal of Language Studies*. Khartoum.
AKM	*Abhandlungen für die Kunde des Morgenlandes, herausgegeben von der Deutschen Morgenländischen Gesellschaft*. Wiesbaden.
AL	*Anthropological Linguistics*. Bloomington IN
ALH	*Acta Linguistica Academiae Scientiarum Hungaricae*. Budapest.
AmSp	*American Speech*.
AO	*Acta Orientalia*. Copenhagen.
AOH	*Acta Orientalia Academiae Scientiarum Hungaricae*. Budapest.
Ar	*Arabica. Revue d'Etudes Arabes*. Leiden
ArOr	*Archív Orientální*. Praha.
AS	*African Studies*.
AUU	*Acta Universitatis Upsaliensis*. Stockholm.
BiOr	*Bibliotheca Orientalis*. Leiden.
BOS	*Bonner Orientalistische Studien*. Bonn.
BSOAS	*Bulletin of the School of Oriental and African Studies*. London.
CHI	*The Cambridge History of Iran*. Vol. IV. *The Period from the Arab Invasion to the Saljuqs*, ed. by R.N. Frye. Cambridge: Cambridge Univ. Press, 1975.
GAP	*Grundriß der arabischen Philologie*. Vol I. *Sprachwisschenschaft*, ed. by Wolfdietrich Fischer. Wiesbaden: L. Reichert, 1982.
GP	*Gepatra Bulteno*. Budapest.
Hemisphere	
HL	*Historiographia Linguistica*. Amsterdam.
IJSL	*International Journal of the Sociology of Language*. The Hague.

Islam	*Der Islam. Zeitschrift für Geschichte und Kultur des islamischen Orients*. Berlin.
JAOS	*Journal of the American Oriental Society*. New Haven Conn.
JNES	*Journal of Near Eastern Studies*. Chicago.
JQR	*Jewish Quarterly Review*. Leiden.
JSS	*Journal of Semitic Studies*. Manchester.
LB	*Linguistische Berichte*. Wiesbaden.
Lg	*Language. Journal of the Linguistic Society of America*. Baltimore.
LI	*Linguistic Inquiry*. Cambridge, MA.
LiLi	*Zeitschrift für Literaturwissenschaft und Linguistik*. Göttingen.
Linguistics	*Linguistics: An International Review*. The Hague.
LS	*Language Sciences*. Bloomington IN.
LSoc	*Language in Society*. Cambridge.
MSOS	*Mitteilungen des Seminars für Orientalische Sprachen, westasiatische Studien*. Berlin.
Orientalia	*Orientalia. Commentarii Periodici Pontificii Instituti Biblici*. Roma.
PCSAL	*Papers from the Conference on Standardization of Asian Languages*, ed. by A.Q. Perez, A.O. Santiago, Nguyen Dang Liem. Manila: Univ. of Manila Press, 1974.
PL	*Pacific Linguistics*. Canberra.
PLCN	*Publications of the Linguistic Circle of New York*. New York.
RČSAV	*Rozpravy Československé Akademie Věd*. Praha.
REI	*Revue des Etudes Islamiques*. Paris.
RRL	*Revue Roumaine de Linguistique*. Bucureşti.
SBAW	*Sitzungsberichte der bayrischen Akademie der Wissenschafte*, phil.-hist. Klasse. München.
SI	*Studia Islamica*. Paris.
SN	*Sociolinguistics Newsletter*.
SO	*Studia Orientalia. Edidit Societas Orientalis Fennica*. Helsinki.
SSASH	*Studia Slavica Academiae Scientiarum Hungaricae*. Budapest.

SSGL	*Studies in Slavic and General Linguistics*. Amsterdam.
TJ	*Travaux et Jours*. Beyrouth.
WI	*Die Welt des Islams*. Leiden.
Word	*Word. Journal of the International Linguistics Association*. New York.
WZKM	*Wiener Zeitschrift für die Kunde des Morgenlandes*. Wien.
ZAL	*Zeitschrift für arabische Linguistik*. Wiesbaden.
ZB	*Zeitschrift für Balkanologie*.
ZDMG	*Zeitschrift der deutschen morgenländischen Gesellschaft*. Wiesbaden.

INDEX OF NAMES

A
Abū ‘Amr ibn al-‘Alā’ 10
Abū l-Aswad ad-Du’alī 10
Alcalá, Pedro de 95
Alexander the Great 20
Algee, J. 69
Alleyne, M. 71, 82, 96, 100, 101, 110n
Ambros, A. 19, 23, 82
Amīn 60
‘Amr ibn al-‘Āṣ 64
Andrzejewski, B. 127n
Anwar, M. 7
Aquilina, J. 33n, 110n
Atatürk 131
Aynor, S. 56n, 149n

B
Badawī, S. 32
Bailey, Ch.-J. 24, 57n, 147
Barth, H. 120
Bauer, A. 96, 107n, 109n, 122, 124
Baum, P. 149n
Baykurt, C. 149n
Beck, E. 10
Behnstedt, P. 108n
Bell, H. 117
Bickerton, D. 33n, 38, 39, 41, 43, 44, 45, 47, 49, 55, 56n, 57n, 84, 85, 88, 98, 99, 100, 101, 107n, 108n, 110n, 117, 123, 127n
Birkeland, H. 26
Bishai, W. 33n
Blanc, H. 15n, 22, 43, 104, 108n
Blau, J. 1, 3, 4, 5, 6, 8, 9, 14n, 15n, 24, 26, 32, 33n, 42, 86, 91, 103, 105, 106, 107n, 108n, 110n
Bloch, A. 28, 110n, 111n
Bodemann, M. 70, 71
Bollée, A. 39, 40, 50, 58n, 81, 82, 91, 98, 107n, 109n, 121, 122
Borg, A. 33n, 34n, 97, 108n, 109n, 110n, 127n
Boris, G. 15n
Bosman, D. 130
Broch, I. 114
Browning, R. 20
Brustad, K. 86
Butler, A. 64
Bynon, Th. 33n, 149n, 150n

C
Cadora, F. 17
Carter, M. 10, 15n
Çelebi, E. 149n
Clark, E. 45
Clark, H. 45
Cohen, D. 1, 20, 22, 23, 24, 26, 27, 82, 87, 107n, 113, 127n
Cohen, M. 82, 127n
Comrie, B. 45, 111n
Cook, M. 13

Corriente, F. 2, 4, 10, 15n, 19, 91, 95, 108n
Cowell, M. 105
Crone, P. 13
Csiszár, E. 56n
Czapkiewicz, A. 89, 93

D
Danner, V. 11
DeBose, Ch. 37, 56n, 71
DeCamp, D. 57n
Declerck, Ch. 56n
Dennett, D. 61
Denz, A. 28, 87, 101, 110n
Diem, W. 6, 14n, 25, 26, 27, 30, 32, 33n, 34n, 42, 52, 58n, 73, 86, 87, 106, 108n, 128n, 139, 149n
Dittmar, N. 57n
Donner, F. 59, 62, 63, 76n
Drechsel, E. 76, 114
Drewes, A. 127n

E
Eckman, F. 57n
El-Tonsi, A. 86
Elizaincín, A. 77n
Enderwitz, S. 62
Erwin, W. 105, 107n, 110n
Escure, G. 76, 149n, 150n

F
Fattal, A. 74, 75, 76n
Fellmann, J. 149n
Ferguson, Ch. 2, 7, 17, 20, 22, 23, 24, 27, 37, 50, 56n, 71, 82, 89, 90, 91, 99, 104, 108n, 109n, 118, 149n
Fischer, A. 14n
Fischer, W. 2, 11, 14n, 15n, 18, 21, 33n, 34n, 82, 90, 91, 92, 95, 97, 98, 99, 103, 104, 106n, 107n, 108n, 109n, 111n
Fleisch, H. 4, 5, 6, 14n, 15n
Forkel, F. 6, 42, 108n, 149n
Fück, J. 3, 4, 5, 10, 13, 26, 76n, 113, 127n

G
Gallagher, Ch. 73
Garbell, I. 9, 25
Georgievits, B. 148n
Gilbert, G. 34n
Givón, T. 56n
Goodman, M. 58n
Granda, G. de 50
Grotzfeld, H. 31, 87, 98, 102
Gumperz, J. 142

H
Hagège, C. 82, 86, 95, 106n, 118, 128n
Ḫalīl 10
Halim, A. 107n
Hall, R. 77n, 109n, 122, 127n, 135, 149n
Hancock, I. 109n, 110n, 115, 117, 118, 119, 127n
Harning, K. 12, 29, 92, 93, 94, 95, 108n
Harrell, R. 29, 105, 106, 110n, 149n
Hazai, Gy. 131, 132, 148n
Heine, B. 13, 44, 45, 49, 50, 81, 82, 86, 91, 98, 99, 105, 106, 107n, 109n, 110n, 111n, 117, 118, 119,

121, 122, 123, 124, 126, 128n
Heinrichs, W. 14n
Hodge, C. 146
Holes, C. 43
Hopkins, S. 15n
Hurreiz, S. 117

I
Ibn Ǧinnī 148
Ibn Ḫaldūn 13, 14, 15n
Ingham, B. 15n, 77n

J
Jahr, E. 114
Janssens, G. 106n
Jastrow, O. 11, 12, 21, 33n, 34n, 82n, 86, 87, 90, 91, 92, 95, 97, 99, 103, 104, 106n, 107n, 108n, 109n
Jespersen, O. 136, 149n
Jiha, M. 102
Johnstone, T. 15

K
Kahane, H. 127n
Kahane, R. 127n
Kähler, H. 115
Kampffmeyer, G. 119
Kay, P. 49
Kaye, A. 23, 82, 87, 90, 91, 104, 106n, 108n, 119, 127n, 128n
Kieffer, Ch. 34n
Killean, C. 127n
Kißling, H. 148n
Koelle, S. 120, 127n
Kornblueth, I. 56n, 149n
Křepinský, M. 135, 137
Kuhn, W. 34n

L
Laberge, S. 57n, 69, 85, 146
Labov, W. 40, 53
Landberg, C. de 110n
Lanly, A. 54
Lass, R. 1
Lazard, G. 66, 76n
LePage, R. 76
Lethem, G. 119, 127n
Liem, N. 69

M
Mahmud, U. 42, 85, 117, 118, 123, 126
Maier, H. 107n
Malaika, N. 110n
Ma'mūn 60, 75
Manessy, G. 50, 84, 104, 106, 107n, 109n
Mantran, R. 59
Maqrīzī 75
Marçais, Ph. 99, 102, 107n
Marçais, W. 64
Marrou, H.-I. 72
Maurer, Th. 15n, 149n
Maymonides 8
Meillet, A. 127n
Meisel, J. 77n, 82, 92, 111n
Miquel, A. 114, 115
Mitchell, T. 88, 101, 106
Molan, P. 7
Mosel, U. 57n
Mühlhäusler, P. 40, 41, 43, 48, 51, 53, 54, 56, 56n, 57n, 58n, 69, 72, 77n, 91, 106n, 146
Muysken, P. 84

N
Nagy de Harsány, J. 148
Naro, A. 46, 56n, 110n, 142, 143, 150n
Nebes, N. 86
Németh, J. 148
Neumann, G. 114, 128n
Newton, B. 34
Nhial, A. 117, 118, 123, 125
Nöldeke, Th. 3
Noth, A. 76n

O
Ó Muirithe, D. 133
Ostow, R. 70, 71
Owens, J. , 107n, 118, 123

P
Palva, H. 12, 108n, 127n
Peeters, P. 66
Pellat, Ch. 76n
Pfaff, C. 77n
Platt, J. 57n
Plautus 8
Poliak, A. 63, 64
Prentice, D. 107n

Q
Quintilian 149n

R
Rabin, Ch. 1, 2, 5, 14n, 26
Reinecke, J. 69, 105, 117, 118, 119
Reinhardt, C. 108n
Rickford, J. 36, 42, 80, 143, 144, 145, 150n
Riego de Dios, I. 100, 105
Roth, A. 95, 99, 102, 105, 110n, 118, 120, 125, 128n

S
Saadya Gaon 9
Salib, M. 98
Samuels, M. 51, 56n, 83
Sankoff, G. 49, 57n, 69, 85, 146
Sapir, E. 33n
Sasse, H.-J. 34n, 87, 106n
Schabert, P. 87, 88, 110n
Schen, I. 103
Schippers, A. 14n
Schlieben-Lange, B. 37, 135, 138, 149n
Schmeck, H. 58n
Schmidt, R. 128n
Schuman, J. 57n
Semaan, Kh. 9
Seuren, P. 57n
Shaban, M. 62, 65
Sībawayhi 10, 14n
Siegel, J. 56n, 57n, 85, 109n
Sieny, M. 102
Singer, H.-R. 33n, 108n
Sīrāfī 11
Sīrat, A. 34n, 111n
Slobin, D. 45, 46, 57n
Sokolova, B. 34n
Southworth, F. 37, 139, 140, 141, 142
Spuler, B. 66
Steinhauer, H. 107n
Sutcliffe, D. 32

T
Ṭabarī 74
Tietze, A. 127n

Todd, L. 50, 130
Togeby, K. 58n
Traugott, E. 56n
Tritton, A. 75
Tsiapera, M. 34n, 108n
Tsereteli, G. 33n
Turner, G. 58n

U
Usāma ibn Munqiḏ 103
'Uṯmān 10

V
Valdman, A. 33n, 34n, 39, 40, 43, 71, 83, 107n
Valiska, J. 34n
Valkhoff, M. 33n, 52, 58n, 70, 76n, 77n, 130, 149n
Vinnikov, I. 109n, 110n
Vollers, K. 2, 5, 28
Vryonis, S. 131, 148n, 149n

W
Wansbrough, J. 5, 14n, 108n
Wartburg, W. von 51
Washabaugh, W. 57n
Watt, W. 61
Webster, G. 69
Weinreich, U. 34n
Whinnom, K. 50, 53, 77n, 127n
Wilson, R. 142
Woolford, E. 48, 57n, 144, 146
Wright, R. 137, 138, 149n

Z
Zarrinkūb, 'A. 65
Zavadovskij, Ju. 12, 108n, 119
Zwettler, M. 1, 4, 14n, 19, 116

INDEX OF SUBJECTS

/'/ 82
/'/ 82, 121

A
/a/ 2, 11, 82
'ā'id bi- 88
accent 12
acquisition, language~, v. language learning
acrolect 32, 41, 126
administration
language of~ 62, 66
adstratal
~influence 109n
~language 30, 34
'aed 88
Afrikaans 33n, 52, 72, 77n, 109n, 115, 130
kitap~ 115
agglutinating construction 81
agreement 21, 103, 104, 105, 125, 126
~markers 85, 126
ahl al-Kitāb 75
Akkadian 51
Albanian 34
allaḏī 99, 110n
allaḏī li- 95
allomorph 82
'ām 102, 110n
'am- 88
'ammāl 88
an 105
analogy 28, 91, 108n
analytical 146, 147
~construction 7, 19, 24, 81, 83, 89, 146
~genitive, v. genitive, analytical
anna 105
anterior 84, 85, 86, 87, 88, 89, 123
Arabic 66, 67, 74, 75, 77n
Abbéché~ 97, 120, 128n
Aden~ 12
'Ādirar~ 120
Afghanistan~ 6, 29, 34, 111n
Algerian~ 92
Algiers Jewish~ 82
Anatolian~ 6, 29, 34, 86, 87, 107n
Ancient South Palestinian~ 108n
Baġdādī~ 15n, 22, 43, 91
Baġdādī Jewish~ 91
Baḥraynī~ 43
Bedouin~ 12, 79, 94, 106n, 127n
Bēṛān~ 127n

Bimbashi~ 117, 125
Bišmizzīn~ 97, 102
Cameroon~ 119
Chad~ 7, 82, 86, 92, 95, 97, 99, 102, 104, 110n, 118, 120, 125, 127n, 128n
Chadian Pidgin~ 118
Christian~ 42
Christian Middle~ 8, 9, 15n
Classical~ 5, 6, 8, 9, 10, 11, 15n, 17, 20, 27, 28, 32, 59, 72, 79, 86, 87, 93, 95, 98, 99, 103, 106, 115, 116, 117, 122, 127n
Classical Standard~ 2
Creole~ 116, 117
Cypriot~ 6, 29, 34, 92, 95, 97, 99, 108n, 109n, 110n, 127n
Damascene~ 111n
Daragözü~ 33n, 91, 95, 108n, 109n
Daṯīna~ 12
Djidjelli~ 82
Ḏofārī~ 12
Eastern~ 2, 5, 14n
Eastern Mediterranean~ 9, 25
Egyptian~ 6, 28, 32, 42, 86, 88, 89, 92, 97, 98, 101, 106, 108n, 109n, 122, 128n, 149n
Egyptian Middle~ 7, 8
Ethiopian trade~ 7, 118, 127n
gilit~ 15n, 92
Gulf~ 15n
Ḥassāniyya~ 12, 108n, 119, 127n
Ḥiğāzī~ 2, 5, 102
'Irāqī~ 34, 88, 99, 101, 105, 110n
Jewish~ 42
Jewish Middle~ 8, 15n, 91, 95
Juba~ 7, 42, 85, 116, 117, 118, 120, 121, 122, 123, 124, 125, 126, 127n
Judaeo~, v. Arabic, Jewish Middle~
Khartoum~ 42, 116, 125, 126
Khuzestan~ 6
Kwayriš~ 87
Lebanese~ 92, 97
Libyan~ 87, 92
Madagascar trade~ 127n
Maghrebine~ 120
Maghrebine Middle~ 7
Maltese~ 6, 29, 33n, 87, 92, 95, 97, 110n
Marazig~ 15n
Mecca~ 12
Middle~ 7, 9, 15n, 32, 86, 99, 103, 106, 110n, 132, 137, 140
Modern Classical~ 17
Modern Standard~ 17, 125, 126
Mongallese~ 117
Moroccan~ 6, 34, 42, 86, 88, 92, 97, 99, 105, 106, 149n
Muslim~ 42, 43
Muslim Middle~ 8, 9
Nağdī~ 2, 15n
Neo~ 15n
New~ 1, 3, 4, 5, 15n, 19, 27, 30, 91, 94, 103

Nigerian~ 82, 87, 92, 119, 127n
North-African~ 89, 101, 102
North-Arabian~ 12
North-east Arabian~ 15n
Nubi~ 13, 31, 86, 98, 108n, 109n, 111n, 116, 117, 118, 120, 121, 122, 123, 124, 125, 126
Old~ 1, 3, 4, 5, 11, 17, 19, 27, 30, 82, 91, 103
Palestinian~ 92, 98
Pidgin~ 7, 50, 85, 95, 116, 117, 118, 119, 120, 121, 122, 123, 124, 125, 126, 146
qəltu~ 15n, 92, 99
Qur'ānic~ 5
Ristāq~ 12
Riyāḍ~ 12
Rural Maltese~ 87, 88
Shuwa~ 119, 120, 127n
sedentary~ 12
Spanish~ 15n, 95
Sudanese~ 42, 92, 122, 126, 127
Sudanese Pidgin~ 117
Syrian~ 31, 86, 87, 88, 92, 97, 102, 105
Syro-Lebanese~ 98
Syro-Palestinian~ 12
Tamīmī~ 2
Tetuan~ 33n
Tunis Jewish~ 87, 88
Tunisian~ 86, 92, 107n
'Umānī~ 108n, 114
Uzbekistan~ 6, 28, 29, 33n, 34, 88, 91, 95, 96, 97, 103, 108n, 109n, 111n
Western~ 2, 14n
Yemenite~ 12, 33n, 87
Zanzibar~ 108n, 114
'Arabiyya 5, 9, 17, 27, 28, 29, 76
Arabs
Christian~ 63, 66, 74
Aramaic 14n, 25, 26, 65, 73, 77n
Aramaic
Neo~ 25
Aramaic/Syriac 139
archaism 1, 31
arḍ al-'Ağam 64
areal influence 149n
article
definite~ 98, 99, 109n, 121, 139
indefinite~ 34, 99, 109n
aspectual
~markers 7, 18, 43, 79, 80, 84, 85, 86, 87, 88, 89, 123, 126, 146
~system 130, 139
asyndetic construction 21, 101, 103, 106, 111n
Auftaktsverb 110n
auxiliary 85, 86, 101, 102, 110n, 150n
semi~ 102
/aw/ 11, 82
/ay/ 11, 82
ayna 110n

B
bə 123
ba'ā 86
back-formation 121
baġā 87

Bahasa Indonesia, v. Indonesian
Bamboo-English, v. English, Korean Pidgin~
Bantu languages 104, 114, 142
Banū Hilāl
invasion of~ 64
base language 143
basilect 32, 41, 76, 138
Basque 136
Bayt al-Ḥikma 73
bbi- 87
Bedouin 3, 4, 6, 9, 10, 11, 12, 14n, 17, 19, 22, 26, 28
~dialect 15n
~speech 28
bedouinization 22, 42
Berber 24, 73
bi- 88
bi gi 123
bilingualism 25
bilinguality 66
bisyllabicity 49, 121
borrowing 31, 33n, 95, 141
btā‘ 93
Bulgarian 34, 139
Byzantine empire 72

C
calque 31
Cape-Malays 115
causality 1, 148
causative 90, 100
Chabacano, v. Spanish, Philippine Creole~
change 35, 36
chronology of~ 9, 14n, 132, 134, 135, 148n
independent~ 26
linguistic~ 56n, 137, 144
mechanism of~ 1, 23, 36, 131, 138
natural~ 48, 147
phonetic~ 137
reducing~ 89
regenerating~ 89, 93
structural~ 130, 132
universals of~ 138, 141
unnatural~ 142
Chinese 57n, 133
Chinese-Russian jargon, v. Russo-Chinese
Chinook Jargon 41
circumstantial clause 103
classicism 120
classicization 32, 33, 102, 105, 106, 127n, 149n
clientage 61
Cocoliche 77n
colonial language 54, 55
common descent 23, 26, 45, 50, 98
comparative 122
complementizer 57n, 144, 146
indirect~ 100
perfective~ 86, 100
completive 84
conditional sentence 110n
conquests
Germanic~ 135, 136
Islamic~ 59, 60, 62, 73, 139
Osmanic~ 131, 132
Roman~ 134
conservatism 11, 12, 15n, 22, 42
constraints 142
contact language 37, 39, 42, 54, 136

context form 149n
context-free rule 81, 82
context-sensitive rule 81
continuum 32
convergence 25, 30
conversion 61, 75
converts 11
Coptic 24, 33n, 65, 73, 146
corruption of speech 9, 13, 14n, 27, 28, 75, 116
creole 38, 39, 40, 47, 57n, 69, 130, 144
early-creolized~ 43, 44, 88
endogenous~ 43, 44, 45, 67
exogenous~ 43, 45, 67
true~ 56n
creolization 38, 39, 40, 41, 43, 47, 48, 52, 53, 56, 57n, 74, 79, 85, 115, 123, 129, 133, 134, 140, 141, 142, 143, 144, 145, 146, 147
creoloid 57n
cultismos 137
cycle
linguistic~ 146, 147
Czech 74, 139

D

d- 93
/ḍ/ 7, 20, 82
/ḏ̣/ 7, 20, 82
da 98
da- 88
daba 86
Dacian 136
dahāqīn 65
Darī 76n
dé 98
declensional endings 4, 11, 19, 149n, 150n
loss of~ 83, 91, 139, 140
decreolization 32, 41, 71, 76, 79, 94, 95, 96, 110n, 115, 116, 125, 126, 127n, 134, 136, 137, 138, 139, 145, 149n, 150n
degeneration 30, 31, 34
deictic system 98, 99
demonstratives 98, 99, 109n
postposed~ 58n
denaskaj esperantistoj 56n
di 98
diffusionist model 137
diglossia 5, 17, 26, 67, 135, 136, 141
ḏimmī 61, 76n
dispensable item 81, 89
divergence 25
dīwān 66
dōl 98
doublet 32
Dravidian languages 37, 140, 141
drift, v. general drift
dual 20, 23, 33n, 89, 104, 139
durative 21, 84, 87, 88, 101, 102
Dutch 33n, 52, 58n, 74, 77n, 109n, 130, 139
Virgin Islands Creole~ 84

E

/e/ 11, 82
earlier marker 84, 85, 86, 100
education 68, 69, 70, 71, 72, 76
Egyptian
Old~ 146
elision 4, 121
emphasis 83, 121
enclaves
linguistic~ 31
endogenous, v. creole, endogeous~

English 96, 139
Belizean Creole~ 149n, 150n
Black~ 80, 143
Chinese Pidgin~ 69, 77n, 107n, 109n
Creole~ 84, 87, 99
Dahomey Pidgin~ 122
Hawaiian Creole~ 84
Hawaiian Pidgin~ 38
Indian~ 54
Irish~ 133
Jamaican Creole~ 32, 41, 42, 84, 96, 100, 108n
Korean Pidgin~ 69
New Guinea Pidgin~ 48, 57n, 58n, 69, 77n, 79, 84, 85, 96, 100, 106n, 109n, 122, 124, 128n, 142, 144, 146
Pidgin~ 50, 95
Samoan Plantation Pidgin~ 107n
Saramaccan~ 101
Sierra Leone Creole~ 100
Sierra Leone Pidgin~ 69
Singapore~ 56n, 57n
Sranan~ 100, 101
Standard~ 32
Surinam Creole~ 96
Tok Masta~ 69, 77n
West-African Pidgin~ 69
Esperanto 56n, 149n
Ethiopian 73
Ewe 58n
exogenous, v. creole, exogenous~
expansion 39, 41, 56, 56n, 80, 146
explicit transmission 81
exponent, genitive~, v. genitive exponent

F
facilitation 68
fʿālil 21
Fanagalo 98, 105, 109n
fard 99
fat 99
fāt 128n
feminine endings 21
final clause 106
first language, v. language learning, first~
foreign workers 70, 71
foreigner talk 38, 45, 46, 68, 71, 81, 83, 96
formation populaire 31
formation savante 31
fossilized form 71, 95, 105
Franks 67
French 146
Creole~ 33n, 34, 50, 82, 84, 87, 96, 98, 110n
Haitian Creole~ 58n, 99, 109n, 122
Indian Ocean Creole~ 50, 85, 122
Mauritian Creole~ 109n
North-African~ 54
Pidgin~ 50, 98
Réunion Creole~ 58n
Seychellois Creole~ 96, 121
Vietnamese Pidgin~ 69, 105, 142
fuʿāl 20
fuʿayyal 21
Ful, v. Peul
fuʿlā 20
functional yield 4, 91
fútu 122

future 84, 86, 87, 88, 123, 146

G
/ġ/ 121
ġa- 86
gá 123
ǧa'ala 90
ġadāk 103
ġadi 107n
Ǧāhiliyya 1, 3, 6, 11, 14n, 19, 22, 26, 62
ǧāk 103
Galgalíya 119
Gallic 136
gām 102
Gastarbeiterdeutsch, v. German, Pidgin~
gender 12, 89, 104
general drift 22, 23, 25, 33n
genitive 141
  analytical~ 12, 18, 21, 24, 28, 92, 93, 94, 95, 133, 139
  ~exponent 18, 92, 93, 94, 95, 97, 122
  synthetic~ 12, 18, 24, 28, 32, 93, 94, 95, 108n
German 31, 34, 70, 74, 77n
  Low~ 52
  Pidgin~ 70, 71, 82, 91, 111n
  Standard~ 91
gi 123
ǧizya 61
glottal stop 5, 7, 21
grammarians 5, 6, 9, 10, 14n, 27, 28, 76
grammar, study of 15n
grammaticalization 81, 83, 89, 121, 146, 147
Greek 30, 34, 66, 73, 131
  Cypriot~ 109n

H
/h/ 121
/ḥ/ 121
ḥa- 86
hā- 98
habitual 87, 88
hāḏā 98
hal 98
ḫalaṣa 86
hana 95
ḥattā 87
Hausa 119
Hawaiian 84
Hebrew 133
  Classical~ 133
high variety 6, 76
Hindi
  Modern~ 141
historical-comparative method 28
Homeric dialect 2, 14n
hyper-correction 9, 149n
hyperurbanism 32
hypotactic construction 103, 105, 106, 110n, 111n

I
/i/ 2, 11, 23, 82
illī 20, 98, 99
illiteracy 73
imāla 11
imperative 85, 123, 124, 128n
imperfect 88
implicational scale 57n
implicit transmission 81
-īn 108n

indefinite marker 15n
Indian languages 57n
Indo-Aryan languages 37, 140, 141, 142
Indo-European languages 33n, 51
Indonesian 107n
Djakartan~ 107n
inflectional construction 81
inflectional endings 19
loss of~ 28
ingressive 101, 102
inherent features 130
inna 105
innovation 12, 24, 25, 26, 30, 42, 48, 50, 51, 72
instruction 56n
interdentals 12, 21, 31, 82
intermarriage, v. marriages, mixed~
interpreters 62, 66
interrogatives 18, 96, 97, 109n
i'rāb 4
iranicization 66
irrealis 84, 87, 88, 89, 123
isolating construction 81
Italian 30, 77n, 114
Ivrit 56n, 133
izafet 34

J
Judaeo-Arabic, v. Arabic, Jewish Middle~
juxtaposition 95, 96, 100, 101

K
ka- 88
kalām arab, v. Arabic, Nigerian~
kàlá(s) 86, 123
kan 123
kān 87
kāna 86
Karamanlides 148n
Khoisan languages 58n
Khuzestanian 76n
Ki-Nubi, v. Arabic, Nubi~
Kjachta Pidgin, v. Russo-Chinese
koine 25, 37
military~ 20, 24, 50
poetic~ 1, 2, 4, 5, 14n, 22, 23, 26
post-Islamic~ 20
sedentary~ 24
koine-theory 7, 20, 24, 99
koineization 26, 50
Krio, v. English, Sierra Leone Creole~
ku- 107n
kūn 107n
Kurdish 30, 109n
kuttāb 73

L
laḥ 88
laḥ- 86
laḥn 10, 75
laḥn al-'āmma 7, 9
language
~as organism 29, 58n, 146
base~, v. base language
~contact 36
contact~, v. contact language
~cycle 146
~encounter 36, 37, 43, 52
literary~ 131, 132, 133
'mixed'~ 77n

natural~ 56
prestige~ 116, 135, 143, 145
source~, v. source language
standard~, v. standard; Arabic, Classical~
target~, v. target language
trade~, v. trade language
unnatural~ 38, 56n, 142, 149n
language learning 36, 38, 43, 44, 47, 48, 55, 56n, 57n, 68, 79, 116, 131, 133, 143
first~ 36, 38, 39, 45, 46, 56n, 57n, 135, 136, 147
imperfect~ 54, 55
second~ 33n, 36, 37, 38, 40, 44, 45, 46, 55, 56n, 57n, 70, 77n, 136, 147
tutored~ 149n
undirected~ 77n, 139, 141
unnatural~ 142, 144
untutored~ 46, 52, 55, 56, 81, 129, 145, 147
latent tendencies 19, 23, 35, 52
later marker 84, 85, 86, 87
Latin 109n, 133, 134
Classical~ 8, 58n, 134, 135, 136, 137, 149n
Pidgin~ 135
Vulgar~ 8, 15n, 57n, 69, 134, 140, 149n
law, study of 15n
lē 95
level of discourse 94
levelling 6, 9, 30, 41, 42, 116, 117, 139, 146
lexicalization 147
lexicon 17
li- 20
lingua franca 37, 41, 50, 65, 114, 136
linguisters 76n
linguistic encounter, v. language, ~encounter
Lithuanian 33n
loanword 31, 114, 149n
low variety 6, 76

M
mā 97
Malagassy 58n
Malay 57n, 58n, 115
Classical~ 107n
kitap~ 115
Pasar~ 107n
man 97
Marathi 37, 140, 141
Old~ 140
marked form 81, 82
marriage law
Islamic~ 61, 75
marriages
mixed~ 63, 66, 68, 70, 74, 75
mašā 87
matā‘ 95, 122
Mehri 73
mesolect 41
military koine, v. koine, military~
military settlements 20, 63, 66, 125
miscogeny, v. marriages, mixed~
míta 95
mixture
heterosystematic~ 147
modal sentence 105, 106
monogenesis 25, 45, 49

moods
    verbal~ 90, 105
mother tongue 38, 39, 40, 68, 114, 126, 147
multi-causality 51
multilinguality 53, 66, 67, 69, 74, 113, 146

N
Nabataean 14n
nās 122
nasalization 83
native speakers 68, 72, 142
nativization 43, 48, 56n, 57n, 129, 133, 143, 145
natural language, v. language, natural~
Negerhollands, v. Dutch, Virgin Islands Creole~
neophytes 61
non-punctual 84, 87, 88, 89, 123
Normans 67
North-American Indian languages 114
Norwegian 74
Nubi, v. Arabic, Nubi~
nunation 12

O
/o/ 11, 82
oblique ending 28, 83
operating principles 45, 46, 47

P
Pahlavī 76n
Panjabi
    Modern~ 141
Papia Kristang, v. Portuguese, Malaccan Creole~
Papiamentu 85, 110n, 149n
papyri, language of 15n
paradigmatic unity 82
paratactic construction 110n
parallel development 24, 25
Parsī 76n
Parthian 76n
passive
    internal~ 12, 21, 90
Pataouète, v. French, North-African~
pausal form 4, 91
perfective 123
    ~complementizer, v. complementizer, perfective~
    ~marker 57n, 101
periphery 30, 32, 93
periphrasis 18, 96, 97, 109n, 140, 141, 146
Persian 24, 30, 34, 66, 73, 75, 149n
    Middle~ 76n
    New~ 76n
    Old~ 76n
personal markers 126
Peul 127n
Phoenician 51
pidgin 27, 35, 37, 38, 40, 53, 56, 57n, 69, 129, 130, 144
    effable~ 43
    pre~ 77n
    pseudo~ 77n
    real~ 71
    standardized~ 70, 71
pidginization 13, 28, 37, 38, 39, 40, 43, 45, 46, 47, 48, 49, 51, 52, 53, 54, 55, 57n, 70, 71, 74, 75, 79, 80, 81, 89, 91, 96, 98, 105, 106, 110n, 113, 115, 124, 125, 129.

ša- 87
šā'a 87
Sabir 37, 50, 115
šāf 15n, 20
Sango 84
Sanskrit 140, 141
sanskritization 141
sāra 87
Sardinian 109n
sawfa 86
schools 72, 73, 134, 135, 136, 145
second language, v. language learning, second~
sedentarization 22
sedentary speech 11, 15n, 22, 43, 73
sejjer 87
selectional criteria 41
semantic primitives 123
Semitic 23
serialization 99, 100, 101, 110n, 130, 142
settlement
    pattern of~ 62, 63, 64, 65
settlements, military~, v. military settlements
Shi'ites 43
simplification 36, 54, 68, 80, 82, 90, 135
Singlish, v. English, Singapore~
slang 56n
Slavonic
    ~languages 31, 139
    Old~ 139
Slovak 74
Slovenian 33n
sociological parameters 43, 53, 54
Soqotri 73
source language 51
South-Arabic 33n, 73
Spanish 77n, 114, 146
    Creole~, v. Papiamentu
    Philippine Creole~ 100, 105
Spanish-Portuguese 77n
speech errors 75
spelling conventions 14n
Sprachinsel 6, 28, 30, 31, 42, 94, 117
Sranan, v. English, Sranan~
standard 41, 42, 48, 53, 77n, 133, 136, 138, 139, 145, 150n
    regional~ 55
    written~ 56n, 57n
standardization 55, 76
status constructus, v. genitive, synthetic~
strategies 39, 44, 47, 48, 49, 50, 70, 79, 81, 123, 145
    facilitating~ 68, 71
    innate~ 47
    learning~ 45, 46
    simplifying~ 74
    universal~ 45, 47, 48, 55, 77n, 116, 131, 148
stigmatized features 128n
stress 106n
subjunctive 105
substratal
    ~influence 24, 25, 47, 49, 50, 51, 52, 110n, 122, 140, 141, 143
    ~language 24, 25, 51, 58n, 73, 74, 75, 141, 142, 145
Sunnites 43
superstratal language 30, 51
suprasegmentals 83

Šu'ūbiyya 62
Swahili 110n, 114
Kenya Pidgin~ 98, 105, 109n, 110n, 111n
Swedish 74
syllable structure 12
syndetic construction 103, 111n
synthetic 146, 147
~construction 81, 122
~genitive, v. genitive, synthetic~
synthetization 89
Syriac 24, 66, 73, 74, 76n, 139

T
ta- 87, 95, 122
tafh̲īm 11, 83
Tajik 29
taltala 2, 20, 22
tanwīn 15n, 107n
target language 31, 38, 39, 40, 41, 42, 45, 46, 47, 48, 49, 51, 52, 53, 54, 56, 57n, 67, 68, 69, 70, 71, 72, 98, 117, 137, 138, 142, 143, 145, 146
taw 86
tawwa 107n
taxation 61, 63, 66
Tây Bồi, v. French, Vietnamese Pidgin~
Tekarir 127n
Tekrour 127n
Tekrur 127n
tél- 95
temm 86
temporal markers 102
Tok Pisin, v. English, New Guinea Pidgin~
Tokoror 127n
Tolai 57n
Toucouleurs 127n
Tourkol 119
trade language 37, 41, 67, 113, 114, 115, 118, 119
Transkriptionsdenkmäler 132, 140
Turkish 34, 111n, 131, 132, 148n, 149n
Christian~ 149n
High Osmanic~ 131, 132, 149n
Osmanic~ 131
Western Balkanic~ 148n
Turku 118
tutoring 41

U
/u/ 2, 11, 23, 82
universal features 49, 84, 106n, 107n
universal strategies, v. strategies, universal~
universal tendencies 45, 47
universality 45, 48, 49, 52
universals 111n
unmarked form 81
unnatural language, v. language, unnatural~
unnatural rules 142
upgrading 119, 127n
Uzbek 29

V
variability 35, 41, 114
variant readings, v. *Qur'ān*, variant readings of~

variation
  linguistic~ 41
  random~ 141
  stylistic~ 57n, 145
velarization 83
verb-modifier 102
verbal measures 108n
verbs
  geminate~ 20, 90, 108n, 124
  IIw/y~ 108n, 124
  IIIw/y~ 20, 23, 90, 91
  imperfect~ 85
  modal~ 21
  ~of motion 100, 101, 103
  passive~ 124
  perfect~ 85
  serial~ 21, 99, 100, 101, 102, 110n
  strong~ 91
  transitive~ 124
  weak~ 90, 91
volitional 87
Volkssprache 2, 28
vowel elision 106n

W
waḥd 99
wāḥid 99
wāqif 88
wave-theory 24, 50
Welsh-Breton 77n
West-African languages 33n, 51, 110n, 122
West-Germanic languages 33n
wōqif 88
word order 21, 103, 104, 106, 111n, 133

Z
zamān 87
Zangi 114
Zoroastrians 75
Zulu 109n
  Pidgin~, v. Fanagalo

17. LIEB, Hans-Heinrich: *Integrational Linguistics*. 6 volumes. Amsterdam, 1984-1985. Vol. I available (Hfl. 125,--/$ 50.00) Vol. 2-6 n.y.p. ca. Hfl. 425,--/$ 170.00

18. IZZO, Herbert J. (ed.): *ITALIC AND ROMANCE. Linguistic Studies in Honor of Ernst Pulgram*. Amsterdam, 1980. Hfl. 98,--/$ 39.00

19. RAMAT, Paolo et al. (ed.): *LINGUISTIC RECONSTRUCTION AND INDO-EUROPEAN SYNTAX. Proceedings of the Coll. of the 'Indogermanische Gesellschaft' Univ. of Pavia, 6-7 Sept. 1979*. Amsterdam, 1980. Hfl. 78,--/$ 31.00

20. NORRICK, Neal R.: *Semiotic Principles in Semantic Theory*. Amsterdam, 1981. Hfl. 80,--/$ 32.00

21. AHLQVIST, Anders (ed.): *PAPERS FROM THE FIFTH INTERNATIONAL CONFERENCE ON HISTORICAL LINGUISTICS, Galway, April 6-10, 1981*. Amsterdam, 1982. Hfl. 135,--/$ 54.00

22. UNTERMANN, Jürgen & Bela BROGYANYI (eds.): *DAS GERMANISCHE UND DIE REKONSTRUKTION DER INDOGERMANISCHE GRUNDSPRACHE. Akten, Proceedings from the Colloquium of the Indogermanische Gesellschaft, Freiburg, 26-27 February 1981*. Amsterdam, 1984. Hfl. 70,--/$ 28.00

23. DANIELSEN, Niels: *Papers in Theoretical Linguistics*. Preface by J. Peter Maher. Amsterdam, 1985. n.y.p. ca. Hfl. 70,--/$ 28.00

24. LEHMANN, Winfred P. & Yakov MALKIEL (eds.): *PERSPECTIVES ON HISTORICAL LINGUISTICS. Papers from a conference held at the meeting of the Language Theory Division, Modern Language Ass., San Francisco, 27-30 December 1979*. Amsterdam, 1982. Hfl. 110,--/$ 44.00

25. ANDERSEN, Paul Kent: *Word Order Typology and Comparative Constructions*. Amsterdam, 1983. Hfl. 73,--/$ 29.00

26. BALDI, Philip (ed.) *PAPERS FROM THE XIIth LINGUISTIC SYMPOSIUM ON ROMANCE LANGUAGES, University Park, April 1-3, 1982*. Amsterdam, 1984. Hfl. 170,--/$ 68.00

27. BOMHARD, Alan: *Toward Proto-Nostratic*. Amsterdam, 1984. Hfl. 100,--/$ 40.00

28. BYNON, James: *CURRENT PROGRESS IN AFROASIATIC LINGUISTICS: Papers of the Third International Hamito-Semitic Congress, London, 1978*. Amsterdam, 1984. Hfl. 145,--/$ 58.00

29. PAPROTTÉ, Wolf & René DIRVEN (eds.): *THE UBIQUITY OF METAPHOR: Metaphor in Language and Thought*. Amsterdam, 1985. n.y.p. ca. Hfl. 140,--/$ 56.00

30. HALL, Robert A., Jr.: *Proto-Romance Morphology*. Amsterdam, 1984. Hfl. 88,--/$ 35.00

31. GUILLAUME, Gustave: *Foundations for a Science of Language*. Translated and with an introd. by Walter Hirtle and John Hewson. Amsterdam, 1984. Hfl. 55,--/$ 22.00

32. COPELAND, James E. (ed.): *NEW DIRECTIONS IN LINGUISTICS AND SEMIOTICS*. Houston/Amsterdam, 1984. No rights for US/Can. *Customers from USA and Canada: please order from Rice University*. Hfl. 100,--

33. VERSTEEGH, Kees.: *Pidginization and Creolization: The Case of Arabic.* Amsterdam, 1984. Hfl. 75,--/$ 30.00

34. FISIAK, Jacek (ed.): *PAPERS FROM THE VIth INTERNATIONAL CONFERENCE ON HISTORICAL LINGUISTICS, Poznan, 22-26 August 1983.* Amsterdam, 1985. n.y.p. ca. Hfl. 175,--/$ 70.00

35. COLLINGE, Neville E.: *The Laws of Indo-European.* Amsterdam, 1985. n.y.p. ca. Hfl. 75,--/$ 30.00

36. KING, Larry D. & Catherine A. MALEY (eds.): *SELECTED PAPERS FROM THE XIIth LINGUISTIC SYMPOSIUM ON ROMANCE LANGUAGES, Chapel Hill, N.C., 24-26 March 1983.* Amsterdam, 1985. n.y.p. Hfl. 125,--/$ 50.00

37. GRIFFEN, T.D.: *Aspects of Dynamic Phonology.* Amsterdam, 1985. n.y.p. Price to be announced.

38. BROGYANYI, Bela & Thomas KRÖMMELBEIN (eds.): *GERMANIC DIALECTS: LINGUISTIC PHILOLOGICAL INVESTIGATIONS.* (working title). Amsterdam, 1985. n.y.p. ca. Hfl. 163,--/$ 65.00

39. GREAVES, William S., Michael J. CUMMINGS & James D. BENSON (eds.): *LINGUISTICS IN A SYSTEMIC PERSPECTIVE.* Amsterdam, 1985. n.y.p. ca. Hfl. 63,--/$ 25.00

40. FRIES, Peter H. & Nancy FRIES (eds.): *Towards an Understanding of Language: Charles C. Fries in Perspective.* Amsterdam, 1985. n.y.p. ca. Hfl. 75,--/$ 30.00

Volumes in preparation include:

POYATOS, Fernando: *Paralanguage: Interdisciplinary Theory and Application.* Amsterdam, 1984. n.y.p. Price to be announced.